THE COMPLETE GUIDE TO HEALTHY
HOUSEPLANTS

THE COMPLETE GUIDE TO HEALTHY
HOUSEPLANTS

WILLIAM DAVIDSON · CLIVE INNES · RAY BILTON

NEW
BURLINGTON
BOOKS

A QUINTET BOOK

This edition published 1990 by
New Burlington Books
6 Blundell Street
London N7 9BH

ISBN 1 85348 041 X

Reprinted 1990
This book was designed and produced by
Quintet Publishing Limited
6 Blundell Street
London N7 9BH

Art Director: Adrian Morris
Editors: Kathy and Fred Gill
Illustrators: Nigel Chamberlain, Chris Forsey, Edwina Keene,
Elly King, Simon Roulstone and John Woodcock
Photographers: Ian Howes, Paul Forrester

Typeset in Great Britain by
Central Southern Typesetters, Eastbourne
Manufactured in Hong Kong by Regent Publishing
Services Limited
Printed in Italy by Fratelli Spada SpA.

CONTENTS

Introduction

People today are becoming increasingly adventurous about the sort of plants they choose to grow indoors – whether in a living room, garden room or conservatory. As interest has grown, professional plant hybridizers have responded by introducing, for general sale, indoor plants once thought of as exotic or rare, but now widely cultivated by amateur growers. Although some are more difficult to grow than others, all repay that little extra care by providing unusual and interesting foliage or flowers – and there is a particular satisfaction to be gained from successfully growing a delicate and beautiful specimen. This book is intended to give growers the information they need to maximize success and minimize failure in growing more exciting plants –

During the nineteenth century, naturalists such as Alexander von Humboldt (**above**) travelled to remote parts of the world in search of exotic plants (**see opposite page**). Those species they discovered were brought back and introduced into the grand conservatories of the day.

from general care and maintenance to the specific needs of particular varieties. The alphabetical list of plants contains many suggestions which, I hope, will encourage amateur growers to try something a little out of the ordinary.

The origin of exotic plants

Almost all the more exciting indoor plants that we know today originated in the tropics. During the nineteenth century there was a passion among botanists for plant-hunting in remote parts of the world. Famous plant hunters, such as Joseph Banks and Robert Fortune, brought back to Britain rare species which, duly noted by the Royal Botanical Society, were subsequently grown in the conservatories of the Victorian and Edwardian upper middle classes.

Plant hybrids Some of the most successful indoor plants are man-made hybrids that bring together the best attributes of the original strains. The example in the foreground shows *Fatshedera lizei,* an attractive hybrid of *Hedera helix* (**top left**) and *Fatsia japonica* (**top right**). The resulting hybrid has the leaf shape and hardiness of the hedera plus the more erect growing habit of the fatsia – an ideal combination.

The pioneering quest for rare and unusual plants has, over the years, developed into a flourishing international trade. Today, the householder need look no further than his local plant centre for species which, a hundred years ago, were to be found only in the depths of the tropical rain forest.

Buying plants: what to look for
This tropical heritage has an important bearing, not only on what to buy, but where to buy. When setting out to grow delicate plants it is of the utmost importance that the plant should be in good condition to start with. And, in order for the plant to be in good condition, the premises of the plant supplier should be something more than an inadequately heated and poorly lit shed. It is important to find a shop that seems warm, well lit and congenial.

The obvious place to start is the established, professional plant supplier, but in recent years department stores, too, have become an important source of plants for the amateur grower. And, surprising though it may seem, purchases from a top department store are often equal, even superior, in quality to plants bought in a plant shop. Department stores often go to considerable trouble, not only to get the right conditions to keep plants healthy, but also to provide trained staff who can offer customers proper advice on plant care. Moreover, as large-scale purchasers, department stores are able to demand high standards of quality from their suppliers.

You should give your retailer an idea of the conditions that the plant will meet in its new home. A good retailer will enquire about the light and the temperature in your home and will then suggest plants that are likely to do well there.

Last, but not least, a good plant supplier will carefully wrap the plant for the homeward journey. On a bitterly cold winter's day you will sometimes see a newly purchased plant, its leaves blowing in the wind, clutched proudly by its new owner, who is muffled to the eyes in protective clothing. Even a brief exposure to cold can irreparably damage a plant, and, if it is cold enough for an overcoat to be worn, you should insist that the plant is suitable wrapped for its protection.

These simple guidelines, no more than common sense, will nevertheless guarantee you the best chance of obtaining healthy plants in good condition. The advice given in the following pages is intended to help you keep your plants looking their best. The book is divided into three sections: a general section on houseplants, with special emphasis on those having ornamental and decorative foliage or flowers, and specialized sections dealing with two of the most popular families of exotic plants – cacti and succulents, and orchids. Each section gives general and specific advice on care and maintenance, together with a list of plants that, with proper attention, can be grown successfully at home.

Reviving a parched plant
If a plant has not received a sufficient amount of water, the leaves wilt and they may drop off (*above*).

The first thing to do for a dehydrated plant is to loosen the top layer of soil (*above*). The water will then be able to permeate to the roots.

If the plant is very parched, it makes sense to spray the leaves with tepid water.

A plant should always be left to drain after watering.

Check for firm, healthy buds that look capable of flowering. If the plant has been left in a cold draught, the flower buds may drop as soon as the plant is moved.

Check for clear, unspoilt flowers. Vigorous plants, such as these begonias, need regular feeding and watering for healthy and profuse flowers. Any browning or wilting points to plant starvation.

Check for strong, well-coloured foliage, free from obvious blemishes. Blister-like spots and brown areas suggest fungus and/or bacterial infection. Rings and mottling may be caused by viruses.

Check for clean, sturdy stems. A white powdery coating may be mildew, caused by keeping the plants in moist, stagnant surroundings.

Signs of health Buying a really healthy plant is the most important step to ensuring indoor gardening success. These beautiful plants of *Begonia hiemalis* 'Rieger' are literally bursting with health – the leaves are firm and glossy, the flowers are sturdy and bright, and the whole plant has a robust appearance. Take the opportunity to look at the surrounds of the plant shop, too. If they are clean and well maintained, chances are that all the plants on sale are in good health. But don't take your chosen plant home until you have checked out the detailed points raised in the annotations above – it could save you disappointment later on.

9

General Care

Almost every plant that is brought into the house will present some challenge to the plant grower. In the first place, no matter how good the environment you provide, it is not the stable greenhouse or hothouse conditions in which the plant has spent the early part of its life. Conditions in the greenhouse are carefully controlled: a moist atmosphere, if that is what the plant requires, good light, and the daily attentions of a skilled gardener, who makes a living keeping plants in top condition. However, if you follow these guidelines in relation to your own houseplants then the risk of failure is very much reduced.

You can pick up some useful tips about the general care of plants from a professional plant grower. Firstly, a nurseryman will take precautions to ensure that the greenhouse is free from pests and disease. The soil he uses for potting will be steam-sterilized, and all pots will be either new or scrubbed clean before use. Almost all plants, and flowering plants in particular, need good light if they are to grow well. The professional grower, while ensuring that the plants have enough light, avoids exposing them to very bright sunlight. If necessary he will cover the glass with a material that provides some kind of shade. Finally, the greenhouse will always be heated to the correct temperature for the particular plants.

The nurseryman, having gone to the trouble of ensuring that plants are healthy, will carefully wrap and box plants so that they arrive at the home of the eventual purchaser in perfect condition – try to keep them that way. It may seem obvious to stress that the plant should be unwrapped as soon as you get it home, but this point is often neglected, with the result that the plant is deprived of the light that is so essential to its well-being. The plants concerned may have travelled hundreds of miles since leaving the nursery and may well have dried out in transit, so you should immediately check to see if they need water; some plants dry out at a surprisingly fast rate.

Given the amount of interest today in growing indoor plants for their own sake, it is not unusual to find rooms that have been entirely given over to plants. With controlled lighting, temperature, watering and humidity, it is possible to grow a very wide range of both flowering and foliage plants.

Pots Natural clay pots are attractive and provide a stable base for large plants. They allow the potting mix to 'breathe' through their porous sides. Lightweight plastic pots, available in many colours, help to retain moisture in the potting mix.

Potting mixes Soil-based mixes, prepared from sterilized loam, provide firm support and longer-lasting natural nutrition. The lightweight 'soil-less' mixes, based on peat, are very convenient for indoor use.

Accessories Just as with outdoor gardening, you'll find such items as gloves, twine, secateurs and scissors essential for good plant care.

Pesticides Aerosol sprays, powders, tablets and liquids are available to ward off pests and diseases. Always follow the label notes for proper and safe application.

Plant foods When the natural food value of the potting mix declines, use a liquid, tablet, granular or 'soil stick' fertilizer to keep plants healthy.

Watering equipment Use a watering can with a long, thin spout to reach into the centre of plant displays. A mist sprayer will help to keep humidity high around indoor plants.

Essential equipment Like most hobbies, indoor gardening needs a basic kit of tools and materials. These are usually on sale 'under the same roof' as the plants, making their selection an extension of the plant-buying process. This is to be encouraged because it is possible to match the plants with the most suitable equipment they require for continued health. Since most of the essential materials, such as potting mixes, are prepared and packaged for use in the home, even the most diffident of beginners should feel encouraged to give gardening a try.

Grouping plants together not only creates an attractive display but also helps the plants by providing group humidity.

Room divider Plants scrambling up a trellis (*below*) form an original and effective boundary between a dining area and lounge.

Plant room Most indoor plants revel in light conditions. In this kitchen/plant room (*bottom*) the bright blooms of geraniums contrast well with the cool greens of ferns and palms.

Window group Where space allows, a large window display of plants (*bottom right*) creates a superb room feature.

Scindapsus aureus (Devil's Ivy; Pothos)

Nephrolepis exaltata (Boston fern)

Dracaena marginata 'Tricolor' (Variegated silhouette plant)

Saintpaulia ionantha (African Violet)

Hedera helix 'Goldchild' (Golden English Ivy)

Leaf Care Dead leaves, such as the ones around the base of this cyclamen (*right*), should be pulled off regularly. However much care and attention they are given, dead leaves will not revive.

Feeding Pellet feeds are pushed into the soil. When the plant is watered, the pellet releases the correct dosage of feed.

Fertilizer sticks are pushed into the soil at the edge of the pot; they are designed to release nutrients over a given period of time.

Liquid feeds can be given to the plant when it is watered. Powdered feed can also be added to the water.

Humidity Many plants require more humidity in the atmosphere than is provided in the average home. If the atmosphere becomes too dry, the plant's rate of water loss increases, which causes it to wilt. You can prevent this by standing the plant on damp pebbles or gravel, or filling the space between the inner and outer pot with damp peat.

Watering

If plants are on the dry side, pour water onto the surface of the soil, from a watering can with a small spout. Pour the water until you can see the surplus draining through the holes in the bottom of the pot. If the plant is excessively dry, then it should be submerged in a bucket of water. Hold the pot with your fingers and place your thumbs on the soil before plunging it in. Leave the pot in the water until all the air bubbles have escaped. If the plant is very thirsty, this exercise can be repeated at every watering (perhaps twice or three times a week).

Rainwater is generally better for plants that object to lime, but it is not essential. It is important not to use very cold water, direct from the tap, when watering tender plants, such as saintpaulias. The best practice is to fill a can and leave it to stand in a heated room overnight, or to place it on a radiator for a few hours. In any event, you should avoid using water that is either very hot or very cold.

Feeding

Your plant has been grown in a nursery where it will have been fed regularly, at least as necessary. If the plant has become accustomed to feeding, the practice must be continued when it is taken indoors, or it will suffer discoloration and general decline.

A very extensive selection of fertilizers, in various forms, is available from garden sundriesmen, and deciding what is most suitable for your plants is very often a question of trial and error. Fertilizer in liquid form is probably the best as the plant can absorb it more easily. You can buy powders that are diluted in water, so forming a liquid feed, or you can use slow-release fertilizers in the form of tablets or sticks. These

Positioning is the key to displaying your plants to best effect. Plants with green foliage will do much better in poor light than plants with variegated or highly coloured foliage, while nearly all flowering plants need good light if they are to do well.

If a room is large and supplied with adequate light, a corner can provide a pleasant haven for a plant requiring moderate conditions of light and temperature. Many types of foliage plant will live happily here, provided the corner is not too dark.

In this position the light in one window is obstructed by a tree outside, but there will be warm, evening light on most days during the summer. Philodendrons, although they thrive best in good light, can adapt to, and tolerate the shade.

Plants needing moderate conditions, but good light, are well placed here. Do however protect plants from the fierce morning sunlight.

This large window will get plenty of light all day, but this includes the hot midday sun in summer, and plants pressed against the window pane may scorch if unprotected by a blind. Flowering and variegated plants thrive in a well-lit position.

The corner of the room that gets no strong light is too dark for flowering plants. Ferns may appreciate the shade if the humidity and temperature are suitable for them.

A shady room has a low light level most of the day and is rather gloomy. Many hardy plants prefer to live in cool temperatures.

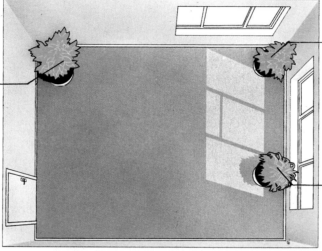

Measuring light intensity (*above*) A light meter can be useful if you are not sure how bright the light in a room is. Set a photographic light meter for film speed ASA 25. Hold a sheet of paper to the plant and the light meter to the paper. Adjust the dial of the meter according to the light reading obtained and check the f stop needed for a shutter speed of a quarter second. f64 or f32 indicates bright, direct sunlight, f16 bright light and f8 medium light.

The direction and level of the light available to an indoor plant considerably affect its growth. A plant placed near a window, against a white wall (*below left*), receives reflected light directly through the window.

Light is also reflected from the wall and this enables the plant to grow straight. A plant placed against a dark wall (*below right*) receives no reflected light and will lean towards the window as the only source of light.

Container sense Strategic positioning of two different plants in the same pot (*above*) makes good sense – the large overhanging leaves of the rex begonias hide the bare lower stem of the upright *Cissus antarctica*. A colourful melee of plants and pots (*right*) makes a superbly informal feature in any room.

Light work If you are really serious about growing your indoor plants under artificial light, then arrange your set-up as shown above. Use fluorescent tubes – ideally ones that produce a balanced light output – and suspend them 6–24in (15–60cm) from your plants (depending on type). A pebble tray will help to maintain high humidity.

Ordinary bulbs If you illuminate your plant displays with ordinary incandescent bulbs, the result may look attractive but the plants may not receive sufficient light or the right sort of light to really prosper. Even so, as an evening supplement to daylight it's worth a try. Try to avoid burning the topmost leaves.

Bowls of light Fittings that combine lamps and plant containers can provide charming displays. Use them with shallow-rooted plants that benefit from some additional light in the evening, such as African Violets. Keep a careful check on the potting mix to prevent it drying out too rapidly, and do not use too bright a lamp.

Potting on Carefully remove the plant, with soil attached, from its pot. The plant should be advanced to a new pot 2in (5cm) wider.

Place about 1in (3cm) of soil in the bottom of the new container, place the old pot inside and fill the space in between the two pots with more soil.

Press down the soil between the two pots and push the inner pot down inside the other very firmly.

The level of the soil between the pots should be at the rim of the inner pot. This empty pot can now be removed by twisting it free.

When the old pot has been removed, it will leave an impression in the soil inside the new container, into which the plant can be neatly placed.

Put the plant into the space left by the old pot, and press the soil around it. Finally, water the soil until the surplus water drains from the bottom.

are pushed into the soil in order to feed the plant over a long period of time and are useful for plants in more inaccessible locations, or for houseplant owners who tend to be forgetful. There are also foliar feeds that the plant can absorb into its system through its foliage, and these are excellent for plants that have sensitive root systems, such as many of the smaller ferns.

Conditioning

A gardener who is preparing borders for a show of summer bedding would not dream of taking plants direct from the greenhouse and placing them into garden soil – unless the temperature outdoors was very mild. Plants should be conditioned to accept changes in temperature; remove them from the greenhouse and place them in a cooler greenhouse or cold frame until they become hardened to the more extreme temperature. A similar practice is required for in-

door plants that have been growing in strong greenhouse light – they should be gradually acclimatized to darker indoor areas.

The elegant Weeping Fig, *Ficus benjamina*, is a plant that appreciates good light, although not direct sunlight. It reacts to poor light by shedding its older leaves, so it is worth remembering, if you want to put this plant in a part of the house which is poorly lit, it should be conditioned, by degrees, to accept a lower level of light. The same rule would apply if you were placing plants in cooler rooms – get them used to the change in temperature by reducing it in the same way that the gardener does with his summer bedding plants.

Temperature

Temperature is critical when caring for plants indoors, but there is no way that most people can provide every plant they own with

ideal conditions. Plants vary in their heating requirements – for example, ivies like to grow in coolish temperatures, while crotons and calatheas prefer warmth. If you are growing a wide variety of plants, you will have to aim for a happy medium.

Plants will generally accept an average room temperature between 60 and 70°F (16–21°C), and it is surprising how well they will do if there is adequate light, and a culture of reasonable standard is maintained.

Light

To satisfy a plant's need for light, natural daylight can be augmented by utilizing artificial light in the evening. Some tougher plants can even be conditioned to survive solely on artificial light. For the latter purpose, warm white strip lights, operating for 12 hours in every 24, will be adequate.

Maintenance

Keeping plants clean and tidy is an excellent practice, but they should not be fussed over constantly. Once their needs are attended to, plants are best left alone to get on with the business of growing. When the leaves of a plant have yellowed and died no amount of attention and encouragement will bring them back to life. However, a good clean-up at the start of the growing season, and again at the end of the season, is a good idea. Spindly growth should be removed, and any straggly pieces should be tied into position – longer canes can be put in if needed. Late autumn is usually a good time for pruning back overgrown branches of plants so that fresh spring growth will quickly come into flower.

Cleaning the naturally glossy leaves of indoor plants can improve their appearance, and there are many chemicals available for this purpose. Larger, tougher leaves, such as those of the Rubber Plant, can be cleaned with a solution of tepid water with a little detergent added.

Potting on

We hear much about potting plants on – when and how it should be done, what soil to use and so on. Almost any time is suitable, except for the middle of winter, when plant growth has slowed almost to a standstill. Spring is probably the ideal time for potting on, but if plants are growing well and conditions are agreeable, there is no reason why they should not be potted on during other months. When large plants in relatively small pots have been purchased, it is sound practice to pot them on immediately, as the plant can starve before the spring comes around. These plants should have their root systems checked as soon

A Wardian Case Wardian cases are miniature greenhouses. They are named after Dr Nathaniel Ward, who discovered, by chance, that ferns need a humid atmosphere and protection from smoke and draughts in order to grow successfully. A keen entomologist, Ward was conducting an experiment on hawk moths, and he accidentally included a seedling fern with a chrysalis that he had put into a sealed bottle, filled with moist earth. The fern flourished and Ward proceeded to build many different fern cases of varying shapes.

as they arrive home and they should be repotted if the root development is excessive. When potting on, it is important not to advance the plant into a pot that is much larger than the one it is coming out of. Very large plants will generally require large pots, but once they are growing in a 7in (18cm) or 19in (29cm) pot they can be maintained simply by regular feeding. They will not need to be repeatedly potted on.

Although plants grow just as well (often better) in clay pots, since the clay retains moisture for a much longer period, plastic pots are light to handle and they drain better.

Soil for potting on

There are now so many different brands of soil available that it is difficult to offer advice on what should be used. However, there is little doubt that almost without exception houseplants of both the foliage and flowering variety do better when grown in mixtures containing a high proportion of peat. In a heavy clay mixture, the roots of indoor plants become less active as they find it hard to penetrate the more compacted soil. If you use the tried and tested mix-

tures favoured by the old gardening school, it is wise to incorporate a good amount of sphagnum peat to lighten the mixture. A few plants will benefit from a heavier mixture – it will keep them more compact and will reduce the risk of the plants becoming top-heavy. An important point to remember when potting plants on is that the plant to be removed from its pot should be watered first. This will blend the old and new soil more effectively and reduce root damage.

Top dressing

There is a tendency on the part of many indoor gardeners to constantly pot their plants on, with the result that many plants end up in pots that are ridiculously out of proportion to their size. As an alternative to potting on, you can 'top dress'. This is the practice of removing the hard crust and top two inches from the surface of the soil. A sharp stick should be used to loosen the soil and eliminate any seed and weeds at the same time. Once this layer of soil is disposed of, the stick can be used to loosen the surface of the remaining soil before you place a handful or two of fresh soil in the pot.

1

2

3

4

5

6

Creating a terrarium Gardening in miniature has a special fascination, particularly planting up a terrarium. Many plants thrive in the humid atmosphere that builds up within the almost sealed glass container. Moisture given off by the plants condenses on the glass and is recycled. Maintenance is minimal – cleaning the glass and pruning is occasionally necessary.

7

1 Terrariums are available in many shapes and sizes. This leaded-glass design lends an appealing 'antique' charm to the plants it displays.
2 Fill the base of the terrarium with a layer of peaty potting mix at least 3in (8cm) deep. Some charcoal pieces and pebbles may be inserted first to assist drainage and to keep the mix 'sweet' for as long as possible.
3 Tap out your chosen plants carefully from

their pots and check the roots for healthy growth at the same time. Water each plant well before transferring it to the terrarium.
4 Insert plants in pre-formed hollows in the potting mix, working from the back towards the front. For an intricate display always plan the arrangement on paper before planting.
5 Use small plants that will not quickly outgrow the terrarium. This small-leaved fittonia (Little Snakeskin Plant) is an ideal choice.
6 Fill in around the plants and ensure that all are firmly embedded in the potting mix before watering again.
7 The final arrangement. The fine markings on the fittonia's leaves are echoed by the delicate fronds of a pteris fern. Height is provided by a small specimen of *Neanthe bella*.

17

Pests and Diseases

It is essential for the grower of indoor plants to maintain a strict programme of pest and disease control if he is going to prevent an epidemic that could devastate an entire crop. Despite the vast sums of money spent each year on pest control, aphids, red spider and mildew are always going to be a problem. In dealing with these pests, there is no substitute for vigilance and swift, effective action. If, for example, red spider mites are allowed to carry on feeding and breeding, they will reproduce at a phenomenal rate and will completely cripple the host plant before moving on to their next breeding ground. Similarly, if the white powdery spores of mildew are not controlled, they will quickly spread over the foliage and eventually kill the plant.

Inspecting plants for pests

Although some pests enter through the open window, it is more likely that they were already on the plant when it was purchased. Inspect any plants that you are considering for purchase very carefully and reject anything that shows obvious signs of pests or disease.

Mildew can be recognized by the white powdery spots. These

Inspecting roots The plant must be taken out of its pot in order to have its roots inspected. Any roots that are brown and unhealthy looking should be gently teased away from the central mass of roots. The outer skin should then be pulled gently to discover if the plant has root rot.

Buying a plant It is worth taking time when you buy a plant. A careful look at the plant's general appearance is essential and quickly reveals its condition. The leaves should be without blemishes and supple, and healthy in colour. In particular, the undersides of leaves should be checked for signs of pests or disease. If possible, check the stems of the plant near the soil for signs of rot.

are usually found on the upper surface of foliage, but appear sometimes on flowers. Aphids are very common pests during the spring and summer months. They feed on the tips of young shoots, so always check the upper section of the plant.

Whitefly can be both troublesome and difficult to get rid of once it has established itself, so keep a watch out for the pest on the undersides of foliage. Two flowering plants that are often hosts are the poinsettia and the hibiscus. Gently touching the leaves of either of these plants will cause the adult whitefly to immediately take flight.

Mealy bugs and scale insects can also be a nuisance; they get onto foliage and between the stems and leaves of plants. Scale insects can be very messy; their excreta falls onto lower leaves, producing a layer of black honeydew mould

that is sticky and looks unpleasant. Both adult and young adhere to the undersides and stems of plants such as *Ficus benjamina* and give the appearance of being part of the plant. Scales can be removed with a fingernail, but if you detect scales when purchasing it is better to select a clean plant, as these insects can be a problem if present in quantity.

Inspecting plants for disease

Inspecting the root system of the plant for problems when purchasing is not practical, but if root damage is at an advanced stage it will show on the leaves. To fully inspect plants that are about to be purchased, it is often necessary to remove the plant from the protective paper sleeve in which it is wrapped, since wrapping can conceal many plant defects. A few discoloured leaves at the base of the plant are generally nothing much to worry about, but plants that have discoloured leaves all over should be rejected. Leaves that are discoloured around the margins indicate that the plant is either suffering from a root disease or has been overfed.

Insecticide

When using insecticide, be sure to follow the manufacturer's directions to the letter. Experimenting is unadvisable as it can be very dangerous to use commercial insecticides that are not recommended for domestic use. Toxic insecticides should not be used anywhere other than in a properly controlled environment. Insecticides for treating indoor plants will have been tested and passed as safe for use indoors. Nevertheless, if plants are portable, it is wise to take them out of doors when spraying insecticide. When applying an insecticide in liquid form, be sure that all the foliage of the

Signs of ill-health Sadly, indoor plants fall prey to a host of influences that sooner or later begin to tarnish the healthy glow that made you buy them in the first place. Sometimes it will be your fault; sometimes you can blame pests and diseases that 'came in through the window'. Whatever the cause, correctly identifying the symptoms is your first step to cure.

Cold and dry Marantas thrive in warmth and moisture; this leaf (*above*) shows the signs that both are lacking.

Leaves on parade This collection of leaves (*below*) clearly demonstrates the classic symptoms of underwatering.

Stem rot The blackened base of this heptapleurum plant (*above*) is a sure sign of stem rot. Overwatering is the usual cause and recovery is unlikely.

Physical damage Obvious signs of maltreatment are easy to recognize, but too late to reverse. This dieffenbachia leaf (*above*) has been chewed by pets and badly scorched.

Undernourished This beloperone leaf (*above*) looks distinctly unwell. The mottled appearance, brown tip and limpness point to a severe lack of nutrients in the soil. If proper feeding is resumed, the plant may respond.

Overwatering A Rubber Plant (*above*) assumes a drooping pose as it slowly 'drowns'.

Potbound This beloperone plant (*above*) is overdue for repotting. When roots run out of soil they grow round in circles.

Cold and damp This sickly codiaeum leaf (*above*) is the sad victim of a damp chill.

Hygiene and Pest Control Provided you keep your indoor plants clean, there should seldom be any need to use insecticides. Hardy plants with glossy leaves (*above*) can be cleaned by sponging the leaves with soapy water. The slightly hairy leaves of the African Violet (*top right*) are delicate and must be treated gently. A soft brush can be used to remove surface dust – no liquid or chemicals should be used. An aerosol insecticide can be very effective provided it is used with care (*bottom right*) and should not be aimed directly at the plant.

plant is treated and not simply the upper areas of the leaves. Most pests, such as red spider and white fly, will be concealed under the leaves, and it is important that the chemical used comes into direct contact with the pest. To avoid breathing in the fumes, a gauze face mask, or a handkerchief, should be placed over the mouth and nose, and you should wear rubber gloves when dealing with chemicals.

When the leaves are saturated, the plant should remain outside until they have dried off and there is no trace of any unpleasant smell. While plants are outside keep them out of direct sunlight, and do not allow them to become cold through exposure to low temperatures. In fact, when treating plant foliage with any sort of chemical, a leaf cleaner for example, it is essential to give it some sort of protection from strong sunlight and low temperatures.

Aerosol insecticides

Insecticides in aerosol form can be very effective for many pests, but such insecticides should be used with care. The spray mist should not be aimed directly at the plant, since it is important to saturate the atmosphere around the plant. It is also important to apply the insecticide before you retire in the evening so that it can disperse before morning. Alternatively, the plants can be taken to a garage or shed for treatment. However, the atmosphere should be still to prevent the mist dispersing too rapidly.

Systemic insecticides

Systemic insecticides are available that offer plants protection from pests over a long period of time. These are very easy to use and come in either tablet or stick form. Simply push the tablet or stick into the soil in the pot. The plant will draw the chemical up through its system, and probing insects will be killed off when they stuck the sap from the plant. Systemic chemicals are ideal for larger plants that cannot be moved around and for plants in hanging containers that are not easily accessible.

Hygiene

When all is said and done, the most effective pest control is hygiene. Good husbandry can make a great deal of difference to your plant's health; clean plants are much less likely to be pest-ridden than those that are neglected, have entangled growth or dead foliage. Insecticides should be used on indoor plants only when absolutely necessary and not simply for their own sake. You will find that recent arrivals of aphids on the topmost soft leaves of your plant can be very easily removed by wiping them off carefully with a soft sponge that has been moistened in soapy water. Soapy water is an old-fashioned remedy for greenfly in particular, and in the country it used to be common practice to throw soapy water over rose trees every other day.

Naturally, you must be a little gentler where smaller plants are concerned. Place a piece of polythene over the soil in the pot to prevent it from falling out, and then submerge the foliage of the small plant in the soapy water. This treatment once or twice a year will give plants a fresher appearance and fewer pests.

Although most indoor plants fail because of indifferent culture rather than because of the presence of pests, it is always helpful to be able to recognize pests when they appear, so that the appropriate action can be taken. The following alphabetical list names the more common pests and diseases affecting indoor plants.

APHIDS	**BOTRYTIS**	**DAMPING OFF**

Botrytis is a fungus prevalent in wet, warm and generally airless conditions. Signs of botrytis are large blotches of wet rot on leaf or stem that will quickly destroy affected plants if not dealt with immediately. Fungicide can be effective in controlling this disease, but the best preventatives are hygienic conditions and good culture.

This is a problem that mainly affects young seedlings; mature potted plants do not generally suffer from it. An obvious symptom is a black discoloration at the base of the stem of the seedling, causing it to topple over and die. To obviate damping off, you should space seedlings a little further apart so that air can circulate around them. It will also help if the soil in which seedlings are growing is kept dry. You can purchase fungicide that will check stem rot in young plants, but be sure to follow the manufacturer's instructions carefully.

Aphids attack many different plants and can multiply at an alarming rate if left unattended. The young tips of growing plant shoots, such as ivy, are a favourite feeding place for this pest, but they may also be found on the undersides of plants. They are not difficult to see and their presence will generally by accompanied by a black sooty mould on leaves below where the pests are feeding. In the early stages a few pests can be wiped off the plant with a soft, damp sponge, but at a more advanced stage it is advisable to use an insecticide that is recommended for the treatment of aphids.

Sooty mould The black marks on this leaf (*above*) indicate sooty mould. This grows on sticky honeydew deposited by aphids and other pests.

Fungus disease Wet, rotting patches and fluffy grey mould on the cactus (*above*) and aglaonema (*top*) indicate botrytis. Cut out the infected areas and spray plants with a fungicide.

LEAF MINERS

These are tunnelling insects that get between the upper and lower surfaces of the leaves of many plants and leave a white trail behind them. The trail will also indicate where the pests are located on the leaf, and if there are only a few present it is easy enough to kill them by squeezing them gently between finger and thumb. Alternatively, there are numerous insecticides available for controlling leaf miners. If pests go unnoticed, the leaves become badly affected in time, and it is then wise to remove leaves and burn them.

Leaf miner This grub leaves a white trail as it burrows between the upper and lower tissue of a leaf (*above*). When the pest is found, pierce its body with a pin.

MEALY BUGS

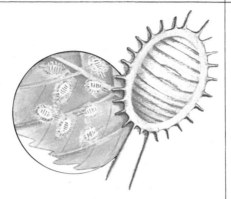

Mealy bugs are generally found on the more inaccessible areas of a plant. They get amongst the twining stems of plants such as stephanotis, where they are difficult to locate. Mealy bugs are very messy, and spraying the leaves of the plant with insecticide does not always eliminate them. The adult bug may be eradicated, but the young are more difficult to get rid of. They are wrapped in a waxy cotton wool-like substance that protects them from the elements and also from insecticide. One of the oldest yet most effective methods of ridding plants of young bugs is to wipe them off with a soft brush (an old toothbrush is excellent). If the brush is dipped in methylated spirit, the cleaning will be doubly effective. Adult bugs are easily seen and can be cleaned from the plant with a piece of cotton wool that has been soaked in methylated spirit.

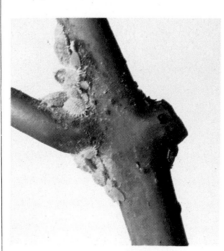

Mealy bug Young mealy bugs are wrapped in a cottony coating and cling to the plant. A thick cluster of them may appear on the stem.

MILDEW

Mildew is another fungal problem that can be treated with fungicide if it is caught early enough. The appearance of powdery white circular spots on the upper surface of leaves is the first sign of mildew. If left unchecked, mildew will destroy the plant.

Mildew White powdery deposits on the leaves, stems or flowers indicate the presence of mildew. Plants with soft growth are particularly susceptible to this disease.

RED SPIDER MITES

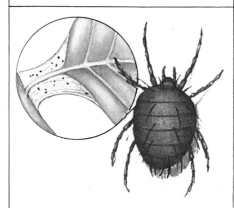

Although they are one of the smallest of plant pests, red spider mites are, without a doubt, the most devastating once they have got a hold on the host plant. Not easily detected with the naked eye, the adults are reddish in colour while the younger ones are flesh coloured.

A damp atmosphere will deter red spider mites, which thrive in hot and dry conditions. Either group the plants together in a trough filled with peat or a tray that is covered with damp gravel, or spray a fine mist around the plants (except the flowering variety).

The first signs of red spider mite will be a pale yellowish-brown discoloration of green foliage around the margin of the leaf and a hardening of growth. Sometimes you will have to use a magnifying glass to locate the pests on the undersides of leaves.

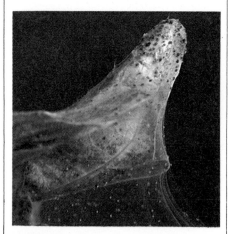

Red spider mites This acalypha (*above*) shows the tiny webs woven by red spider mites on the undersides of leaves.

ROOT MEALY BUGS

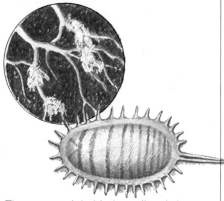

These pests inhabit the soil and show up as a white powdery substance around the roots of the plant when it has been removed from the pot. A sign of their presence is a general debility of the plant. Root mealy bugs are much smaller than the ordinary mealy bugs, but they are similar in shape. You can control them by drenching the soil with insecticide.

Root mealy bug This cryptanthus (*above*) has been infested by root mealy bugs, small insects often covered with a fuzzy white coating. Cacti and succulents are particularly suspectible to this pest.

SCALE INSECTS

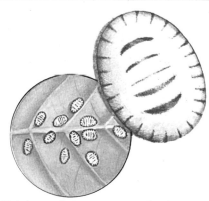

This is another messy pest that leaves a black sooty mould on the leaves underneath the feeding place. The adults are dark brown and the young are flesh coloured; both cling to the leaves and stems of plants like miniature limpets. Spraying frequently with a malathion solution will control them, but it is often better to don rubber gloves and sponge the plant with a solution of malathion liquid. Scale insects cling very tenaciously to their anchorage points and must be cleaned off very firmly.

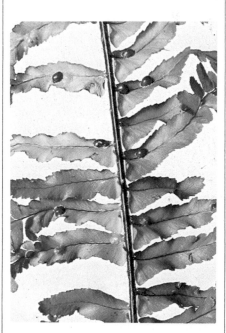

Scale insect Plants with woody stems offer them camouflage, but when they appear on green foliage (*above*), these yellow or brown pests are easy to detect. Scale insects suck the sap from a plant, causing it to wither.

SCIARID FLY	SLUGS	SPRINGTAILS
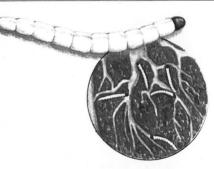		
Sciarid flies, sometimes called fungus gnats, are soil-borne pests that sometimes appear if the mixture in the pot becomes stale. Maggots in the soil develop into small black flies and these jump around when the plant is watered. You can control this pest by watering the appropriate insecticide into the soil in which the plant is growing.	Large holes in the leaves of plants can often be traced to slugs, lurking amongst the lower growth at soil level. Locating and subsequently disposing of these pests is no problem. If you prefer not to remove them by hand, they can be killed off with slug pellets placed on the surface of the soil.	These are small white insects that jump around when the soil is watered. They do little harm, as they feed off decaying matter in the soil. Treat them by watering with insecticide, making sure that the water flows right through the pot.
	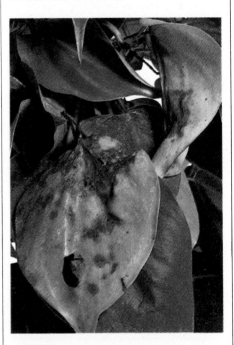	
Sciarid fly This calathea (*above*) is a victim of sciarid fly. Maggots have attacked the roots of the plant, causing it to droop.	**Slugs** Slugs have eaten through the leaves of this philodendron (*above*). To eliminate these pests, apply a slug repellant to the base of the plant.	**Springtails** These pests, which resemble small, cream-coloured centipedes, gnaw at roots. The dieffenbachia (*above*) is infested with them.

THRIPS

Streaks of silver on the flowers of an indoor plant are a sign that thrips are present. Though tiny, these can be detected on the upper surfaces of leaves. They are either black or pale yellow in colour. Treat them with an appropriate insecticide at the first sign of their presence.

Thrips These pests can disfigure plants and stunt their growth. Streaked or spotted foliage or flowers, like the leaves on this plant (*above*), indicate their presence.

WHITE FLY

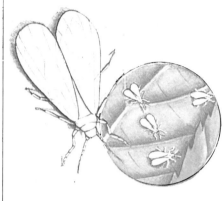

White fly is a common indoor plant pest that is mostly found on the undersides of leaves. The flies are easily detected and can be brushed from the leaves of the affected plant. Many plants, and particularly poinsettias and hibiscus, suffer from white flies so they should be inspected prior to purchase. Since these flies are difficult to eradicate, you must be persistent with the recommended insecticide — one application will not be enough.

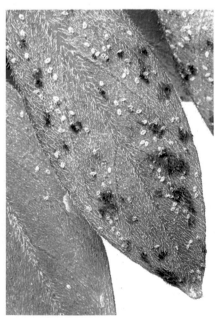

White flies The greenish scales on this plant (*above*) are the larvae of white flies, which live on the undersides of leaves and suck the sap from the plant. Leaves drop off when plants are badly infested.

WORMS

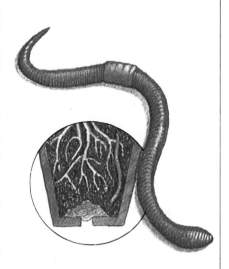

Sluggish soil that is slow to drain can be due to the presence of worms in the pot. You can get rid of them by using a worm killer or you can remove the plant from its pot and dispose of the worms by hand.

Worms The leaves of the *Dracaena deremensis* (*above*) are wilted and discoloured. Worms have interfered with the drainage in the pot.

Plant problem solver

Problem	Give the plant food	Water the plant	Reduce watering	Move the plant out of direct sun	Put the plant in better light	Repot in fresh soil or larger pot	Change the position of the plant	Protect the plant from draughts	Look for pests in leaves or soil	Look for caterpillars or earwigs	Examine the leaves for botrytis	Watch for signs of virus infection
Plant growing slowly	●		●		●				●			
Wilting leaves		●										
Mottled leaves									●			●
Browning on leaf margins			●	●			●					
Flower heads dropping				●			●					
Leaves bruised or broken							●					
Leaves falling				●						●		
Rotting in stems or leaves			●								●	
Leaf colour too pale	●				●		●					
Small leaves spindly growth	●								●			
Leaves turning yellow				●					●	●		
Holes in the leaves									●	●		

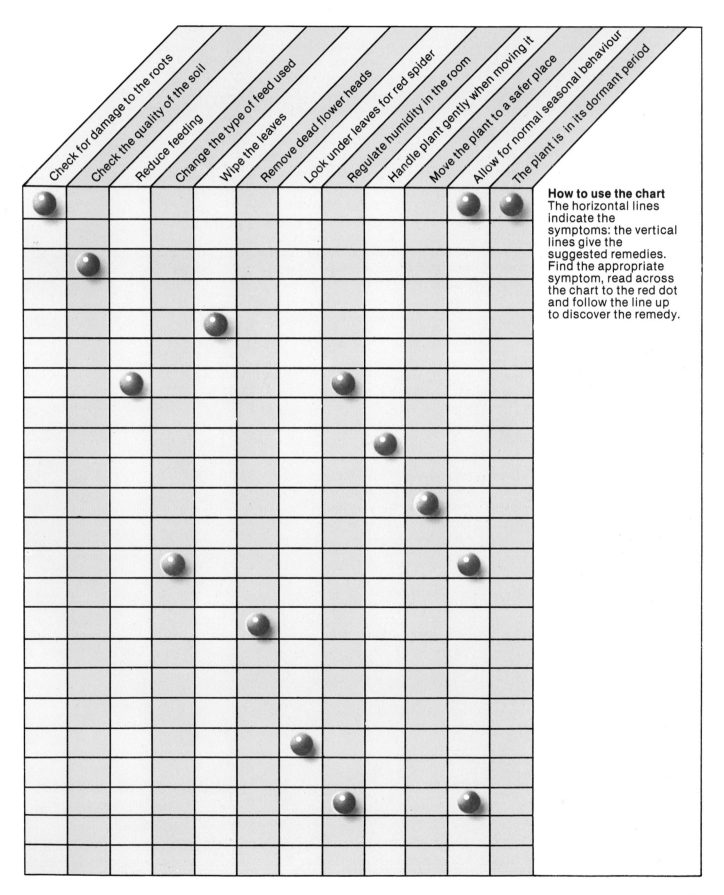

How to use the chart
The horizontal lines indicate the symptoms: the vertical lines give the suggested remedies. Find the appropriate symptom, read across the chart to the red dot and follow the line up to discover the remedy.

Conservatories and Garden Rooms

There can surely be no greater pleasure than creating and stocking your own garden room, where plants can flourish in conditions ideally suited to their needs. The main problem with growing exotic or tender plants indoors is that you cannot re-create the moist and humid conditions of their natural habitat – in a conservatory or garden room that is entirely given over to the plants, you can come closer to creating the right environment.

During the nineteenth and early twentieth centuries, the conservatory, with its palms, ferns and orchids, provided a natural adjunct to every elegant house. Many fine examples of the work of conservatory designers of the time still remain, although many more have long since disappeared.

At today's exorbitant prices, it would be difficult for all but a few to emulate the grand conservatory designs of the Victorian age, but there is no reason why similar results cannot be obtained with more modest constructions. If the modern conservatory is warm, light and adequately heated, then

you should be able to grow palms, ferns and orchids just as successfully as the gardener of the past.

Locating the conservatory

Siting the structure is not a major problem, as it is seldom a question of locating the conservatory in the ideal position. Most conservatories are simply tagged onto the house in a position that will be most practical. However, if there is a choice, then the conservatory or garden room should go on the sunny side of the house, as the plants will get the heat from the sun. Do, however, make sure that the plants receive adequate protection from bright sunlight so that they do not get scorched.

Constructing the conservatory

The most important factors to consider when building a conservatory are height, ventilation, light and flooring. Many garden room plants attain a height of around 10ft (3m) and they will become distorted if they come into contact with the glass roof, so make sure your construction is tall enough to house them. Ensure at

The ideal conservatory A place of peaceful beauty, a conservatory was the traditional plant-filled extension to Victorian houses. Today, its sumptuous elegance is still aspired to by many a green-fingered householder. If possible, build the conservatory on the sunny side of the house. In that position the only problem you should encounter is providing sufficient shade at the height of summer. Since the conservatory is designed to be a show-place for your plants, furnish it with style in mind, not utility. Then you can sit back and enjoy it as a welcome refuge from the cares of the world.

Ponds For something a little different, why not install a pond? Build it above ground for convenience. A fountain adds welcome sound and movement to the scene.

Heating Low-consumption electrical heaters are an ideal source of warmth for chilly winter nights.

Flooring Ceramic or stone tiles laid on a solid concrete base will provide a suitable water-resistant flooring. Rugs will soften their 'hard' appearance.

Doors Try to locate the doors away from prevailing winds to prevent draughts and to allow the doors to be used for extra ventilation in summer.

Conservatory pond Water forms a focal point in any garden situation and so is an ideal addition to the conservatory. Water lily leaves float on the surface of this pond (*left*) with the stunning blooms of *Clerodendrum thomsoniae* adding a colourful accent among the fan palms and dieffenbachias around the edges.

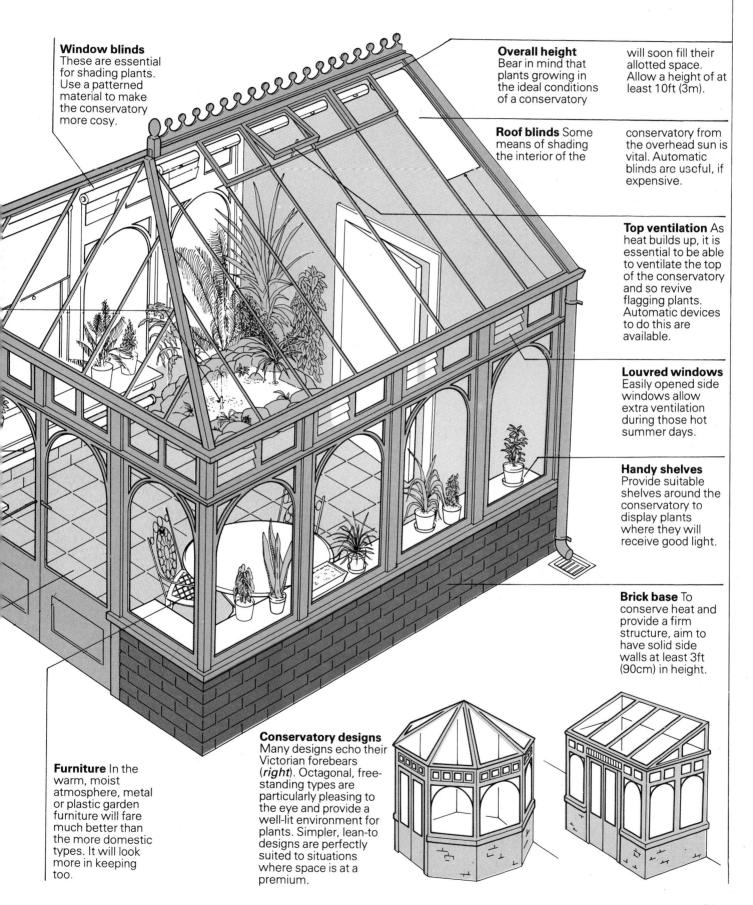

Window blinds These are essential for shading plants. Use a patterned material to make the conservatory more cosy.

Overall height Bear in mind that plants growing in the ideal conditions of a conservatory will soon fill their allotted space. Allow a height of at least 10ft (3m).

Roof blinds Some means of shading the interior of the conservatory from the overhead sun is vital. Automatic blinds are useful, if expensive.

Top ventilation As heat builds up, it is essential to be able to ventilate the top of the conservatory and so revive flagging plants. Automatic devices to do this are available.

Louvred windows Easily opened side windows allow extra ventilation during those hot summer days.

Handy shelves Provide suitable shelves around the conservatory to display plants where they will receive good light.

Brick base To conserve heat and provide a firm structure, aim to have solid side walls at least 3ft (90cm) in height.

Furniture In the warm, moist atmosphere, metal or plastic garden furniture will fare much better than the more domestic types. It will look more in keeping too.

Conservatory designs Many designs echo their Victorian forebears (*right*). Octagonal, free-standing types are particularly pleasing to the eye and provide a well-lit environment for plants. Simpler, lean-to designs are perfectly suited to situations where space is at a premium.

an early stage that the structure is adequately ventilated. Initially the principal concern is to conserve as much heat as possible and you are unlikely to give much thought to the opening of heat-losing ventilators. However, overheating a confined space during the warmer months of the year can be just as damaging to some plants as exposure to cold in winter, so be sure to have vents in the roof, and in the side walls, if possible. If the door of the building can be located away from prevailing winds, it can provide additional ventilation when the temperature is high.

Garden rooms must have sufficient light to enable the plants to grow properly, but there is a difference between good light and

Classic conservatory In this superbly planted conservatory (*above*) it is possible to feel 'at one with nature'. Everything enhances the mood – the green canopy of vines, the mixture of plants, even the cane furniture.

blisteringly hot sunlight streaming down on plants all day long. Plants that are close to the glass are particularly vulnerable. Therefore, when furnishing a garden room, be sure to provide some shade. Internal blinds that can be opened and closed as the weather conditions demand are an excellent idea, and enhance the atmosphere of the sitting-room-cum-garden room.

Choosing suitable flooring can be difficult. If the plants are the main consideration, then you should have a solid floor, prefer-

ably tiled. However, if you plan to use the room as an occasional sitting area, colourful rugs on the tiled floor make a good compromise.

You may also want to consider including a fountain or pool in the garden room. If there is sufficient space for building a pond, be sure to give plenty of thought to its location, since it will be difficult and expensive to remove if you later change your mind about the site. It is probably best to opt for a pool that is built up from floor level, rather than dug and sunk into the floor. The sunken pool will inevitably be the more attractive, but the pool that is built up can easily be removed when it outlives its usefulness.

Finding space in a garden room for plants, furniture and people can be a problem during the summer months when the room is in peak demand. A patio outside the garden room is the ideal place to put some of the less tender plants when the weather is fine.

Greenhouses
For a garden room to be really successful it should be combined with a more conventional greenhouse, set in another part of the garden. Thus you can bring on young plants to a certain stage in the greenhouse and then transfer them to the garden room. This also prevents you from forever falling over the pots and other paraphernalia that are an essential part of plant propagation. In addition, the greenhouse can serve as a hospital area for plants that have lost their sparkle and are not quite up to standard for the 'showplace' garden room. You can also prepare hanging baskets and other types of containers and give the plants a little time to settle before moving them into the conservatory.

Hanging and Climbing Plants

In recent years the range of containers that can accommodate hanging plants of all shapes and sizes has increased. However, when you are aiming for a really bold display of colour there is still much to be said for the old-fashioned moss-lined wire basket. The only drawback with these is that when the container is watered, the surplus drains through onto the floor below, so an outdoor location is preferable when moss-lined baskets are in use.

When planting in a hanging basket, use soil that contains a reasonable amount of loam, as mixtures that are composed almost entirely of peat tend to dry

Muted comfort The juxtaposition of 'sensible' stone-flagged flooring and inviting sofas provides this garden room/ conservatory (*below*) with just the right mix of beauty and utility. Natural clay pots containing palms, dracaenas and the odd flowering plant reflect the muted colours. Climbing plants soften the ceiling line.

out excessively – a common problem with plants that are suspended overhead. When the basket is past its best, the old soil should be disposed of and new soil used for the following season's plantings.

As the basket is lined and soil is introduced, a few plants can be put in position around the sides of the container so that they will fill out the basket and trail down. Almost any of the conventional basket bedding plants will do for this purpose – hoyas, columnea, stephanotis and *Begonia semperflorens* will all give a splendid show.

There are many fine plants that may be put in hanging containers and suspended from the roof of the garden room. The more exotic ones will need to be kept at a temperature ranging from 50° to 65°F (13°–18°C). Throughout the colder months of the year, few plants will survive the combination of wet and cold conditions, so be

especially careful not to overwater. Some of the best plants for indoor hanging baskets are mentioned below.

Aeschynanthus speciosus
This species, commonly called the Basket Plant, is shown to best advantage in a hanging basket. It has fleshy leaves of a pale green colour and an abundance of trailing stems. The *Aeschynanthus speciosus* normally has a summertime flowering season that produces striking, tubular orange flowers.

Begonia Tuberhybrida
These are among the most spectacular of all flowering plants in pots, and there are many fine-coloured varieties to choose from. Besides the upright growing types, there are excellent pendulous forms that may be grown in tubers, available in winter for planting in early spring. When

Cascading beauty The columnea (*above*) provides a superb display of scarlet flowers on long trailing stems. Keep it almost dry in the winter for summer blooms.

Basket plants The *Begonia tuberhybrida* (*above*) will grace any hanging basket with its exquisite flowers. Another good candidate for an eye-level, brightly lit location is the hoya (*below*). Grow it undisturbed; repot every two years.

well established, the young plants should be placed in hanging containers filled with loam-based soil.

Columnea banksii

This species has changed little since it was introduced into the Victorian conservatories in the nineteenth century. The cascading flowers are a rich shade of orange and they will completely cover the plant if it is flourishing. To encourage later flowering, the plant should be in a cooler temperature, around 50°F (10°C), during the

winter months. The soil should remain on the dry side.

Hoya bella

This is a summer-flowering plant. It has pale to dark-green leaves, attached to wiry stems that fan out almost horizontally from the container in which it is growing. The branches do not hang pendulously as you would expect with a hanging plant, because the flower clusters form on the underside of the branches. The *Hoya bella* is a plant that should be suspended

about head level so that the beauty of the waxy flower clusters and the delightful fragrance can be fully appreciated. Be sure to provide it with some shade in summer, avoid overwatering and be careful when applying insecticides.

Climbing plants

Climbing plants are a particularly useful category of plants. Not only are many of them extremely attractive, adding decorative interest wherever they are placed, but climbing plants can also emphasize – or mask – architectural lines and serve as sun or wind screens. All climbing plants need some kind of support to which they can attach themselves. This may be either a trellis, bamboo cane or the wall of a garden room. If the latter, place climbing plants against a solid wall (most garden rooms will have at least one wall that is part of the house) rather than against walls that form the glass exterior of the garden room; the plants will appear to much better effect. Either prepare a border filled with good soil into which the climbing plants can be freely planted or extend the floor of the garden room to the base of the wall and establish the climbing plants in large containers. Small containers will be of little use since most indoor climbing plants produce an abundance of growth, and such plants cannot be sustained by the limited amount of nourishment contained in small pots of soil. The following plants are suggested for use as suitable climbing plants.

Allamandas

There are a number of allamandas, mostly with rich-yellow trumpet flowers, that can be used as climbers in a room heated to 60°F (16°C). Attaining a height of 8ft (2.4m), *A. cathartica* has soft-

Hanging baskets All stages of planting in a hanging basket are a pleasure to perform. The growing medium is easy to handle; the plants are small and the choice wide; and the final result can be truly hailed as 'all your own work'. This series of photographs demonstrates the essential steps in creating a hanging garden that will provide colour and interest throughout the whole season. Several types of containers are available, ranging from pottery to wickerwork; some are solid plastic with built-in drip trays to make watering less of a hazard for people underneath.

1 First line the base of the basket with a generous layer of damp sphagnum moss. This provides a firm foundation for the growing medium and plants.

2 Add more moss and arrange it carefully around the sides of the container. This layer will form a semi-waterproof barrier and help to retain moisture.

3 Make sure you bring the moss layer right up the sides to cover the wire framework. You can trim off any excess later when the planting is complete.

4 Fill the centre with peaty potting mix, liberally laced with extra drainage material such as perlite. Damp it first with a weak liquid feed.

5 Insert each plant firmly in the mix, making sure there are no air pockets around the roots. Have a layout in mind before you start.

6 The heather, *Erica hiemalis,* is an ideal plant for a cool-season hanging basket; its tubular flowers provide colour through the winter months.

7 Bolder splashes of colour can be provided by planting pansies. These charming flowers are available in winter- and summer-flowering types.

8 A red primula adds a contrasting shade to the emerging pattern. Be sure to keep these flowering plants moist for their relatively brief flowering period.

9 When the planting is complete, trim the moss as necessary to tidy up the basket, and double-check that all the plants are firmly tucked in place.

10 The finished result looks a little sparse but that is intentional; as the plants settle in and grow a little the gaps will disappear. Hang the basket at eye level for easy maintenance.

Not all indoor plants have to be grown in pots. The bromeliad (*above*) has been grown on a mossy log. When tying plants to a stake it is important to use the right material. Plain wire will corrode and may damage the plant; string may rot in time. Plastic-coated or cardboard-covered wire is the best thing to use (*below*).

Supporting plants Plants can be supported in many different ways. A trellis (*above*) is an effective method of staking, or plants can be trained round a piece of plastic-covered wire (*top right*). Pieces of wood can be tied into decorative supports (*right*).

yellow flowers and will need to be tied to a support. The rare variety *A.c. 'Grandiflora'* has flowers almost 5in (13cm) across.

The species *A. neriifolia* has woody stems that can be trained to a support (these are also very fine free-standing plants). The flowers are small, bright-yellow and trumpet-shaped. They do not have a particular season, but will flower throughout the year if conditions are moist, warm and shady. The soil should be wet all the time, and a moist atmosphere is also important for these plants.

Clerodendrum thomsoniae
This plant has thin leaves of mid-green colouring and clustered flowering bracts that are bright red and white in colour. Although the stems are stout and woody, *Clerodendrum thompsoniae* is not a natural climber and will have to be trained to be seen at its best. It will reach a height of 8ft (2.4m) in time, but this vigorous plant is easily contained by pruning.

Hoyas
These are natural climbing and trailing plants, as they have stems

that twist and twine around everything in sight. They can grow several feet tall and are usually grown on indoor trellises, or wound around stakes. They are very easy to manage. Two fast-growing climbers are *H. carnosa* and *H. australis,* which are both summer flowering and produce clusters of star-shaped white flowers.

Stephanotis floribunda

Stephanotis is from the same family as the hoyas, and has the same twining habit. It has oval-shaped, dark-green leaves that are set opposite one another, and an overpowering and delicious fragrance that permeates every corner of the room. The flowers are creamy-white and are borne in clusters of five or more. They will appear at intervals over a lengthy period throughout the spring and summer months. If flowers clusters are removed, they can be taken indoors and inverted in a dish of water, where they will last for several days.

Plumbago capensis

This is a plant that will grow quickly and produce lovely flowers throughout the summer and well into the autumn. Small leaves are attached to twiggy branches that will grow vigorously if conditions and culture are reasonable. The flowers are a lovely powder-blue in colour. There is also a white form, *P. capensis 'Alba',* but it is not quite so showy as the blue variety. If both varieties are planted together, the combination of the blue and white flowers is most attractive. Over-active growth of *Plumbago capensis* can be trimmed to shape at any time. At the end of the flowering season, you should cut the plant down to a foot or two from the base if it is very vigorous.

Colourful climbers No indoor plant display is complete without its fair share of climbing plants. *Clerondendrum thomsoniae* (**above**) is a vigorous twining plant that needs to be kept in check and properly trained to look its best. The delicate blue flowers flowers of *Plumbago capensis* (**right**) are borne on straggly stems that benefit from being tied neatly to supports.

Golden trumpet This common name echoes allamandas' bright yellow flowers. Even this young specimen is bursting with bloom. As it matures, the plant will need a suitable support and plenty of warmth and sunlight to develop fully. Superb for a large plant window.

Tubs and Containers

An excellent way to display plants is in mobile, free-standing tubs. There is a wide range to choose from, made from many different materials. The plant containers that are now fitted with castors can be pushed around and re-arranged quite easily, either singly, or in groups, for a bolder effect. These containers should be completely watertight, but when watering the plants, check that there is no build-up of water in the bottom of containers that have no means of drainage. This can be difficult with plants growing in soil, and it may be necessary to insert a piece of tubing into the soil to drain liquid at the bottom of the container. You can then use a cane to check if there is an accumulation of water and, if there is, it can be siphoned out.

Self-watering containers

Many of the better containers have self-watering devices. The self-watering unit has a base on which the soil rests and a water reservoir between the soil and bottom of the container. Water is drawn from the reservoir via a nylon wick and the water level in the base is controlled by means of an indicator. The water-level indicator must remain at minimum for at least one week between each topping-up operation so that the soil becomes properly aerated. The major benefits of these units is that plants can be left unattended for a period of up to a month without needing water.

Almost any kind of indoor plant can be grown with comparative ease in these containers if both temperature and light are correct, but it is better to grow more mature plants, rather than very small ones. Mature palms, philodendrons and ficus plants are among the best subjects, with plants such as aglaonemas and dieffenbachia to fill the base.

Plant containers Indoor plants can be grown in a wide range of containers (*above*). The original – and some say still the best – are the clay pots. Plastic pots are suitable for many plants and decorative 'pot hiders' are available in a plethora of styles and materials.

Self-watering pot This ingenious pot (*above*) allows you to leave plants unattended for some time. Moisture reaches the soil from a basal water reservoir (1) by means of a nylon wick (2).

Hydroponic growing

The practice of growing plants in water, with only a nutrient added, has become increasingly popular in recent years.

Commercial gardens usually handle the first stages of water cultivation. When plants are a good size and showing strong, firm roots, the plant is taken from its pot and all the soil is removed by washing it clean under running water until no toxic particles of soil remain. The plant roots are then surrounded with clay granules in a pot with open sides before being placed in a trough of gently flowing water in a warm greenhouse. The granules are there simply to support the roots, and the plant will start to grow on its more succulent water roots in about two months' time. The plant is then usually considered sufficiently established to be sold.

You will find that most water-culture units have an indicator similar to the self-watering planter. It is important that the water level remains at the minimum mark for at least one week before the container is recharged. This ensures that the roots are well aerated – an important requirement for all plants that are growing with their roots restricted to pots.

To sustain the plant, a special slow-release nutrient is placed in the water. The nutrient is activated and made available to the plant as the water goes through its various chemical changes. In order for a chemical change to take place, the water surrounding the plant should come from the domestic water supply.

If you follow the directions that come with the plant and offer reasonable cultural conditions, the plants that are grown by water-culture methods will generally be of much better quality than similar plants grown in soil.

Hydroponics Plants growing with their roots in water need a special type of slow-release fertilizer. First add a dose of this to the outer container.

The inner pot houses a water-level indicator that extends to the base of the outer pot. Slits allow roots to grow into the fertilizer solution.

Finally, pour in more granules to fill the space between the two pots (*above*) and provide a tidy top surface.

Next pour in a layer of the expanded clay granules to provide support for the inner pot containing the plant. Add water to dissolve the fertilizer.

Insert the planted pot in the centre, resting its base carefully on the layer of granules, with the rim just below the level of the outer pot.

The finished pot (*right*), in this case sporting a stately *Yucca*, has a neat appearance with the all-important water-level indicator, a vital clue to its hydrocultural status. When the float in the indicator falls to the minimum level, leave it there for about a week before adding more water. This will allow the roots a beneficial 'breather'. The fertilizer should keep the medium-sized plant well nourished for about six months. It works by releasing the nutrients in balance with the plant's needs; an ordinary fertilizer would provide too much 'food' all at once. Hydroponic displays are useful for reception areas and offices.

The
Plant
Finder

A colourful guide to over 100 exotic plant species. For easy reference, it is arranged in A–Z order, according to the genus of the plant.

A healthy example of *Belperone guttata* (**opposite page**), commonly called 'Shrimp Plant' on account of its shrimp-like bracts.

Abutilon

Abutilons are free-growing plants with either green or variegated foliage and pendulous bell flowers that appear in the summer. These are easy plants to care for if given adequate light, and may be planted out of doors during the summer months of the year. Older plants can be hard-pruned in the autumn, and it is usually best to discard abutilons after two or three years. Propagate from top sections of stems about 5in (13cm) in length.

The two species commonly grown for indoor use are *Abutilon thompsonii* and *Abutilon sevitzia*. *A. thompsonii* (sometimes called *A. striatum*) has a reddish-orange bloom and grows to a height of 5ft (1.5m). It requires ample water and feeding during the growing season, and needs good light to retain its bright foliage colour.

A. sevitzia attains a maximum height of 6–7ft (1.8–2.1m) when grown in a pot of sufficient size, but can be kept to more manageable dimensions if pruned regularly. Pendulous apricot-coloured flowers bloom in summer, but the species' principal attraction is its green and white foliage.

Abutilon Colourful foliage is a principal feature of these plants, but bright light is necessary to ensure that colouring does not revert to green. As cool conditions will not be unduly harmful, plants can be placed out of doors during the warmer months of the year and can make fine central features in more elaborate bedding islands and borders. At the end of the summer, plants can be trimmed back to a more manageable shape. They will do better over winter if the soil is kept dry and no feed is given.

ABUTILON

Light and position

These plants do well in light locations, and can be placed out of doors in the summer, in a partially shady spot.

Temperature
Cool — Intermediate — Warm
Keep the plant cool, particularly in winter when the temperature should be between 50° and 60°F (10-16°C).

Watering

Water is essential when the plant is in active growth — it can be sprayed with a mist occasionally.

Feeding
Be sure to feed the plant well during the growing season — spring to late autumn. Give a dilute liquid feed regularly.

Seasonal care
Winter | Spring | Summer | Autumn
Many of these fine plants become quite substantial in time and will need potting on, using loam-based soil, when a matted root ball develops. Propagate stem cuttings or seeds in the spring.

Soil
The ideal soil is loam-based, free-draining.

EUPHORBIACEAE

Acalypha

This genus includes decorative plants with highly coloured foliage in the numerous varieties of *A. wilkesiana,* and with interesting and pendulous bracts in *A. hispida.*

The wilkesiana varieties are not too difficult to manage if temperatures in the region of 65°F (18°C) can be maintained and a sharp eye is kept for red spider mites on the undersides of leaves. These plants are grown entirely for their exotic foliage colouring, which is usually mottled and highly coloured, ranging from red to yellow to deep bronze. Many of the varieties of wilkesiana have a mixture of many colours in a single leaf. If plants are grown in good light, they will have much better colouring and will also be more compact. Plants grown in pots around 8in (20cm) in diameter will grow to about 3ft (91cm) in height with similar spread.

With drooping rattail of red bracts that may be 18in (46cm) or more in length, *A. hispida* is impressive when well grown, but it is not the easiest of subjects. Large leaves are pale green in colour and coarse in appearance. They are not of great significance, although they do help to set off the vivid colouring of the bracts when they appear.

Rich, loam-based soil is essential, and pots not less than 7in (18cm) in diameter will be needed for plants that are intended to become specimens of larger size. Moist conditions and regular feeding are important, and watch for red spider mites, especially around the young leaves that are forming at the tips of each branch.

Acalypha hispida (*main picture right*), with its drooping tail-like red bracts, is a particularly striking plant despite its dull-coloured leaves. By contrast, *A. wilkesiana* (**inset**) is grown for its decorative foliage, for in several varieties there are many colours in a single leaf.

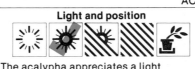
ACALYPHA

Light and position

The acalypha appreciates a light position, but not one which is continually exposed to bright sun.

Temperature range

Cool   Intermediate   Warm

A fairly warm temperature range is required, no lower than 60°F (15°C) and up to 70°F (21°C). Cuttings and young plants require the higher temperatures in the range.

Watering

The plant will flourish if the soil is kept quite moist at all times, which means extra water in summer,

Feeding

This is a voracious plant during the active summer months and it will require plenty of food.

Seasonal care

Winter	Spring	Summer	Autumn

The acalypha is difficult to grow unless the right conditions of warmth and humidity can be maintained.

Soil

Cuttings do well in small pots filled with fresh peat. When repotting becomes necessary, use a loam-based mixture which can sustain the plant during the growth periods.

Aechmea

Originating from tropical South America, this is not only one of the most exotic flowering houseplants, but also one of the most durable. Its foliage is very coarse and edged with quite vicious spines, and its colouring varies from light grey to dark red. The recurving and overlapping leaves form into a natural watertight urn shape, which gives the plant its common name of Urn Plant. In the plant's natural jungle habitat this urn fills with rainwater or heavy dew, which can sustain the plant for many months in the event of drought.

Perhaps the most spectacular time in the life of the aechmea is when, after a number of years, it produces its fascinating bracts. These may vary in shape, but they all reach their high point when they become studded with tiny flowers that are mostly intense blue. Another characteristic of this plant is that it is epiphytic, which means that it grows on trees, by becoming lodged between branches, or around rotting stumps, for example.

Although the commercial grower propagates aechmeas from seed in optimum conditions, this is generally not a very rewarding method for someone with limited indoor facilities. It is much better to remove offsets from the base of mature plants that have flowered and to pot these up individually in a very loose mixture composed almost entirely of peat and leaf mould.

VARIETIES AND PURCHASING

The greenhouse culture for aechmeas is highly specialized and they can take as long as five years to flower. Because the plants occupy space in the greenhouse for so long they are quite expensive to buy. Smaller, cheaper plants which are not in flower can be found but are less attractive. Choose a plant that has bracts showing above the urn shape formed by the leaves, but not one which is so advanced that it is flowering from the bract. **A. rhodocyanea** This variety, also known as *A. fasciata,* is the most suitable for growing at home, having grey-green foliage and a fist-sized bract in a true, clear pink which is dotted with tiny flowers of an intense blue. The great benefit of this plant is that the bract remains colourful for a full six months. When the plant has flowered, the main rosette dies off and smaller plants develop at the base of the main stem. These can be removed and potted up individually, but it may be a year or even longer before a plant propagated in this way will flower. An attractive way of displaying an aechmea is to wrap the roots in damp sphagnum moss and wire it to a natural or chiselled hollow in a piece of bark. **A. fulgens 'Discolor'** This is a much smaller plant than *A. rhodocyanea,* with a more open rosette and leaves with a dull green upper surface, but red underneath. The scarlet bract is also more open, but if it is put in a group of plants, it produces an interesting contrast of colour, shape and texture. The flowers are purple, spread along the stem.

AVOIDING PROBLEMS

Light and position

The Urn Plant is a bromeliad and these usually object to a dark location. In good, strong light with partial sun it will be found that the leaf colouring is bright and attractive. Although the plants are tough, do not place them in draughts or near heating appliances.

Temperature range

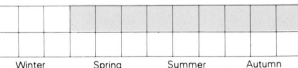

Cool   Intermediate   Warm

The plant is not especially fussy about temperature, and a moderate to warm range of 60°-70°F (15°-21°C) suits it very well. A slight change at either end of this scale will be tolerated but do not subject the plant to extremes of heat or cold. It has no special requirements for humidity but the method of watering will tend to encourage a moist, rather than dry, atmosphere.

Watering

Leave about 1in (2.5cm) of water in the central rosette, changing it every three weeks. Rainwater can be used for this, as the plant is kept moist in the wild by rain collecting in the leaves and running into the urn. Keep the soil just moist.

Feeding

It is not essential to feed this plant, but an occasional liquid feed added to the water will do it no harm. If something seems wrong, do not resort to extra feeding. Check the temperature and look for pests.

Seasonal care

Winter	Spring	Summer	Autumn

Despite its exotically tropical appearance, the Urn Plant is quite easy to care for, requiring only regular, but not excessive, attention to watering. As the plant develops, the old flower bract can be cut away and in time the parent rosette can also be discarded. New rosettes are put into small pots and may be repotted before flowering. The plants are usually trouble free throughout the year, but spotting may be caused by the use of household aerosols in the vicinity of the plant.

Soil

It is vital to provide free drainage through the soil so use an open mixture. Equal parts of fairly coarse leaf mould and peat, worked together with a little fresh sphagnum moss, will be ideal. The plants should not need potting on more than every other year.

PESTS AND DISEASES

In keeping with the general tolerance and easy care of this plant, it is rarely visited by pests.
Mealy bug This may attack older bracts on a mature plant, but is uncommon. Gently remove the bugs with a small toothbrush dipped in methylated spirits.

The leaf texture of an aechmea (*left*) naturally varies. A mottled texture appearing to cut across the leaf is interwoven with broken stripy markings down the length. The heavy green marks, like scratches, which can be seen here are due to rough handling and may also be caused by a cat brushing past the plant and bruising the leaves. Never use a chemical leaf shine on this plant.

Discoloured bract After about seven weeks in flower the bract may darken slightly. Any bad discoloration may mean that the plant is too cold.

Healthy leaf This should be firm and even, arching gracefully from the central stem of the plant.

Healthy plant The curving leaves should be tough, greyish green, and the bract a clear pink with no sign of browning. A fully grown leaf may be 12in (30cm) in length.

Browning leaf A leaf which is becoming brown or shrivelled at the edges or tip may be suffering from conditions that are too hot and dry. Check the moisture in the urn and if the plant is in direct sun, move it to another position.

Aeschynanthus

These are natural trailing plants that produce an abundance of branches to which are attached leathery leaves that are a metallic glossy green in colour. To show them to their best advantage, grow plants in small hanging pots or baskets and confine the planting to one variety of aeschynanthus per pot, rather than combining different varieties or including other kinds of plants.

Cuttings root with little difficulty if placed in a warm propagator. It is best to place five or six cuttings in pots 3in (8cm) in diameter, and to then put three of these plants in a small hanging basket. The result will be a full plant with lots of cascading branches.

Aeschynanthus lobbianus is one of the most popular species and perhaps the easiest to obtain. During mid- to late summer, the branches will carry lovely dark red flowers emerging from interesting cup-shaped calyxes that are a sooty red in colour. Red flowers have a yellow throat, and make for a very attractive plant. There are numerous other species with similar habits and attractive and quite varied flower colouring.

Aeschynanthus lobbianus (*top above*) is ideal for hanging baskets. The beautiful red and yellow flowers (*detail above*) appear in mid- to late summer.

AESCHYNANTHUS

Light and position

These plants like plenty of bright light, but they should not be exposed to direct sunlight for more than 2-3 hours a day.

Feeding

Liquid fertilizer, applied regularly, is desirable.

Temperature range

Cool	Intermediate	Warm

Keep at normal room temperature, as long as the humidity is high. Mist-spray the plant on a daily basis during the flowering season.

Seasonal care

Winter		Spring		Summer		Autumn			

Following summer flowering, these plants may be pruned to a more attractive shape, but it is wise not to be too severe when cutting back. Cuttings a few inches in length can be propagated at any time while the plants are not in flower.

Watering

Water plants plentifully during active growth, moderately at other times.

Soil

Use a peaty mixture when potting plants into large containers.

Aglaonema

Most aglaonema plants are compact and low-growing, with congested leaves borne on short stalks that are produced at soil level. *A. pseudobracteatum* has a more branching habit and is much less common, and therefore more difficult to acquire. An important quality of most aglaonemas is their ability to grow where there is very poor light.

New plants can be propagated at any time by splitting large clumps into smaller sections and potting them independently.

VARIETIES AND PURCHASING

When buying, avoid plants with brown leaf margins, as this shows that the plant has been raised in poor conditions and kept in too cold a temperature. It is best to select a young plant with firm leaves.

A. modestum This is the true Chinese Evergreen, but it is a rather dull plant.
A. crispum **'Silver Queen'** This has blotched silver and green foliage.
A. treubii This has cream and green mottled leaves.

Healthy plant *A. crispum* 'Silver Queen' is an excellent plant for indoor use. It gains its name from the silvery markings of its foliage. Its leaves are usually between 5in (12.5cm) and 6in (15cm) long. The plant looks extremely attractive. Although it does require warm conditions, it will tolerate a very shady location. 'Silver Queen' is one of the most popular aglaonemas, and is well suited to hydroculture.

Types of leaf This leaf from *A. crispum* 'Silver Queen' (***below left***) shows the characteristic silver and green colouring on the foliage. The cream and green leaves of *A. trewbii* (***below***) should be densely packed on the healthy plant.

Healthy plant *A. treubii* (***above***) has mottled cream and green markings on its leaves. Although it is perhaps not so exciting to look at as *A. crispum* 'Silver Queen', it is still relatively popular with house plant enthusiasts.

PROPAGATION

Remove plant from its pot.

Use thumbs to gently divide plant.

Separate into plantlets with more than two leaves.

Pot up shoot in open peat-based compost and cover with a clear pastic bag.

Aglaonema may be propagated in a number of ways. The most popular and the one that probably causes the least amount of damage to the plant is to separate sideshoots from the base of the plant.

In mid-spring to early summer remove the plant from its pot and remove side-shoots that have several leaves. Do not remove any that have only two leaves and, where possible, try to acquire some root, preferably attached to the shoot. A sharp knife may ease the process.

The shoot should then be potted in an open peat-based compost in a 3½in (9cm) pot and covered with a clear plastic bag to conserve moisture. Rooting will take several weeks, even up to a couple of months. Keep the plant at a temperature of 68–70°F (20–21°C) out of direct sunlight.

Apart from being raised from seed propagated at around 75°F (24°C) from late spring, aglaonema can also be propagated from sections of the stem. This technique is suitable for overgrown, untidy and leggy specimens that have outgrown their usefulness.

Stems sections measuring 1½–2in (4–5cm) can be pressed into the surface of the compost until about one-quarter to one-third of the stem is buried. Maintain a temperature of around 75°F (24°C) and keep the compost moist, potting up the plantlets when they are large enough to handle.

PESTS AND DISEASES

Mealy bug The congested leaves and stalks of the aglaonema provide ideal conditions for mealy bug. Rather than spraying with insecticide as normal, it is better to mix the insecticide (malathion) in a watering can and apply through a coarse rose.

Root mealy bug These small pests can only be found by removing the plant from its pot. Apply insecticide solution into the soil. Endosulfan is recommended.

Botrytis This leaf (*left*) shows signs of botrytis. Spray with an appropriate fungicide.
Leaf spot For leaf spot diseases (*below*) spray the plant with an appropriate fungicide.

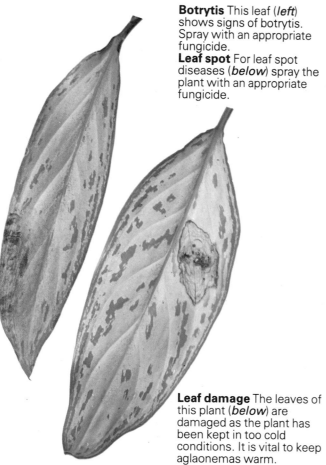

Leaf damage The leaves of this plant (*below*) are damaged as the plant has been kept in too cold conditions. It is vital to keep aglaonemas warm.

AVOIDING PROBLEMS

Light and position

The aglaonema will tolerate poor light with no ill effects, but must not be exposed to direct sunlight as this may scorch the leaves. It is seen to best effect when grouped with other more colourful plants.

Temperature range

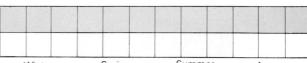

Cool · Intermediate · Warm

This plant must not be placed in cold conditions. A warm room anywhere between 60°-70°F (15°-21°C) is suitable, but an aglaonema will grow more vigorously if the temperature is even higher than this. Any slight chill may cause leaf discoloration. Humidity can be increased by placing trays of moist pebbles under the pots.

Watering

Aglaonemas should be watered regularly so that the potting mixture stays moist. Only the very surface should dry out between waterings. In the winter months the plants will require slightly less water. If the roots become too wet the leaves will begin to wilt.

Feeding

Established plants should be given a liquid feed each time they are watered if they are to flourish well. Again, less food is necessary during the dormant winter period. The fertilizer should be administered in a fairly weak solution.

Seasonal care

Winter · Spring · Summer · Autumn

If kept in suitable conditions, aglaonemas tend to stay healthy. They are susceptible to oil and gas fumes however, and should not be exposed to them. Unsuitable household aerosols used in the vicinity of the plant may cause spotting on the leaves but this can probably be removed by wiping the leaves gently with a damp sponge. Aglaonemas should be kept away from windows and draughts throughout the winter months, and whenever the weather is very cold.

Soil

A peaty mixture is needed for aglaonemas, and repotting should be avoided in winter if possible. The pots that are used should not be too large, as these plants grow best when their roots are confined in quite small containers.

47

Allamanda

Allamandas are very attractive flowering plants with dark green leaves and rich yellow trumpet flowers. They are natural climbing plants but thrive only in the room heated to not less than 60°F (16°C).

With soft yellow flowers, *A. cathartica* will attain a height of some 8ft (2.4m) and will need to be tied to a support – the variety *A.c.* 'Grandiflora' has flowers almost 5in (13cm) wide, but is rare.

With woody stems that can be trained to a support (it is also a very fine free-standing plant), the species *A. neriifolia* produces small bright yellow trumpet-shaped flowers that have no particular season. Foliage is not particularly attractive, but the plant will flower for almost the entire 12 months of the year if moist, warm and shaded conditions are provided. The soil should always be wet, and moisture in the atmosphere is also important. These plants must be fed regularly. Propagate tip cuttings in early spring in a mixture of equal parts peat moss and coarse sand.

Allamandas are shrubby or climbing plants that grow vigorously in warm, moist, shaded conditions. Many species need to be trained to a support, and they are seen at their best when growing against the wall of a garden room or greenhouse. Like all allamandas, *A. cathartica* (*below*) produces clusters of eye-catching trumpet-shaped yellow flowers (*detail right*).

ALLAMANDA		
Light and position  Allamandas like bright light, but they should not be exposed to more than 3-4 hours a day.		**Feeding** Feed established plants regularly, but not in winter when growth is inactive.
Temperature range Cool Intermediate Warm Although plants will tolerate a lower temperature in summer, it is important to maintain a minimum of 65°F (18°C) at other times. Humidity is essential.		**Seasonal care** Winter Spring Summer Autumn Any potting on should be done in the spring or early summer, using a loam-based potting soil. In winter cut plants back by as much as two-thirds.
Watering Keep soil moist at all times. Water moderately during active growth and sparingly in winter.		**Soil** Never allow the soil to dry out excessively.

Anthurium

Anthuriums belong to the same family as the philo-dendrons, which is a reasonably sure indication that they will enjoy moist, humid and warm conditions in preference to dry and cold. There are many different anthuriums, but only three that are really suitable for growing in room conditions. These three – *A. andreanum, A. scherzeranum* and *A. guatemala* – have broadly arrow-shaped leaves that are carried on slender stalks. They all have exotic flowers that remain colourful for many weeks, even when used as cut flowers.

The commercial grower raises new plants from seed. However, this requires special skill and conditions and is not often within the scope of the amateur grower with only limited facilities.

Healthy plant A well-tended anthurium makes a handsome houseplant. A white pot contrasts well with the dark leaves.

AVOIDING PROBLEMS

Light and position

Anthuriums require good, bright light, but if placed in a window they must be protected from the glare of direct sun. The plants are spectacular and one or two varieties become quite large when mature, so can be given a spacious, individual position.

Temperature range

Cool   Intermediate   Warm

Even, warm temperatures of 65°-70°F (18°-21°C) are necessary for a healthy plant and a radical change in the conditions, in winter or at night, will not contribute to its comfort. These are originally tropical plants, so they like high humidity as well as adequate warmth.

Watering

Keep the plant well watered in summer and during the main growing period. Less water is required in winter, but do not allow the soil either to dry out, or to become waterlogged as this will cause the plant to wilt.

Feeding

Give the plant a liquid feed weekly while it is active and reduce the feeding as the growth slows down towards winter. If the plant is dormant in winter, no nourishment is needed.

Seasonal care

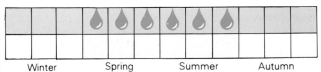

Winter   Spring   Summer   Autumn

Anthuriums are not easy plants to grow, and it is vital to maintain the correct temperature and humidity and to shield them from draughts. Provided these conditions are met, and the plant is neither overwatered nor allowed to thirst, it should do well. Rainwater is preferred when possible and may also be sprayed on the leaves. These may also be cleaned occasionally with a soft sponge, but do not handle soft, new leaves.

Soil

An open potting mixture is needed, composed of equal parts of peat, sphagnum moss and partly rotted leaf mould. To allow the soil to drain properly, place crocks in the pot before filling it.

Natural and unnatural deaths
The *A. churchurianus* (**above**) died naturally; the *A. scherzeranum* (**below**) is suffering from the fungus disease, botrytis brought on by cold and damp. Though anthuriums love moisture, problems will soon arise if very wet conditions are allied to a low temperature.

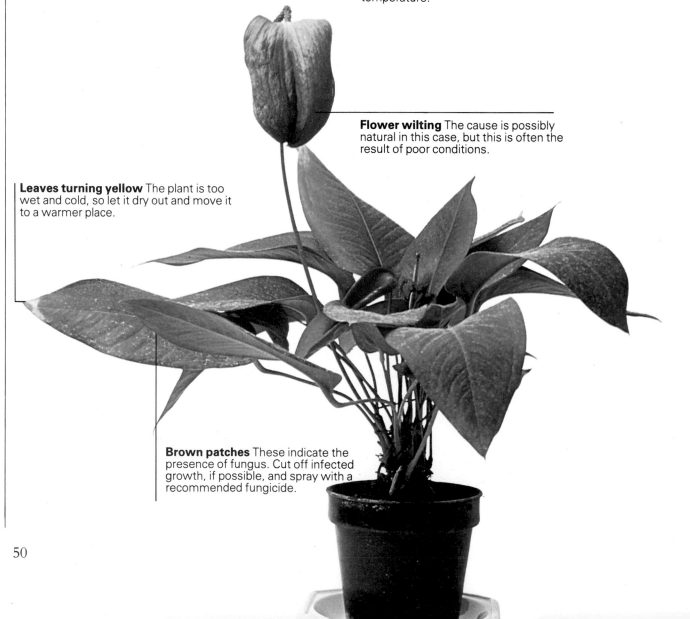

Flower wilting The cause is possibly natural in this case, but this is often the result of poor conditions.

Leaves turning yellow The plant is too wet and cold, so let it dry out and move it to a warmer place.

Brown patches These indicate the presence of fungus. Cut off infected growth, if possible, and spray with a recommended fungicide.

Aphelandra

Having greyish green foliage with silver markings, the aphelandra is one of the more attractive foliage plants. Its appearance is further enhanced when colourful yellow bracts are produced at the top of each growing stem. The small, yellow, tubular flowers are fairly insignificant, but the bracts remain colourful for many months, making the aphelandra a spectacular, long-lasting plant. There are now two worthwhile varieties of the original plant, which is indigenous to Mexico. *A. squarrosa* 'Brockfeld' is the more robust plant, while *A. squarrosa* 'Dania' is more compact and if anything flowers more prolifically.

New plants are propagated by removing the top section of the stem with two opposite pairs of leaves attached, or by removing a pair of lower leaves with about 1in (2.5cm) of stem above and below where the leaf stalk is attached. Use peat and sand mixture and ensure the temperature is not less than 70°F (21°C) and the atmosphere is humid.

PROPAGATION

Aphelandra may be propagated from stem or tip cuttings in mid-spring to early summer for best success, although it is possible to root cuttings through the summer.

Tip cuttings measuring up to 3in (7.5cm), or stem cuttings consisting of a pair of leaves with about 2in (5cm) of stem below the leaves, may be used.

Dip the base of the cutting in hormone rooting powder and insert one per pot into a 4¼in (11cm) pot in a peat-based potting compost. If the leaves of the stem cutting are too large, trim off the tips with a sharp pair of scissors.

Cover the cutting and pot with a clear plastic bag and keep out of direct sunlight at a temperature of around 70–75°F (21–24°C) for up to about six weeks while the cutting is developing a root system.

Once rooted, remove the bag and grow the plant on, keeping the compost moist and potting on as required.

Tip cuttings tend to produce a more balanced plant with a single stem, whereas stem cuttings can sometimes produce a plant that may look a little out of balance if one side-shoot develops before the other.

AVOIDING PROBLEMS

Light and position

The aphelandra is an exception among flowering plants in that it does not require full light in order to flourish successfully. Good light is needed, but not full sun. The plant should be given plenty of room in which to spread its leaves.

Temperature range

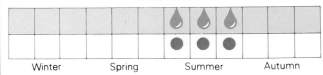

Cool   Intermediate   Warm

Warm temperatures of 65°-70°F (18°-21°C) are essential and this is a plant which is particularly vulnerable to a cool environment. A humid atmosphere is also appreciated and the pot can be packed with moist peat or left to stand on a tray of pebbles if the room is normally dry.

Watering

The aphelandra must be watered regularly, although overwatering may encourage botrytis and should be avoided. If the plant is allowed to dry out the leaves will rapidly fall. Less water can be given for a few weeks after flowering to allow a period of rest.

Feeding

This plant produces a mass of roots and is a heavy feeder. Liquid fertilizer should be supplied through the soil and it is possible to double the recommended strength of the feed without harming the plant.

Seasonal care

Winter   Spring   Summer   Autumn

The only real variation in the treatment of this plant is after the flowering, when it can be kept at the cooler range of its preferred temperatures and given less food and water while it rests. It is not a plant which can survive neglect but provided its basic needs are satisfied, it is not as difficult to keep as is sometimes imagined.

Soil

Pot on an aphelandra soon after purchasing, using a potting mixture with a high proportion of loam. The plant must be firmly potted and at a later stage can be potted on at any time of year other than the coldest winter months.

VARIETIES AND PURCHASING

***A. squarrosa* 'Dania'** This is the most readily available type of Zebra Plant. It is also the variety best suited to normal room conditions as it needs less care and growing space than some of the other kinds of aphelandra. It is quite difficult to make *A. squarrosa* 'Dania' flower, but the dark green leaves have very pretty silvery markings.
***A. squarrosa* 'Louisae'** (*see illustration left*). The leaves of this plant are 8–12in (20–30cm) long and it has broad, conspicuous orange-yellow flower bracts. When buying this variety (which is also known as Saffron Spike) make sure that the flowers are not too far advanced. The actual flowers should not be visible along the edge of the bract.
***A. squarrosa* 'Brockfeld'** This is a compact plant with dark green leaves.
A. chamissoniana The variety has close-set leaves which are 4–5in (10–12.5cm) long. Its flower bracts are yellow, narrow and pointed.

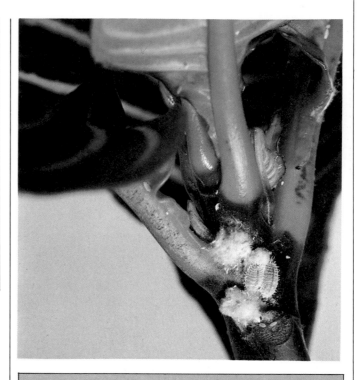

Scale insects These pests (*below*) are encased in a white waxy coating. They suck the sap out of the plant.
Botrytis Aphelandras must not be kept in wet and airless conditions or they may contract this fungus (*bottom*). This can be controlled by improving the general conditions and applying a suitable fungicide.

Diseased leaves Mealy bugs (*right*) sometimes attack the stems and roots of aphelandras. They are distinctive for their white woolly looking coverings and can be removed with insecticide.

PESTS AND DISEASES

Despite its tough appearance, the aphelandra is vulnerable to a number of pests and should be examined regularly to make sure it is pest free.
Scale insect These look like miniature limpets and are skin-coloured when young and dark brown or yellow when mature. They attach themselves to the undersides of the plant's leaves and to its stem. Excreta falling on lower leaves encourages sooty mould fungus. This blocks the pores of the leaves and considerably weakens the plant. Scale insects can be removed by wiping the leaves with a firm sponge dipped in a pesticide solution.
Alternatively, the plant can be sprayed with malathion. This should be done outdoors as malathion has an unpleasant smell.
Aphids These are frequently found on the bracts of the aphelandra. They can be removed fairly easily with one of the standard insecticides.
Sciarid fly These tiny insects are commonly known as fungus gnats. They tend to occur when the potting mixture becomes excessively wet and sour, depositing their larvae in the soil. Most of them are not harmful but one or two kinds may damage the roots of the plant. Dispose of them by drenching the soil with a liquid insecticide such as malathion. More than one application may be needed.
Springtails These pests are so called because they jump about on the top of the soil. They are white, wingless insects, usually harmless but occasionally gnawing at the stems of young plants. They can be removed in the same way as fungus gnats.
Red spider mite This is not a common problem, but red spiders will attack aphelandras that are growing in very hot and dry locations. They can be controlled by spraying the undersides of the leaves with insecticides.
Black leg This is a fungus that attacks cuttings at rooting stage. Affected plants should be thrown away.

Healthy plant Avoid buying plants which have a yellow look to their foliage (*right*). The bracts tend to attract greenfly and the leaves scale insects so both should be checked.

Aralia elegantissima

This plant is also recognized by another name – *Dizygotheca elegantissima,* which is often called the False Aralia. The common name is also confusing as it belongs to at least one other very popular indoor plant. However, despite the problems of its name, *A. elegantissima* is one of the most distinctive and attractive houseplants when it has been well grown. The foliage is very dark green, almost black, and it has a delicate 'filigree' appearance. The plant's leaf stalks are attached to stout central stems and the leaves appear evenly around the plant as it increases in height. It is quite possible for plants to reach a height of 10ft (3m) even though their roots are confined to pots that are little more than 10in (25cm) in diameter.

New plants are grown from seed that is easily germinated in a temperature of around 70°F (21°C). An odd characteristic of this plant is that delicately constructed leaves are produced at the seed stage and are retained by the plant until it reaches a height of about 7ft (2m). A complete change then takes place as each new leaf produced has a much coarser and less attractive appearance. This is the stage at which the plant develops its more tree-like habit. Nevertheless, due to the rather delicate nature of this plant, it rarely achieves tree proportions while confined to average room conditions.

PESTS AND DISEASES

Scale insect These are waxy, shell-like creatures, dark brown in colour. The insects may be hard to spot as their colour blends with the woody stem of the plant, but it is important to treat them promptly as the plant may become very badly infested. They suck vital juices from the plant and it will eventually wither. The most effective method of treatment is to wipe the insects away firmly with a sponge soaked in malathion. Wear rubber gloves for protection when handling insecticides. Spraying is difficult on a plant with such an open arrangement of leaves.

Mealy bug These pests are white and similar in shape to small woodlice. They can be treated in the same way as scale insects (*see illustration right above*).

Root mealy bug These are also white bugs which, as the name implies, attack the roots of the plant within the soil. They may be unnoticed for some time, but if the plant becomes mysteriously unwell, remove the plant from its pot to check for root mealy bugs. Soaking the soil thoroughly with malathion solution is the best remedy. The insecticide can also be sprayed directly onto the bugs, but this may not be quite as effective. A solution of pirimiphos-methyl can be used instead of malathion for soaking the soil.

Aphids These are small, soft insects, light green in colour. They cluster on the stems and new leaf growth of the plant, sucking out the sap. This undermines the vitality of the plant and will cause weak or distorted growth. To remove aphids, run a finger and thumb along the stem or leaf firmly enough to dislodge the insects, but be careful not to damage the tender new growth of the plant.

AVOIDING PROBLEMS

Light and position

Small plants may be placed on a windowsill, provided they are not exposed to direct sunlight and the position is not subject to draughts. Larger, mature plants may prefer a place on the floor or a table in a room which receives plenty of light and is fairly warm.

Temperature range

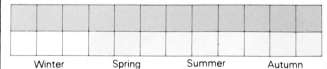

Cool   Intermediate   Warm

This plant generally prefers warm conditions and should be kept in a minimum temperature of 65°F (18°C). It may survive in cooler temperatures but will not maintain a continual healthy growth. Neither does it enjoy dry surroundings so humidity must be maintained, by standing the pot in a tray of damp pebbles if extra moisture is needed.

Watering

Water the soil regularly but not to excess. The top two thirds of the soil can be allowed to dry out before more water is needed. The watering may be evenly distributed throughout the year and occasional spraying of the leaves can be beneficial.

Feeding

Give the plant weak, liquid feeds at the same time as watering. It will need less food during the winter. The time when it needs the most care in this respect is during the period of active growth in summer.

Seasonal care

Winter	Spring	Summer	Autumn

There is very little seasonal variation in the treatment of an *Aralia elegantissima.* It should be kept moist all year round but should not be subjected to any excessive conditions, whether wet or dry. A plant which is kept in a window should be moved during the hottest summer months to avoid direct sun.

Soil

Repot established plants in early summer, using a peaty mixture for the soil. This plant is slow growing and should be transferred to a larger pot about once every two years. When it has reached a 10in (25cm) pot, simply top it up with peat mixture each spring.

Mealy bug This is a small, white pest which is common and persistent. The bugs appear like tiny lumps of cotton wool on stem joints and the undersides of leaves. Mealy bugs multiply quickly and must be dealt with thoroughly. Pick off as many of the bugs as you can. Because the aralia has an open framework of narrow leaves, wear rubber gloves and sponge the malathion onto the plant to ensure it gets to the right places.

Healthy plant The *A. elegantissima* is very attractive when it is well grown. Each leaf has a delicate filigreed appearance (*inset*). When buying, choose a plant which has dark green foliage right down to the surface of the soil. This is a sign of careful cultivation.

Araucaria

In its natural home and throughout the tropics this coniferous tree can reach the majestic height of around 100ft (30m), and is one of the most handsome examples of plant life. With roots confined to a pot, a maximum height of 10ft (3m) can be expected after about 10 years if the plant is being grown indoors. The leaves, produced in layers at the top of the plant, are a bright green and they look like typical pine needles. All commercial plants are grown from seed that is exported from New Zealand.

PESTS AND DISEASES

Aphids The Norfolk Island Pine may suffer from these. They will settle on the soft top leaves of young plants, but can be easily eradicated with most insecticide sprays.
Mealy bug These are easy to spot on the araucaria's open foliage and can also be treated with insecticide spray. Alternatively, they can be wiped from their perches with a cotton wool swab that has been soaked in methylated spirits.

Healthy plant Also called the Norfolk Island Pine, this plant (*left*) was originally discovered in the South Pacific island of that name. It is an attractive evergreen conifer with fairly heavy branches that stick out horizontally from the central stem. Araucarias can be used as miniature Christmas trees, but any decorations used should not be too heavy or they may damage the plant. The new foliage will be a glossy bright green that darkens slightly as the tree ages. Needles can grow to ¾in (19mm) long, forming groups that make up the tiers of each frond. In a healthy plant, the central stem should become tough enough to support the weight of all the branches, without the need for any artificial supports. Large araucarias are often displayed in porches, halls or on landings, where they can look very striking. They tend to be less popular for mixed displays.

Unhealthy plant Araucarias tend to lose some lower leaves as they age. If the plant is drooping as well as dropping leaves (*right*), it is likely to be suffering from too much water, too much heat or lack of light. A plant in this condition should also be checked thoroughly for evidence of pest infestation.

56

VARIETIES AND PURCHASING

Araucaria plants are usually sold in small pots when they have reached a height of about 10in (25cm). Larger ones are sometimes available, but they tend to be much more expensive. Select plants that look fresh and free from blemishes. *A. excelsa* is the only variety that can be grown inside, but it has a very well-known cousin, the *A. araucana* or Monkey Puzzle Tree. This is often found in gardens and has more prickly foliage.

AVOIDING PROBLEMS

Light and position

Good light is essential to this plant, but take care to protect a young plant from direct sunlight. At an early stage an araucaria may enjoy the company of other plants, but it will grow to quite a size and a mature plant makes a feature if displayed alone.

Temperature range

Cool   Intermediate   Warm

The plant requires cool, though not draughty, conditions in a temperature range of 50°-60°F (10°-15°C). In a higher temperature the needle growth becomes thin and weak, whereas in a cool atmosphere they will look healthy and stand out proudly from the stem.

Watering

Araucarias prefer soil on the dry side so be careful not to overwater them. Let the soil almost dry out between waterings. Water at the top of the pot so the moisture drains freely through the soil.

Feeding

Feed the plant with weak fertilizer each time it is watered, rather than giving a heavy feed at less frequent intervals. If the plant continues to grow through the winter it can be fed continually, but leave it alone if it seems dormant.

Seasonal care

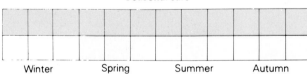

Winter   Spring   Summer   Autumn

This is quite a hardy plant and provided it is not kept in an atmosphere which is too warm and dry it should not give problems. It follows the usual pattern of many plants in needing the most attention during a growing period in spring and summer, but minimal food and water in the winter. When the plant has grown to a height of about 4ft (1.3m) it will shed the lower branches. A leggy plant can be cut back and the cuttings used for propagation.

Soil

A loam-based potting mixture is essential at all stages of growth. The plant can be kept in a small pot for the first year, transferred to a 5in (12.5cm) pot for two years and so on up to a 10in (25cm) diameter pot, when it can be sustained by feeding.

Aspidistra lurida

In the business of houseplants, new varieties come along from time to time, eventually making the grade and being retained, but the aspidistra is a plant that, although popular in Victorian times, now appears to be out of favour. It is very easy to care for, but is slow to mature, and so is not a commercial proposition for plant suppliers. Luckily there are still many aspidistras around, a number of which have actually survived since the Victorian era.

New plants are made by dividing up established clumps and potting them individually. Either single pieces or clusters of leaves can be potted, the latter producing better plants more quickly.

VARIETIES AND PURCHASING

Choose a plant of full appearance with lots of stems and an elegant arching shape. Do not buy plants with split or speckled leaves or leaves that have been cut back.

A. lurida (or *A. elatior*) This is the only species in cultivation and is known as the Cast Iron Plant because it will survive in tough conditions.
A. l. 'Variegata' Very like the parent plant, this has white or cream stripes on some of the leaves.

Healthy plant Seen at their best, as lone specimens in an attractive china pot, aspidistras provide a fine display of dark green or green and white striped arching leaves. They need little care and in particular should never be polished with chemical leaf shine.

AVOIDING PROBLEMS

Light and position

Aspidistras will grow in very little light but will do best in a moderate light – in a window with not much sun, for example. The striped variety will need more light but neither type of plant should be placed in direct sunlight as this will soon scorch the leaves.

Temperature range

Cool | Intermediate | Warm

These plants will usually thrive in a wide range of temperatures – between 55°-70°F (13°-21°C) – and they can therefore be kept almost anywhere in the house. They will even survive below this range provided that they are kept free from frost.

Watering

Water these plants moderately throughout the year, allowing the top two-thirds of the soil to dry out before watering again. Water less in the winter months.

Feeding

These plants do not require much feeding. Apply liquid fertilizer once every two weeks in the growing period but stop feeding for the rest of the season if the leaves start to split.

Seasonal care

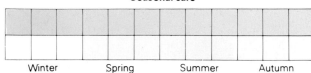

Winter | Spring | Summer | Autumn

One of the main advantages of the aspidistra is that it requires much less care than most other houseplants. Water it a little more frequently in the growing period and feed it occasionally. The plant will need less water in winter.

New plants can be grown by splitting off clumps of stems in the spring when the pot is overcrowded. Each section of the rhizome will need at least two leaves. Do not feed the new plants until the following spring.

Soil

Use a loam-based mixture. Aspidistras rarely need repotting and can be top-dressed once they reach the best size for the pot for several years. Very old plants are best left in their original pots. Remove new shoots and some roots if necessary.

PESTS AND DISEASES

These plants rarely suffer from pests, which normally find the leathery leaves too tough to penetrate.
Mealy bug These may occasionally attack this plant. If white woolly patches appear remove them one at a time with a piece of cotton wool dipped in methylated spirits or spray with a systemic insecticide.
Red spider mite These will cause the leaves to turn brown and will produce white webs on their undersides. Spray with systemic insecticide. Most leaf problems are caused by too much sunlight or overfeeding.

Damaged leaves The Cast Iron Plant's leaves will split if the plant is overfed. If this happens stop feeding for the rest of the season and start again the following year, cutting down the amount given to half that originally recommended.

The brown mark on the leaf (*above*) is caused by direct heat from a radiator. Make sure that these plants are protected from heat sources and too high a temperature.

Azalea indica

There is nothing that can compare with *A. indica* as a specimen plant in full flower. The oval-shaped leaves are small, coarse and evergreen; the flowers, which grow at the ends of branches, may be either single or double, with their colour ranging from pristine white to dull red. There are also splendid multi-coloured varieties. Most of the better plants start their life in Belgium, from where they are shipped all over the world. Azaleas are always potted and grown on to flowering stage before being despatched to the retailer.

Healthy plant One of the most beautiful of the winter flowering plants, many azaleas (*left and opposite*) naturally flower in spring but are often forced into bloom for the Christmas season. They are very slow growing plants, which is one reason why they are often expensive to purchase. Whether situated indoors in individual pots, or outside in large groups, azaleas always look attractive with their rich clusters of pastel or deeply hued colours displayed against deep green foliage.

VARIETIES AND PURCHASING

If carefully tended, the azalea can be one of the most rewarding of all the flowering houseplants. Because they are one of the few plants which flower in winter, they are usually seen in abundance in florists' shops from late autumn onwards. Selecting a healthy specimen is important if the plant is to survive. A healthy plant will be clean and bright in appearance. Some of its flowers should be open, but there should also be an abundance of buds. Tempting as it may be, avoid plants which have opened entirely. On the other hand, avoid those with small, under-developed buds, or no buds at all. When lifted, the pot should feel heavy and wet, which is how it should remain for the rest of the plant's life.

A. indica This is a common azalea and the one which is most easily available. It includes many variations of colour and is usually chosen for this quality and its general decorative appearance. *A. indica* needs a humid environment and should be sprayed with lime-free water every day.
A. obtusa This plant is known as the Japanese Kurume. It is not as easy to force into bloom as *A. indica* and is thus not available in shops until its natural flowering period in late winter. *A. obtusa* has small flowers that nestle among the leaves of the plant. It makes a fine potted plant with its clear, pink flowers. It can be put in the garden following indoor flowering, whereas *A. indica* must be carefully guarded from frost.

1 Remove 2–3in (5–7.5cm) tip cuttings.

2 Carefully remove lower leaves.

3 After dipping base of cutting in hormone rooting powder, insert one per 2¼–3½in (6–9cm) pot.

4 Cover cutting with clear plastic bag.

PROPAGATION

The Indian azalea is not that easy to propagate successfully, but is worth attempting from late spring to early summer.

Dip 2–3in (5–7.5cm) tip cuttings into hormone rooting powder and insert one per 2¼–3½in (6–9cm) pot of a peat-based seed and cutting compost or low-lime compost with a lower pH (higher level of acidity).

Cover each cutting with a clear polythene bag or, alternatively, mist regularly to reduce water loss from the foliage. Maintain a temperature of 68–70°F (20–21°C), keeping the cuttings in light shade.

Rooting may take up to three months, after which the rooted cuttings may be potted up in a 3½–4¼in (9–11cm) pot of a peat-based low-lime compost, watering where possible with rainwater to avoid the damaging effects of calcium deposits in tap water.

AVOIDING PROBLEMS

Light and position

Azaleas can be grown both indoors and out, and in both cases need a light location out of direct sun. If there is danger of frost, azaleas must be brought indoors.

So they will survive from one year to the next, azaleas should be put outside during the summer months.

Temperature range

Cool   Intermediate   Warm

Azaleas prefer cool temperatures of between 50°-60°F (10°-15°C) which will ensure that the plants continue to flower abundantly.

When moved indoors, the temperature in the room should not be allowed to rise above 60°F (10°C) or the plants will dry out.

Watering

When in flower, azaleas need copious amounts of lime-free water which should be given every two days. Never let a plant

dry out; check it at least twice a week. If dry, plunge into a bucket of tepid water until beads of moisture appear on the topsoil.

Feeding

A weak liquid fertilizer given at regular intervals will help maintain lush, green foliage, but

avoid heavy applications. When in flower, add fertilizer to the water about every two weeks.

Seasonal care

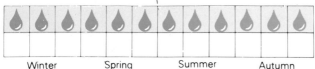

Winter   Spring   Summer   Autumn

Much greater than the danger of pests and diseases is that of neglect, especially neglecting to water the plants adequately. At all stages of development, whether indoors or out, the roots of the azalea must be kept wet. In late

spring the plants can be moved outside. Plunge the pots to their rims in a bed of wet peat in a shady location. Bring the plants indoors before the first frost. Avoid pruning as this will result in fewer flowers the following year.

Soil

Potting should be done in the spring with a mixture of peat with a small amount of rotted leaves which make the mixture acid

rather than alkaline. Press the mixture very firmly around the rootball, water it thoroughly and place the plant in a shady location.

PESTS AND DISEASES

Azaleas are prone to few pests and diseases, which makes them easier to care for than other plants. There are, however, signs of ill-health which should be heeded. If the leaves dry and fall, the environment is too hot and dry. Spray the plant with lime-free water and move it to a cooler place. Buds which fail to open mean the plant is either in a draught or waterlogged. Move to a new location and water less frequently.

Dehydration This will quickly kill an otherwise healthy azalea. It is essential that these plants be adequately watered at all times of the year. Symptoms include faded and wilting flowers and leaves. Move the plant away from heat and direct sun. If badly affected, plunge the pot to its rim in a bucket of tepid water and let it sit until beads of moisture appear on the topsoil. Remove the plant and allow it to drain.

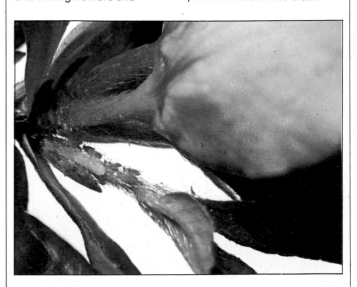

Aphids These may be found on the soft, new leaves of an azalea, but they are not very troublesome and can be easily controlled by spraying with any one of several insecticides, including malathion or pirimiphos-methyl, which will usually destroy the pests very quickly. Remember that a plant newly sprayed or dusted with insecticide must not be exposed to full sunlight.

Beaucarnea

There is only one houseplant in the *Beaucarnea* genus. A relative newcomer to the European indoor-plant scene, *Beaucarnea recurvata* is a tough plant that will tolerate much ill-treatment (though not low temperature) without being unduly affected.

B. recurvata is indigenous to Mexico. Its common name in America is Bottle Palm; in Europe it has become known as the Pony Tail plant. The first name refers to the bulbous bottle base that older plants develop, while the name Pony Tail derives from the way in which the stiff, recurving leaves bend over in a way that is not unlike the tail of a well-endowed pony. Leaves are narrow, brittle, dark glossy green in colour.

This species is accustomed to growing in very arid conditions. Water plants well during the spring and summer, but because they hold moisture in their bulbous stems, give little or no water during the winter. No fertilizer is necessary during the summer, but mature plants must be fed at weekly intervals during the summer months. Mealy bug can occasionally be a problem.

BEAUCARNEA

Light and position

Grow plants in bright indirect light; some direct sun is beneficial.

Temperature range

Cool — Intermediate — Warm

Beaucarneas will flourish in average room temperature. A minimum temperature of 50°F (16°C) is necessary in winter.

Watering

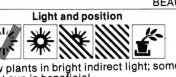

Water thoroughly, then leave until compost is moderately dry. Do not overwater.

Feeding

Plants do not demand much feeding. Provide a weak liquid fertilizer in spring and summer.

Seasonal care

Winter — Spring — Summer — Autumn

These are easy-care plants and require little attention. Repot them in spring if necessary.

Soil

Use a loam-based compost.

Beaucarnea recurvata (*above*) is a tough plant with an unusual appearance. The stiff, brittle leaves grow up out of a bulbous base, giving the plant its two common names of Pony Tail and Bottle Palm. This houseplant suffers from few problems and is undemanding as long as it is kept at a reasonable temperature.

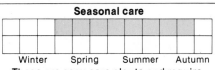

Begonia

Among the most exotic of all foliage plants, the *B. rex* can have many colour combinations on the upper sides of its leaves, while the undersides are mainly reddish brown. The leaves remain healthy for a reasonable time after they have been cut from the plant, making them useful material for inclusion in more colourful flower arrangements.

New plants can be raised from leaf cuttings, for which there are two methods of preparation. The first and simplest way is to remove a firm and unblemished leaf and cut the veins on its back in several places with a sharp knife, scalpel or razor blade. The leaf should then be placed, plain side down, on a bed of moist peat and sand in a shallow box or pan, with a few small pebbles on the leaf to hold it in position. The new plants will grow out of the knife cuttings. The other method is to cut up the mature leaf into sections about the size of a large postage stamp and place these about 1in (2.5cm) apart on a similar bed of peat and sand. From then on, the temperature must not fall below 70°F (21°C) and the atmosphere should be moist but not heavily saturated.

Healthy plant A *B. rex* (*left*) is kept for the beauty of its colourful leaves, and for these to show to best advantage, the plant should have a compact shape. The effect is undermined by straggling stems and untidy, formless growth. If the soil is kept too wet (*below*) the leaves droop and turn brown. This is more likely to happen in winter, when temperatures are low and the plant needs less water as it is not so active.
Botrytis (*right*) is a fungal disease which develops when conditions are generally too damp and stagnant. Cut away affected leaves and remove mouldy compost from the pot. Spray the plant with dichloran.

with just a few plants you can make a highly decorative display. The colours range through dark red to delicate pink, dark and light green and subtle silvery greys. They can be combined with other foliage plants to provide interest in a predominantly green arrangement, or with flowering plants which will complement the varied hues. Some of the common names given to these plants are descriptive of their festive appearance – Yuletide, Merry Christmas, Silver Queen – and although the individual plants are not long lasting, with the proper care they will give about two years of healthy growth and can be propagated quite easily from leaf cuttings. The common name of the *B. rex* is Fan Plant.

Foliage begonias These exist in such a variety of colour combinations and different leaf markings that

VARIETIES AND PURCHASING

When buying a begonia of any type – whether foliage, those with woody, trailing stems known as the cane types, or a flowering variety – always look for a clean, unblemished plant, making sure there is no sign of pests or root damage.

B. rex The varieties of these attractive foliage types are too numerous to mention. Visit a retailer with a good selection and choose the most pleasing. If the plant is quite large and crammed in a small pot, be sure to repot it as soon as possible or the plant will deteriorate through lack of nutrition from the soil.

B. glaucophylla This is one of the cane-type begonias, a plant of natural trailing habit, with light green leaves. In late winter and early spring it produces clusters of orange flowers.

B. haageana Another cane variety, this plant has brownish leaves with a hairy texture and pale pink flowers. The plants are easy to manage, becoming very bushy and reaching a height of up to 6ft (2m) in time. The flowers appear almost continuously.

B. 'President Carnot' This is probably the best of the cane-type begonias. It has brownish green leaves and during many months produces large clusters of pink flowers. Properly cared for, it can achieve a height of 6–8ft (2–2.5m).

B. hiemalis 'Reiger' This is a flowering begonia with soft and brittle growth which is easily damaged. Inspect the leaves to make sure there is no sign of botrytis and choose a plant with plenty of buds and only a few flowers fully open, so that the best is still to come.

B. Tuberhybrida These can be bought as pot plants or as tubers to be potted. Select firm tubers which are clean and healthy. If choosing a growing plant, look for one with a few buds about to open so the colour of the flowers can be determined. A mixture of unnamed varieties can be bought quite cheaply. To take up serious cultivation of these plants, take advice from a specialist grower and go to see the plants at their best in a good, comprehensive flower show.

There is a large variety of begonias which creep or climb and almost all of them have decorative foliage and long-lasting, colourful flowers. Many can grow to a height of 6–8ft (2–2.5m), while others are shrubby or trailing plants. These begonias are not popular with the commercial grower in spite of being easy to grow, probably because they are rather difficult plants to pack and transport.

Given proper care, there are few plants that can produce flowers quite as spectacular as the tuberous begonias when they are grown as pot plants. The best of these are invariably grown from tubers, and good-quality, named varieties can be very expensive. Tubers are started into growth in early spring in boxes filled with moist peat, at a temperature around 65°F (18°C). When clusters on the shoots and a few leaves have formed, the young plants are transferred to 5in (12.5cm) pots filled with a peaty mixture in which they may be grown for the season, or more vigorous plants can be advanced when they are well rooted to pots of 7in (17cm) in diameter.

Healthy plant Flowering cane-type begonias (*above left*) are beautiful plants, with their rich leaves and clustering, delicate flowers. The begonias need regular feeding and sufficient water or they may suffer from starvation. The leaves of a starved *B. Tuberhybrida* (*above*) wither and become yellow, with brown, curling edges, and the flowers also suffer from browning. Discoloration of the leaf tips and the deterioration of the flowers are also seen here in *B. solonanthea* (*left*). Mildew (*far left*) may form on plants in a badly ventilated environment. It is not too damaging but is unsightly on the plant. Remove badly affected parts and spray the plant with dinocap or dichloran.

Healthy plant *B. hiemalis* 'Reiger' (*above right*) is an exotic, colourful variety which, given good care, will flower consistently during its life. The heavy green leaves give a rich contrast with the luxurious red flowers. Botrytis (*right*) attacks a plant which is kept in conditions which are too damp. It is an unpleasant grey mould which forms on leaves and stems. Cut away the most heavily affected leaves and spray the plant with dichloran. Also, remove any dank or mouldy compost and replace it with fresh. Flower petals which drop into the leaves and remain there to rot (*far right*) also cause this sort of disease in the plant, so they should be cleared away from leaves and soil regularly.

There is a completely new strain of begonia that goes variously under the names of 'Reiger' or 'Schwabenland'. As the names suggest, it originated in Europe. Initially, they were mostly red with single flowers, but now they are available in many colours with both single and double flowers. The foliage is glossy green and very dense, so that there are many branching stems, all of which bear flower clusters providing a rare wealth of colour. They are ideal room plants that can flower throughout the year, though fewer flowers are produced in winter.

New plants are raised from cuttings. These should be from the top of the stem with two or three leaves attached and all the flowers removed. A mixture of peat and sand and a temperature of around 70°F (21°C) are needed.

AVOIDING PROBLEMS

Light and position

Fibrous-rooted and rhizomatous begonias, grown primarily for their foliage, require bright light but not direct sunlight.

Windowsills which are not too cold are best. Tuberous begonias need bright, indirect light all the year round.

Temperature range

Cool Intermediate Warm

In active growth periods, fibrous-rooted, rhizomatous, and tuberous begonias all do well in normal room temperatures of around 60°F (15°C). Those with winter rest periods should be kept at the same level, but no lower. In winter, dormant

tuberous types should be kept at 55°F (13°C). In normal conditions, cane types should be kept at 55°F-70°C (13°-21°C); *B. hiemalis reiger* around 60°F (15°C); *B. rex*, 60°-70°F (15°-21°C), and *B. tuberhybrid* 55°-65°F (13°-18°C).

Watering

Begonias do not like dry air. The plants can be stood in their pots on moist pebbles, or, if hanging, saucers of water can be suspended beneath. During

active growth, water moderately allowing the top inch (2.5cm) of soil to dry out. Reduce watering as growth slows down.

Feeding

For actively growing plants, apply a standard liquid fertilizer every two weeks. Cane types should be liquid fed, erring on the side of too

much rather than too little. *B. hiemalis, B. rex,* and *B. tuberhybrid* should all be fed a weak mixture with each watering.

Seasonal care

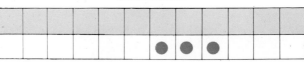

Winter Spring Summer Autumn

In winter, *B. rex* requires limited watering. Cane types require year-round attention with dying petals and leaves removed to avoid fungus. *B. hiemalis reiger* needs less watering in winter, but avoid overwatering at all times. When older plants have passed their prime, trim them and use the

pieces for propagation. After flowering in late summer, *B. tuberhybrid* should have the foliage removed and the corm stored in a frost-free place in dry peat until early spring. When in leaf, the plant requires copious watering.

Soil

For *B. rex*, use peaty mixtures and keep the plants in pots large enough for new growth. *B hiemalis reiger* does best in

mixtures without soil; avoid repotting into pots too large. With cane types, use a loam-based mixture.

PROPAGATION

Remove mature leaf with sharp knife.

Carefully cut leaf into postage stamp-sized pieces.

Having cut leaf, lightly dust undersides of leaf pieces with hormone rooting powder.

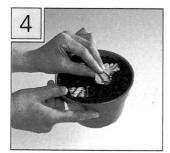

Lay leaf pieces gently on surface of compost.

Use sharp knife to remove 3–4in (7.5–10cm) tip cutting.

Hold stem gently and dip in hormone rooting powder.

Insert cutting, one per 2¼–3½in (6–9cm) pot.

Cover cutting with clear plastic bag.

The **Begonia rex** may be propagated by a most unusual procedure. During spring and summer the plant may be propagated by selecting a mature leaf, taking care not to use a leaf that is too old. Using a very sharp knife, cut the leaf into roughly postage stamp-sized pieces, taking care not to bruise the tissue or cut any fingers.

Dip the cut surfaces across the main veins into hormone rooting powder. The pieces may then be laid on the surface of a seed tray or 5½in (14cm) pan filled with seed and cutting compost or gently pressed into the surface, ensuring that the cut vein is in close contact with the compost.

Cover the leaf pieces with clear plastic, glass or polythene and maintain a temperature of around 70°F (21°C) until rooting has taken place and small plantlets have formed. Regularly inspect the leaf squares and rapidly discard any that are showing signs of rotting off. If this occurs you may need to use a fungicide to avoid further losses.

Once growth occurs the cover may be removed and the plantlets grown on until about 1½in (2.5cm) tall. They may then be gently separated and potted up singly in a 3½in (9cm) pot of a peat-based potting compost.

Begonia Elatior may be propagated from tip cuttings with a small section of stem attached.

The tip cutting may be prepared by using a sharp knife to cut cleanly to remove a tip cutting of 3–4in (7.5–10cm). The cut surface should then be lightly dusted with hormone rooting powder and dibbled one per pot into a 2¼–3½in (6–9cm) pot of seed and cutting compost. Although not really necessary, support may be supplied by a small stick to keep the leaf secure while rooting takes place.

A clear plastic bag placed over each cutting will help to increase humidity and more rapid rooting.

Keeping the cutting at 68–70°F (20–21°C), rooting should take place within about a month, after which the cutting will grow to produce plantlets.

If you wish to build up your stock the plantlets may be separated once large enough to handle and potted up singly in a 3½in (9cm) pot, using a peat-based potting compost, and grown on before being potted on in the final pot.

Alternatively, the clump of plantlets may be potted up into a 4¼in (11cm) pot, although this may tend to lead to a crowded plant of varied habit.

Take cuttings in spring or summer. Plants propagated in spring will flower the same year.

Beloperone Guttata

The only plant in this genus widely grown indoors is the world-renowned plant *Beloperone guttata*. Commonly called the Shrimp Plant, it is a bract-forming plant that offers a great profusion of colour almost all year round, though fewer bracts appear in winter. Thin, insignificant green leaves are attached to wiry stems that will attain a height of some 6ft (1.8m), but branches can be trimmed to a more compact shape at almost any time. The actual flowers are off-white in colour, but add little to the plant's appearance and can be a nuisance since they fall in all directions. The bracts, however, are a rich autumnal shade on top and an attractive lime green on their undersides. They have a distinctly shrimp-like appearance, hence the plant's common name.

B. guttata needs full sun and rich loam-based potting soil. Keep plants moist, and feed at every watering after they have become established in their pots. In the plant's early stages of development, remove bracts as they appear in order to promote stronger growth. Prune to shape leggy and unattractive growth. Cuttings of young shoots a few inches in length will root at almost any time, but remove any bracts that may be attached to the cutting. No pests seem to attack the plant.

Beloperone guttata (*right*) is a tall bushy plant which grows leggy if not cut back to retain its shape. The noticeable feature of this popular houseplant is the reddish overlapping bracts (*above*) which resemble shrimps in appearance.

PROPAGATION

Beloperone may be successfully propagated by either tip or stem cuttings from mid-spring to early summer, when conditions favour more effective rooting.

Remove tip cuttings measuring up to 3in (7.5cm) or stem cuttings of about 2in (5cm), using a sharp knife or scissors, and dip each cutting into hormone rooting powder. Dibble each cutting into a pot, ensuring that tip cuttings and stem cuttings are kept together if you wish to produce a bushy plant, unlike the more 'leggy' specimen pictured above.

Dibble three cuttings to a 3½in (9cm) pot and five cuttings to a 4¼in (11cm) pot, using a seed and cutting compost. Cover the cuttings with a plastic bag and maintain a temperature of around 68–70°F (20–21°C) until rooting has taken place, for up to a couple of months.

Keep the cuttings in good light, but out of direct sunlight to avoid scorch.

As soon as the cuttings have rooted, remove the plastic cover and if the cuttings have started actively to grow, commence feeding.

Beloperone can grow to be extremely straggly and regular pruning will be required after propagation to train the plant accordingly. Commercially grown beloperone are treated with a chemical growth retardant to produce a more compact habit of growth.

Failure to remove the bag cover may result in the new growth becoming etiolated, which will require early trimming to form a better-shaped plant.

AVOIDING PROBLEMS

Light and position

The Shrimp Plant needs plenty of light to maintain the colour of its bracts and encourage flowering but, in common with many plants, must be protected from direct, hot sunlight. It will not tolerate continual shade or a cold, draughty position.

Temperature range

Cool   Intermediate   Warm

The plant is fairly tolerant with regard to temperature, enjoying a range between 55°-70°F (13°-21°C). Extreme conditions of heat or cold are not usually good for any houseplant, and the Shrimp Plant is no exception. It will prefer the cooler end of the temperature range during winter.

Watering

Water can be added to the soil from the top of the pot. This is a plant which likes moist conditions, but not saturation. If the soil is allowed to become too dry, on the other hand, the leaves will quickly droop, so watering should be frequent in summer.

Feeding

Frequent, regular feeding is essential for a well-established plant. If the plant develops yellowing, curled foliage, it is probably suffering from chlorosis (iron deficiency) and should be treated by watering the soil with a special iron solution.

Seasonal care

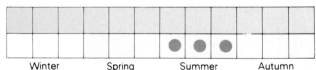

Winter   Spring   Summer   Autumn

Active plants require ample watering during summer months, and may need almost as much during the winter, since the soil must not be allowed to dry out. The Shrimp Plant has a tendency to become rather spindly, and this can be countered by pinching out the growing tips of a young plant to encourage bushiness. When the plant needs pruning, this can be done following the main summer flowering, or in the spring when it moves into a more active period of growth.

Soil

It may be necessary to repot a strong, young plant twice in its first year, and in general, frequent potting on is essential. Use a loam-based potting mixture and pot the plant firmly. For propagating top cuttings, use a peat and sand mixture.

be sluggish, although it may have plenty of light, warmth and food, and the soil in the pot will dry out more quickly than usual. The plant must then be repotted to give it more room. The Shrimp Plant needs frequent feeding and signs of starvation appear in the leaves when it is undernourished. The leaf of a plant which has not been fed enough will look limp and go brown at the tip (*below*).

A pot-bound plant (*above*) It may be possible to recognize a pot-bound plant simply when the roots emerge through the drainage holes of the pot. Even before this happens the growth of the plant will

PESTS AND DISEASES

Aphids These greenfly are found on the softer top leaves of the plant. Their activity weakens the plant and in addition they secrete a sticky substance called honeydew, which is unsightly and unpleasant. The flies should be easily disposed of by spraying the plant with malathion.

White fly This common and persistent pest attacks the undersides of leaves to suck sap from the plant. They multiply quickly and treatment must be repeated to be effective. Spray the plant with diazinon at least four times, with four-day intervals between each spraying. If white fly persist, change to another insecticide.

Red spider mite These flourish in warm, dry conditions. They must be treated at an early stage, but they are difficult to see with the naked eye. Look out for mottled, dropping leaves which indicate the presence of mites on the plant. Isolate the plant to prevent the problem spreading and spray the undersides of the leaves with malathion or dichloran. Unfortunately, if the mites have really taken hold and formed small webs it is too late to treat the plant with any insecticide and it is better to remove and burn the badly affected areas or, indeed, the whole plant if necessary.

Mealy bug These little insects are like woodlice with a white, floury coating. On a Shrimp Plant the bugs are easily visible and accessible and can be removed with a sponge soaked in methylated spirits. Direct contact with this kills the bugs immediately. A malathion spray may be effective in killing the adult insects, but wiping should also remove the protected young, freeing the plant completely.

Black leg This is a fungus which may attack cuttings of this plant, if they are allowed to get too wet before roots have formed. The only sensible remedy is to remove and burn the affected cuttings and treat the surrounding soil with streptomycin.

Bougainvillea

In their natural tropical environment the brilliant flowers of the bougainvillea can outshine almost everything in sight. Its strong stems have vicious barbs and carry thin and insignificant foliage, but the defects of the plant are more than compensated for when it flowers throughout the summer. It would be misleading to suggest that the bougainvillea is the ideal houseplant. It can be most frustrating as it is very reluctant to produce flowers in a situation that offers only limited light. However, they can be grown successfully in a conservatory or bay window.

New plants are raised from cuttings taken in spring, using sections of 3in (7.5cm) stem, with a heel of older wood attached. A minimum temperature of 70°F (21°C) is essential if the cuttings are to survive.

Healthy plant (*above and right*) The decorative papery bracts of the bougainvillea make it a most attractive plant. If the plants receive plenty of light, they can make a very effective display, especially if trained to wind round a tall framework. Choose clean plants with some open flowers and clusters of flowers about to open.

Diseased leaves Sooty mould (*above*), caused by aphids, is not only very unsightly but also harmful to the leaf. It blocks the pores and eventually the plant goes brown and dies. Mealy bug (*left*) can be identified by its grey-white woolly coat. The bugs can be removed by wiping with methylated spirits or spraying with insecticide.

PESTS AND DISEASES

Bougainvilleas are fairly tough plants and do not suffer a great deal from pests. However, it is as well to watch out for the following.

Aphids These can quite often be found on the tips of new growth. They suck the plant's sap, making the leaves go yellow and, in extreme cases, causing distortion. They also secrete a sticky substance called honeydew upon which an ugly sooty mould may grow. Aphids also carry incurable viruses. They can be removed with an application of malathion or diazinon, sprayed on the leaves.

Mealy bug This often attacks older plants in the greenhouse but is less frequent indoors, unless it is actually brought in on the plant. The open leaves of the plant make detection of mealy bug an easy matter. The adults are a powdery-white and resemble woodlice. The young are wrapped in a protective waxy coat and tend to be attached to the more inaccessible parts of the plant where the branches intertwine.

VARIETIES AND PURCHASING

Bougainvilleas should be bought in flower. The mature ones will usually be wound round a frame, but they can be unwound and put on a different frame if desired.

B. glabra This is the species most easily obtained in nurseries and shops. It has purple bracts which appear in summer and autumn. There are several variegated sorts, including *B.g.* 'Harrisii', which has leaves streaked with cream, and

B.g. 'Sanderana Variegata', which has cream-bordered leaves.

B. buttiana This is the original parent of several hybrid bougainvilleas which are now very popular, as it is easy to train them into shrub form. They can best be kept in 6–8in (25–30cm) pots. They are happy in most indoor locations and they are therefore more suitable as houseplants than the original species.

Light and position

Maximum light is vital to the bougainvillea, so place it in a sunny window, right against the windowpane. There is a chance that it will be scorched by the sun, so keep an eye on the leaves. However, it cannot flourish in poor light and scorching is a minor risk.

Temperature range

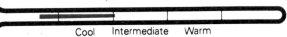

Cool   Intermediate   Warm

Temperature is not crucial during the plant's period of active growth, but should probably remain at 55°F (13°C) or above if possible. While the bougainvillea is dormant in the winter, a cooler temperature of 50°F (10°C) is preferred. Although it requires plenty of light and enjoys the sun, it will not be the better for being allowed to bake.

Watering

Water the plant from the top of the pot, but do not leave it standing in a full saucer. The soil should be moist while the plant is in active growth, but it will not require water during the winter until new growth begins to appear.

Feeding

Suitable feed for the bougainvillea is fertilizer containing a high proportion of potash. Again, this is not necessary during the winter dormancy, but is vital in spring to encourage new growth. Use a liquid feed when the plant is watered.

Seasonal care

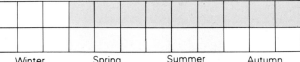

Winter   Spring   Summer   Autumn

The pattern of seasonal care to be observed is dictated by the summer growth period and winter dormancy, as explained above. Whereas many plants need less food and water in the winter, the bougainvillea may go for two or three months without any nourishment and then requires further attention when new growth starts in early spring. If the plant becomes straggly it can be gently pruned in the autumn, but flowering is better if growth is wound around established stems and tied back.

Soil

Potting mixtures without soil are useless to the bougainvillea. It requires a loam-based compost and can be potted on in spring once new growth has begun. A pot of 8in (20cm) diameter is ample and when the plant has reached this stage, sustain it by feeding.

Bromeliads

Bromeliads are perhaps the most fascinating of all tropical plants, and are indigenous to South America.

Almost all are easy to care for and will tolerate considerable neglect. Many plants in the family are epiphytes and make their precarious anchorage in trees, depending on the elements and passing birds for much of their nourishment and moisture. Some of the plants, such as the many and varied cryptanthus, are terrestrial and grow among the rocks and fallen trees at ground level. Others are virtually weeds.

The larger bromeliads produce rosettes of leaves that overlap at their base and make perfect water reservoirs. Flowering bracts appear from the centre of these urns – some to stand out from the leaves, others to barely emerge from the water in the urn. Heavy

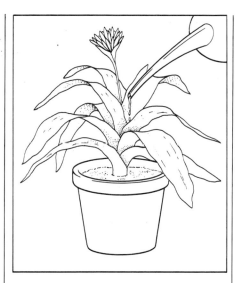

Watering bromeliads Larger bromeliads should have water poured directly into their urn. This reservoir is formed by the overlapping bases of the rosette of leaves.

dew or rainfall will fill these urns when plants are growing in habitat. Because plants can derive their

water requirements from this source, they are able to withstand the most difficult conditions. These urns also provide water for the many birds and small animals that frequent tropical trees, and whose droppings provide a certain amount of nutrition for the bromeliad plants.

Although bromeliads vary in size from tiny tillandsias to majestic vrieseas, all are similar in their requirements. Most are within the scope of the reasonably competent gardener. Those plants that form water urns should have the urn filled to capacity all the time; very little water should actually be poured into the soil. The water in these urns will become stagnant in time, especially after plants have produced their bracts, so tip the old water away periodically and replenish the urns with fresh water, preferably rainwater.

Bromeliad tree An established bromeliad tree (*above*) is an attractive addition to any indoor setting.

Smaller tillandsias are particularly good plants to place on a bromeliad tree. They are very durable and will come to no harm provided the tree is sprayed over with water occasionally. Another fine bromeliad to place on the tree is *Billbergia nutans*, or Queen's Tears, which produces pendulous bracts of spectacular colouring at regular intervals throughout the year.

For the finest-looking tree possible, it is best to include other plants as well as bromeliads. The soft green foliage of small ferns provides a contrast to the tillandsia. The miniature ficus, *F. pumila*, is another good plant for a bromeliad tree. The firm, oval-shaped leaves will twine around the branches of the tree.

Moist sphagnum moss is wrapped around the base of each rosette, covering any roots.

Pieces of cork bark are placed around the moss base and the whole thing is then attached to the branch of the tree with reel wire.

Aechmea

This genus provides numerous majestic plants, many of which are used often for decorative purposes. The bright cream-and-green foliage and striking rosettes of growth produced by *Aechmea caudata* make it one of the best display plants.

Perhaps the best known of all the bromeliads as far as decorative plants go is *A. fasciata* (also called *A. rhodocyanea*, or *Billbergia rhodocyanea*), which has large powdery silver-grey foliage and superb pink-coloured bracts from which appear small intensely blue flowers. The leaves are broad and upright and have black spines along their margin, and the bracts remain colourful for several months, making this one of the finest of all exotic indoor plants. With softer leaves of wine-red colouring, *A. fulgens* is a pleasing plant that produces small bracts. *A chantinii* has vicious spines along the margins of the leaves, so must be handled with care.

Ananas

The only bromeliad that is of any commercial value to the world is the ananas, which provides us with the pineapple of commerce. Most ananas are not grown indoors, but *A. comosus* develops small pineapples when roots are confined to pots, though the result is a very insignificant little fruit. The hard green leaves are not particularly attractive, but there are variegated forms of ananas, *A. bracteatus* 'Striatus' being one, that have special value as decorative plants, both for their striking foliage and for the majestic appearance that the plant assumes when

This bromeliad tree shows the variety of genera that can be included, each plant firmly secured in a fork or angle of the branch.

the bright-pink pineapple fruit is produced. All the ananas are easy-care plants, but become large, with spines along the leaves, and need ample space in which to grow.

Billbergia

The more common *B. nutans* (Queen's Tears) and the broader-leaved *B.* × *windii* are among the most tolerant of indoor plants, putting up with much mistreatment without too many ill effects. Flowering bracts are highly colourful and naturally pendulous, so plants are seen at their best when they are raised on a pedestal or planted in small hanging containers. The foliage is not of any great merit, but flowers are likely to appear at any time. Both *B. nutans* and *B.* × *windii* make thick clumps of growth that can be separated to make additional plants at any time other than when in flower.

B. pyramidalis 'Concolor' is a plant that is reluctant to produce offsets for propagation and is consequently rarer. This is a more tender plant than *B. nutans* and *B.* × *windii*, and has longer tubes of leaves from which appear bracts of the most spectacular colouring, a combination of crimson-red, purple and blue. The bracts are also broader and more upright than those of *B. nutans*, and in common with other billbergias, the bracts are short-lived. One common name for the plant is Summer Torch.

Cryptanthus

Plants in this genus have thick fleshy leaves that form rosettes in the shape of flat stars. In their natural habitat, they grow at ground level. They do well in shallow pans or pots provided with drainage material and holding soil that is very open and free to drain. Plants rarely, if ever,

reach any great size and, in fact, lose much of their appeal when they have formed into heavier clumps of foliage. The best method of growing them is to regularly split the bolder clumps and to use the offsets for propagating fresh plants.

C. bromelioides 'Tricolor' has bright pink and cream coloured foliage and pushes its leaves up much higher than most cryptanthus. As a result, the plant appears less star-like than other cryptanthus. With very small rosettes that are olive-green in colour with contrasting bands, *C. bivittatus* 'Minor' is one of the smallest plants in the entire bromeliad family. Small rosettes become very crowded in their pots, and it is quite common for individual rosettes to be virtually pushed out of the way by other developing rosettes. One result is that they can be found rooting into almost anything that will give them a reasonable foothold.

The aristocrat of this genus must be *C. fosteranus*. The leaves are very fleshy and are shaped like large flat stars. The remarkable marking on them has given the plant the common name of Pheasant Leaf. This plant is generally difficult to obtain, but it belongs in every good collection of bromeliads. The species *C. zonatus* is similar in colour, with leaves that are gently waved, but it lacks the distinction of the Pheasant Leaf.

Guzmania

With rosette-forming foliage that is less vicious than many of the larger-leaved bromeliads, guzmanias are well worth acquiring. *Guzmania lingulata* is an epiphytic species. It has metallic-green leaves, red and yellow bracts and yellow-white flowers. Another easy-care plant that is in this genus is *G. monostachya*, which produces

Billbergia pyramidalis (*above*) and *B. nutans* (*below*) have spectacular bracts from which emerge spikes of flowers. But, as with all billbergias, they do not last long.

Guzmanias have softer foliage than many of the larger bromeliads. *G. lingulata* (*above*).

slender rosettes of yellowish-green leaves in large free-growing clumps with stiff multicoloured bracts.

A product of Belgium, where much has been done to popularize bromeliads, G. 'Omar Morobe' has a somewhat insignificant bract, but more than compensates with foliage that is bright pink and cream in colour. Rosettes should mature to a reasonable size before you pull them from the parent plant and root them in an open mixture as individual plants.

Neoregelia

By far the most popular species of neoregelia is *Neoregelia carolinae* 'Tricolor'. Plants make flat cart-wheel rosettes of splendid colouring, with the added attraction that the centre of the plant around the water reservoir changes to the deepest red as bracts form just below water level. Bracts are insignificant, and the parent rosette dies after it has produced its bracts. The old rosette is cut away when it has lost its attractive appearance. The small offsets that appear at the base of the plant should then be removed and rooted as individual plants.

Tillandsia

Plants in the *Tillandsia* genus range in size from tiny lichen-like plants to plants with very large rosettes of leaves. Almost all are easy to care for and can go for weeks on end with no water or feeding whatsoever – many seeming to exist virtually on air. Most tillandsias grown as houseplants have little or no roots and will do best on a bromeliad tree or fixed to a piece of cork bark and tied with a little sphagnum moss.

Tillandsia cyanea has recurving rosettes of hard green leaves, and spectacular pink bracts that produce bright blue petunia-like flowers.

Tillandsia usneoides, commonly known as Spanish Moss, consists of threadlike stems covered with minute grey scales. When growing in the wild, it hangs from trees and rocks in great curtains of grey, choking the life of everything around it. Under controlled conditions, however, Spanish Moss can be a very striking addition to a bromeliad tree.

Vriesea

There are many splendid plants in this genus, all of them forming large rosettes of leathery leaves with an attractive pattern and colouring.

The best known is *V. splendens*, which produces a brilliant red bract that is spear shaped and stands proudly away from the leaves, which are banded green and brown in colour. Bracts are long-lived and plants require good light in which to grow. The urn formed by leaves must always contain water. Only the minimum of water should be given to the soil, and feeding is not necessary. Plants will not flower until several years old.

Other vrieseas, such as *V. hieroglyphica*, or *V. fenestralis*, which has a netted pattern to its leaves, produce very large and majestic rosettes of leaves that may be 3ft (91cm) or more in diameter. However, these are plants for the connoisseur and will not often be available for sale.

Vriesea splendens is a fine plant. Its principal feature is the erect sword-like bract that emanates from the rosette of leaves. The yellow tubular flowers that emerge from the bract are of little consequence. In common with many species of bromeliad, the leaves of this one overlap at their base and form a rosette that is a water-tight urn. The urn should at no time be allowed to dry out, although it is advisable to dispose of existing water and to replenish with fresh water periodically.

Cryptanthus plants Also known as the Earth Star, these grow in rocky cracks and on tree stumps or roots in the wild. Their leaves are often edged with prickly spines and striped or barred in a broad range of colours from white and pale pink to purple and yellow. Healthy plants often have a whitish bloom called 'scurf' on their leaves, which gives them a silvery look. *C. bromelioides* (**left**), the Rainbow Star, has white-edged leaves. Unlike most of the genus it grows upright, sending out stems carrying plantlets which, if rooted, will become new plants.

Aechmeas include some of the largest and most magnificent bromeliads. *A. fulgens* (**above**) shows wine-red colouring and has scarlet bracts with purple flowers.

Tillandsia plants (**below**) are highly suited to bottlegardens. They have huge rosettes with colourful flowers.

PROPAGATION

Ananas comosus 'Variegatus' may be propagated by two methods, using the rosette from the top of the fruit and the offsets that form around the base of the plant. The former is much more difficult, whereas offsets offer the best chance of success.

In order to root the rosette, carefully cut off the top of the fruit as well so that about ½in (1.5cm) is attached to the base of the rosette. Allow this to dry for a day or so out of direct sunlight and then dip it into hormone rooting powder and lightly press into a 4¼in (11cm) pot filled with seed and cutting compost, covering the plant and pot with a clear plastic bag.

Maintain a temperature of 75–80°F (24–27°C) until rooting has taken place; this can take up to two months or more.

Ananas (*above*) is not a particularly attractive bromeliad, but it is interesting for the fact that the genus is the source of pineapple fruit, and some species develop tiny fruit when grown in a pot.

When offsets are 4in (10cm) they may be carefully pared from the parent with a sharp knife and potted singly in a 3½–4¼in (9–11cm) pot filled with seed and cutting compost. Remember to dip the base of the offset in hormone rooting powder first.

Cover the plant and pot with a plastic bag and keep the compost barely moist at a temperature of around 75°F (24°C) to enable rooting to take place. Again, this may take up to two months.

As relatively high temperatures are required, propagation of ananas is best left until mid-spring to mid-summer, when ambient temperatures should be higher. Avoid too much direct light during the initial stages of propagation.

The colourful **neoregelia** may be treated in a similar way to the aechmea.

Propagation is relatively straightforward, but requires great care to ensure that you do not damage and, therefore, possibly increase the chance of losing the offsets when they are produced.

Start work in mid to late spring. Choose a plant with off-sets measuring approximately 6–8in (15–20cm), having moistened the compost thoroughly first. Tease away some of the compost to expose the lower root of the offset and, using a sharp knife, make a clean cut close to the mother plant.

The offset may then be potted in a peat-based seed and cutting compost complete with as much as possible of its root system into a 3½–4¼in (9–11cm) pot. For the first month, or even up to two months, enclose the offset in a clear plastic bag and keep it at 70°F (21°C) in reasonable light, but out of direct sunlight.

Once the root system starts to develop, the plant may be removed from its cover and grown on, feeding with a reduced-strength liquid fertilizer both onto the compost and into the central vase, ensuring that water is also applied in the same way when the plant needs watering.

As the young plant develops, it may be potted up into a 5in (13cm) pot in late spring, probably the season after, in order to give it sufficient time to establish before the autumn and winter.

Healthy plant The *Neoregelia carolinae* 'Tricolor' (*top*) is a plant which will grow to 2ft (60cm) in width. Its rosette of cream-striped leaves will turn brilliant red at flowering time and remain so for months if the centre is kept full of water.

Cryptanthus plants usually have leaves that form flattish, star-shaped, rosettes. Two decorative species are *C. tricolor* (*above*), and *C.* 'Foster's Favourite' (*right*).

VARIETIES AND PURCHASING

Bromeliads present a wide range of leaf and flower shapes of remarkable colour and will often grow during the whole year. Many types, though tree-growing in the wild, may be bought in pots, but it is important to see that all small plants do have roots. Several types can also be grown on mossy logs and are ideal for a bottlegarden. The flowers are usually short-lived, but the leaves often take on brilliant hues which last for several months.

Aechmea This is the best known of the bromeliads (*see page 46*).

Ananas comosus The Pineapple Plant belongs to this group, but is almost too large for growing indoors.

A. bractatus 'Variegatus' The most popular type, this is a far prettier plant than the common pineapple. It has green and cream striped leaves, which turn pink as the flower develops, and a rich reddish-pink pineapple.

Billbergia This is the easiest and most adaptable bromeliad. It has a rosette of leaves in a range of colours from red-bronze or grey-green to white or purple. The flowers, too, take on many shapes and display a wealth of brilliant colours.

B. nutans The Friendship Plant or Queen's Tears has an arching fountain of olive-green leaves, which may turn red if kept in sunlight. It produces flower heads with striking pink bracts rather like exotic ears of wheat.

Cryptanthus The Earth Star is one of the most popular bromeliads.

C. acaulis The Starfish Plant is small and easy to grow. Varieties have leaves suffused with pink.

Tillandsia These are available in a wide range and are particularly good for growing on branches.

Vriesea This is a genus with sword-shaped leaves and flower spikes standing on tall stems and composed of colourful bracts.

V. splendens The best-known species, called Flaming Sword, has 15in (45cm) long dark green leaves with purple and black bands and a tall flower spike of brilliant red bracts encasing the tiny yellow flowers.

G. 'Omar Morobe' (*above*) is an attractive species.

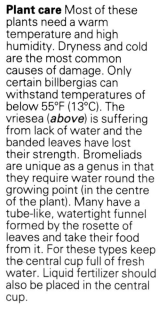

Slug Bromeliads with their tough leaves are resistant to pests. Because of the need to keep the central funnel of many of these plants full of water, however, they will sometimes attract slugs (*above*). Empty the stale water regularly.

Plant care Most of these plants need a warm temperature and high humidity. Dryness and cold are the most common causes of damage. Only certain billbergias can withstand temperatures of below 55°F (13°C). The vriesea (*above*) is suffering from lack of water and the banded leaves have lost their strength. Bromeliads are unique as a genus in that they require water round the growing point (in the centre of the plant). Many have a tube-like, watertight funnel formed by the rosette of leaves and take their food from it. For these types keep the central cup full of fresh water. Liquid fertilizer should also be placed in the central cup.

Dying plants The cryptanthus (*left*) has been badly affected by root mealy bugs, which nest in the roots and stunt the growth of the plant. For a small plant, treat by washing the mixture from the roots, cut away the worst infected parts, and soak the rest of the roots in a solution of insecticide. Then repot in fresh mixture. The tillandsia plants are suited to bottlegardens. They have huge rosettes with colourful flower heads. *T. cyanea*, the most popular species, has grey-green leaves 12–18in (30–45cm) long and a flower spike of delicate pink bracts from which small violet flowers emerge. As the flowers fade (*above*) the foliage still remains attractive.

AVOIDING PROBLEMS

Light and position

For neoregelias, good light is essential, even direct sunlight. With a selection of plants, a light location ensures bright colouring, but avoid direct sunlight.

All the other bromeliads need good light but it should not be too strong. Position them where they can be viewed from above as they are best seen from this angle.

Temperature range

Cool   Intermediate   Warm

Bromeliads thrive in warm room temperatures of between 60°-70°F (15°-21°C). Some types will not survive in temperatures lower than 60°F (15°C). A constant

level of warmth and humidity is necessary in the active growth period. When temperatures rise above 65° (18°C), spray the foliage daily with tepid water.

Watering

Water bromeliads moderately allowing the top inch (2.5cm) to dry out between waterings. During winter rest periods, water only enough to keep the top soil

slightly moist. Avoid using hard water which can leave deposits on the foliage. Rainwater or distilled water are preferable.

Feeding

When in active growth, apply fertilizer as recommended by the manufacturer. Liquid fertilizer can be splashed over the leaves. Plants grown in mixtures with

peat moss require extra feeding throughout the year. Those grown in soil should not be fed during winter rest periods.

Seasonal care

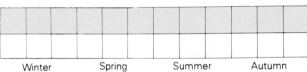

Winter   Spring   Summer   Autumn

Bromeliad selections should be watered twice a week in summer, once in winter. Cryptanthus should also be watered twice a week in summer and once a week at other times. When

watering neoregelias, the urn part of the plant should be topped up with tepid water and this should be changed regularly throughout the year.

Soil

All bromeliads require an airy compost. A recommended mixture is half sphagnum peat, half rough leaf mould, and a small amount of sand. Avoid potting

into large pots and pot on only when the plant seems out of proportion to its pot. Clay and plastic pots can both be used.

Cacti and Succulents

Succulent plants have many rare and unusual features, developed during a long and slow evolutionary process. One of their principal characteristics is the ability to adapt to harsh conditions, conditions which would cause most other plant groups to perish. The various peculiarities associated with succulents, cacti in particular, probably result from this. Thus we find the intriguing shapes, some bordering on the grotesque but beautiful nevertheless, evidenced in over 50 different plant families – these include over 350 genera, of which about 250 belong to the Cactaceae.

The shapes and sizes of succulent plants are well-nigh endless. Their common feature is a fleshy inbuilt structure that is apparent in their stems, leaves or roots. This structure enables them to store moisture and helps to protect them against environmental conditions and changes.

Succulent plants are to be found growing almost everywhere in the world – even in the much more unpredictable weather and temperature conditions that prevail in many northern parts of Europe, Asia and America. Cactaceae, which are distinguished from other succulents in having a growing point called an areole, have their habitat almost entirely in the Americas. The larger succulent plant families – Euphorbiaceae, Mesembryanthemaceae, Asclepiadaceae – are to a great extent natives of the Old World, particularly Africa and Arabia. Australasia also has its indigenous succulents.

There is a saying that 'cactus thrive on neglect'. However, this aphorism is utterly false. Succulents *may* survive, but certainly not thrive. After all, nature never intended plants to grow in pots in houses or greenhouses; plants have been introduced to and forced to accept whatever provisions are made available for their care and protection. So give due attention to detail. Monitor your plants' response to treatment given, and use personal initiative and enterprise.

The number of succulents suitable for indoor culture is enormous. Comparatively few are mentioned in these pages, but those described are representative of hosts of others that will add brightness and interest to the home. Obviously, some are not as easy to grow as others. Those from equatorial regions often demand more warmth than those from tropical and sub-tropical areas, so should not be lumped together with incompatible plants.

Caring for cacti

Not all succulents are from arid or semi-arid regions. A great number are jungle or rain-forest plants, some growing in trees just as many orchid species do. These forest plants require a somewhat different culture from desert succulents. Probably the most well-known cactus houseplant is *Schlumbergera* × *buckleyi* – the popular Christmas Cactus. There are a few of its close relations referred to later, and those things necessary for the care of the Christmas Cactus – sun, water and fertilizer – also apply to these.

Light and Temperature

Place plants in a bright location, not in full sun, or scorch could affect them at certain times of the year.

Give plants the appropriate temperature. You can't water, fertilize or even wisely repot if the air temperature is very much below 55–60°F (13–15°C). During growing and flowering times in particular, plants demand higher temperatures. Failure to supply such conditions may cause either leaves to wither or buds to drop.

Compost and Potting

Provide plants with a really rich compost that consists of thoroughly decomposed leafmould, peat and sharp sand in equal parts. In some instances, additional humus may be advisable. It is vital that the compost be porous. If extra humous prevents this, add more sand.

Potting is important. Never use a container that is too small or too large – both are equally unsuitable.

Cacti and Succulents (*above*) come in many different shapes and sizes. While all succulent plants have a swollen, fleshy structure in either their roots, stems or leaves that enables them to store moisture, cacti, the largest group of succulent plants, also have an areole. This round or elongated cushion of hairs is the growing point from which develop any offsets, branches or spines. Flower buds are produced from the upper area of the areole.

By definition a succulent is a plant which stores moisture in its leaves, stems or roots. The echeveria (*left*), with its fleshy leaves, typifies a leaf succulent.

Cacti are succulent plants belonging to the Cactaceae family. All cacti have a growing point called an areole — a cushion-like area from which grow the spines and flowers.

85

Repotting should be done soon after plants have flowered, certainly not just before, or a year's flowering could be lost.

Watering

With jungle plants, it is not necessary, and probably not advisable, to allow the soil to dry out completely at any time. During the growing season, water freely but never permit the soil to remain drenched, which will cause root rot. Good crocking of the pot should prevent excess water accumulating.

Fertilizing

Once new growth is observed, or flower buds appear, fertilizing is essential. If throughout these periods plants are fertilized when watered – always in a weak, liquid form – plants will often prosper. An old-fashioned method of guaranteeing a good flowering plant is to introduce thoroughly decomposed cow manure into the compost. This is still a first-class method and does away with the need to use artificial fertilizers.

One further point on fertilizers and fertilizing: there are numerous brands offered in stores, but very few have been specifically prepared for succulent-plant culture. The majority contain nitrogen and potash. These are essential ingredients, but too much nitrogen will encourage growth as opposed to flowering. There are fertilizers that contain these two elements plus trace elements – iron, manganese, magnesium, copper, boron, molybdenum. Use these fertilizers, and you are well on the way to success. Never fertilize when plants are not in growth or when they look sickly, dehydrated or generally off-form.

Disease

Excessive watering, particularly to the root structure, causes many diseases. If your plant shows signs of disease, examine the roots, cut away any damaged parts, dust the plant with sulphur powder, and repot in fresh soil. Black rot may attack certain plants, such as stapelias and some epiphytes, usually at soil level. Black rot is caused by bacteria getting into the plant's system and turning the tissues black and soft. The affected parts should be cut out very thoroughly. Dust the cut with sulphur powder, and keep the plant on the dry side until the cut is healed. A copper-based fungicide applied occasionally will help to restrain the problem. Damping-off primarily affects young seedlings. A good fungicide will remedy this; use one containing captan or zineb.

Propagation

Charts of the following species of succulents discuss propagation by seeds. A little guidance is necessary here. It is obvious that all plants can be propagated from seeds. Unfortunately, some seeds are difficult to obtain. The majority are available, but must be obtained from reputable sources. The process of sowing is simple.

Propagation Many succulents can be propagated from cuttings, which may also improve plants' shape and encourage basal growth. The red lines on the opuntia (*below left*) and echeveria (*below right*) show where the cuts can be made. Let the cuts heal before rooting offsets in a mixture of equal parts peat and sharp sand.

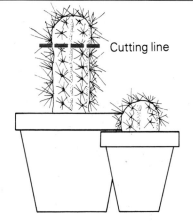

Cutting line

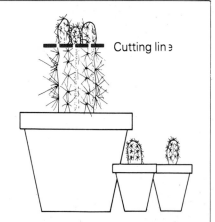

Cutting line

Because they have their own internal water supply, succulents are not so disturbed by a temporary stoppage in water flow and lend themselves readily to vegetative propagation by division, offsets, suckers, cuttings or grafting.

This globular cactus can be increased two ways. The top section may be cut off (*above left*) and the cutting left on an airy, light shelf until a protective callus has been formed over the wound. (Some growers recommend dipping the cut in a rooting powder.) After callusing has taken place, insert the top section in a new pot. To prevent rot, do not bury the base too deeply.

The plant that has been divided will grow new offshoots (*above right*) from the top of the stump. These may also be cut off and rooted in smaller pots. Use a rooting compost of equal parts sifted sharp sand and peat.

With few exceptions, the soil can be the same as that recommended for plants in the individual charts, but extra-sharp sand should be added. Succulent seeds germinate readily, but if soil is not porous they may rapidly rot. It is common practice to cover the seeds with just a sprinkling of fine-sifted sand to a depth equivalent to the size of the seeds. If seeds are dust-like seeds, carefully sprinkle them onto the sandy surface of the container and, even more carefully, water them in. Soak the containers thoroughly. Drain them completely and keep in a shaded but warm area until germination. Then provide more light gradually. After about three months, place containers in a very bright position, but not in full sunshine until the seedlings have assumed their characteristic forms.

Caring for desert succulents

With plants from more arid surroundings, there can be slight variations to the guidelines listed above. With few exceptions, these plants are sun-lovers; place them in the sunniest spot available. Much the same type of soil will suit many – in a few instances it may be wise to add a little lime or substitute loam for peat. It is possible to purchase ready-prepared composts. Many brand-name soil-based composts can give excellent results, but it is often necessary to add additional grit to ensure they are porous. Soil-less composts have gained in popularity in recent years, and there is much to commend them, but 30 per cent or more sharp sand should be added to the bulk. Nutrients have already been added to these prepared composts. These nutrients may only last for a limited period of time – succulent plants usually prove to be very hungry plants – so remember to fertilize.

SUCCULENT FAMILIES

Succulent plants come from all parts of the world and range in size from tiny weeds to enormous trees. The family Cactaceae is the largest succulent family, with other 250 genera and approximately 3,000 species and varieties. There are 50 other plant families that have species possessing some degree of succulence. In many cases, however, only a very few species in a family are succulent. All the plants in the section that follows belong to one of these families. Plants are classified according to genera, each of which can be found in this chart.

Apocynaceae
Most species of this family of about 180 genera are non-succulent shrubs or climbing plants found in tropical or sub-tropical countries. Though few in number, succulent genera such as *Pachypodium* and *Plumeria* contain some of the most exotic plants in the world. Flowers are beautiful and fragrant – seedpods appear in the form of horn-shaped fruit.

Asclepiadaceae
There are over 200 genera in this large plant family, including *Ceropegia, Hoya, Huernia, Luckhoffia, Stapelia* and *Stultitia*. Succulent species originate from Africa, Arabia, the Far East and Australasia. Flowers are usually beautiful and colourful, and are often sweetly scented.

Cactaceae
Plants in the best-known and biggest family of succulents are largely native to the Americas. The many thousands of species vary tremendously, but all bear an areole, a distinguishing feature not known in any other plant family. The areole is the round or elongated cushion of 'felt' or hairs that is the growing point from which develop any offsets, branches or spines.

Convolvulaceae
Species in this gigantic 'bindweed' family are found in many parts of the world. Their habit varies tremendously; plants may be shrubs, trees, climbers, trailers, even parasites. Succulent species generally have large colourful flowers. They are represented in the genera of *Ipomoea, Turbina* and *Merremia*.

Eurphorbiaceae
There are over 400 genera in this plant family, but only a few contain succulent plants. *Euphorbia, Jatropha, Synadenium* and *Monadenium* are the principal succulent genera. The

structure of the inflorescence distinguishes plants in this family: flowers are either all-male or all-female. Hence, pollination is best guaranteed where there are colonies of the same species.

Crassulaceae
This is a family of succulent genera and includes *Crassula, Echeveria, Graptopetalum, Sedum, Tacitus* and *Cotyledon*. Species are mainly native to temperate Europe, Asia, Australia and America.

Geraniaceae
This well-known plant family contains about 800 species, which are distributed among a small number of genera. The two genera that contain succulents are *Pelargonium* and *Sarcocaulon*; plants are native to South Africa.

Liliaceae
This large family of plants has over 3,000 species. Succulent genera include *Aloe, Haworthia* and *Gasteria*; most plants are native to Africa and Madagascar.

Aizoaceae
This is the largest family of succulent plants after the Cactaceae, numbering about 125 different genera (among them *Conophytum* and *Lampranthus*) and several thousand species. Most species are native to South Africa, though a few originate in Australasia, Arabia and the Atlantic islands.

Pedaliaceae
This Old World family of plants contains only 12 genera and probably no more than 50 species. They are all from tropical or sub-tropical regions, primarily Africa. Plants in only two genera, *Pterodiscus* and *Sesamothamnus*, are considered perennial succulents.

(*Right*) Puya alpestris

Astrophytum/Cryptocereus/Disocactus

Astrophytum

This is an important genus and the comparatively few species in it are among the most sought-after of plants. The generic title derives from Latin and means 'star-plant' – the starry aspect is evidenced by the numerous star-like scales completely covering the epidermis.

Astrophytum myriostigma 'Nudum' is spherical in shape, sometimes becoming slightly cylindrical when fully matured. The body is more or less spineless and has five to six symmetrical ribs running from crown to base, furrowed in between. The mitre-like shape created amply justifies the common name – Bishop's Cap.

This plant has a characteristic not shared by other varieties within the species – namely, the distinctive green colouring of the body. Other varieties are mainly grey. From north-central Mexico, it grows in the limited shade provided by native scrub, at altitudes of around 2,300ft (700m).

Flowers are bright yellow and have a silk-like lustre. They appear near to or in the crown of the plant. Blooms appear when specimens are a few years old.

ASTROPHYTUM

Light and position	Feeding
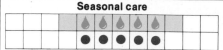 Astrophytums require good light at all times and an airy position. Full sun can scorch, and draughts are dangerous.	In growing season, feed plants with weak fertilizer at each watering.

Temperature range

In winter, keep temperatures at 50°-55°F (10°-13°C). In summer, plants will accept high temperatures.

Seasonal care

	Winter	Spring	Summer	Autumn

Keep plants completely dry and free from draughts in winter. Repot in spring if necessary. Never over-pot or under-pot.

Watering

 Water above or below, but only when the soil has dried out. Then soak and allow soil to drain thoroughly.

Soil

A porous, sandy soil is essential. Use a mixture of equal parts peat, leaf-mould and sandy gravel, plus a little lime.

Astrophytum myriostigma var. nudum (*above*) has symmetrical ribs running from crown to base and furrowed in between.
Cryptocereus anthonyanus (*right*) has some of the most colourful flowers of all epiphytic cacti and an attractive rick-rack stem.

CRYPTOCEREUS

Light and position	Feeding
 *Cryptocereus anthonyanus* needs good light or semi-shade.	 Apply weak fertilizer with each watering.

Temperature range

Keep plants in a minimum temperature of 50°-60°F (10-16°C) during winter, when a slightly moist condition is beneficial. In summer, the plants will accept high temperatures as long as shade is provided.

Seasonal care

	Winter	Spring	Summer	Autumn

In winter, temperature must never drop below 50°F (10°C). Plants must never really dry out, or branches will begin to dehydrate. Take cuttings early summer; cuttings must callous before setting.

Watering

    This epiphytic plant needs moisture all year-round. Water regularly and well.

Soil

Use a mixture of leaf-mould, peat and sharp sand in equal parts, plus a little dried cow manure.

Cryptocereus

This is a small genus of epiphytic plants. The generic title means 'hidden cereus', for the flower bud is hidden in the notched and lobed, flattened stems of the plant. It has what is often termed a 'rick-rack' stem, which in itself is a pleasing feature. The branches can attain 6ft (2m) or more in length.

Cryptocereus anthonyanus is a comparatively recent discovery. In fact, it was first located growing on a native's hut, and some time elapsed before its actual habitat was confirmed. It is a true epiphyte and grows in trees. The aerial roots produced on the stems enable the plant to anchor safely in the tree branches, from which it hangs pendent. This Mexican plant from the forest regions of Chiapas is easy to cultivate. Grown in a well-placed hanging basket, this plant will flourish either in a shaded area of the home or in a greenhouse.

The brick-red sepals and yellow throat combine to make this an exceptional flower within the Cactaceae family. Flowers open in late afternoon and remain so throughout the night. They have a light, pleasant scent.

Disocactus

Only a few species can be said to truly belong to this genus. All are somewhat similar in habit and appearance, but differ in quite obvious features. Stems are long, often 12in (30cm) in length and 1–2in (3–5cm) wide. They are notched or serrated, have a tendency to twist slightly, and are rather pointed at the tips. Flowers can be quite numerous. They are produced in the upper portion of the stems, are about 2in (5cm) long, carmine-red and trumpet shaped. The protruding style is an important feature.

Disocactus eichlamii is a very interesting and unusual epiphytic species that comes from the forest areas of Guatemala. It has flattened stems and branches, similar to but more dwarfed than those plants in the genus *Epiphyllum* to which it is related. Plants are somewhat bushy, branching out from the base of the plant, but eventually develop the pendent habit characteristic of all epiphytes.

There is little problem in growing *Disocactus eichlamii* satisfactorily. Plants require much the same treatment as the well-known Christmas Cactus. Flowers occur rather late in the year, hence the

need to maintain a temperature of around 53°F (12°C) for good results. Plants are suitable for home or greenhouse culture and can grow either in pots or hanging baskets. It is wise to keep plants slightly moist all the time.

Disocactus eichlamii (*above*) is an epiphytic species native to the forest areas of Guatemala. An array of vivid-coloured flowers is produced quite late in the year, the blooms persisting over a period of several weeks. Stems are long, notched or serrated, and have a tendency to twist.

DISOCACTUS	
Light and position 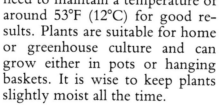 Disocactus needs good indirect light or semi-shade. Fresh air is essential, but keep plants away from draughts.	**Feeding** 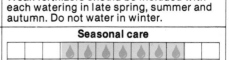 Weak fertilizers should be included with each watering in late spring, summer and autumn. Do not water in winter.
Temperature range 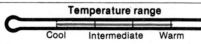 Flowers need a minimum temperature of 55°F (13°C) at all times. Plants will take a high temperature in summer and early autumn as long as they are shaded.	**Seasonal care**  Take cuttings in spring, which is also the time any pruning should be done. Repot in spring. Watch for pests at all times.
Watering  Keep plants just moist at all times. In hot weather, occasionally spray plants with water.	**Soil** An acid compost - decomposed leaf-mould and sharp sand in equal parts, plus a little peat - will give good flowering results.

Echinocereus/Echinopsis

Echinocereus

Plants in this genus are diverse in their characteristics – they may be cylindrical, globular, erect or prostrate – but all bear medium to large colourful flowers. The generic title is from the Greek 'echinus' and means 'hedgehog' – a reference to the many-spined bodies of the plants. Certain species do indeed merit the term 'Hedgehog Cactus'. Echinocereus species are found in southwestern areas of the USA and in northern and central Mexico.

One of the better-known species in the genus is *Echinocereus pentalophus*. Many varieties of this plant develop offsets – some elongated, others short, but all eventually becoming prostrate and forming large 'cushions' or 'mats'. *E. pentalophus* 'Procumbens', a plant from northern Mexico, is one of the best examples of the group. Stems are somewhat slender, less than 1in (about 2cm) wide, frequently 5in (12cm) or more long. The few ribs develop a spiral effect, with the white areoles bearing a few brown spines. The prostrate or 'procumbens' aspect is vividly displayed and when in full bloom with its large, glistening flowers,

ECHINOCEREUS PECTINATUS		
Light and position  Full sun is advisable; continual shade can prove detrimental to growth and flowering.		**Feeding**  Provide regular feeding with each watering, but do not feed at all from early winter to late spring.
Temperature range Cool Intermediate Warm Plants will tolerate very high temperatures in the growth period, but in winter they will accept temperatures of 45°-50°F (7°-10°C) if kept completely dry.		**Seasonal care** Winter Spring Summer Autumn Maintain plants in vigorous growth during the growing season by providing them with warmth, fresh air, adequate water and nutrients. Repot in spring. Take cuttings in the summer; do not under-pot.
Watering 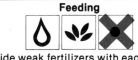 Water abundantly during the growing season, but keep totally dry in winter.		**Soil** A good compost for these plants is composed of loam, leaf-mould and sandy gravel in even parts. The addition of a little lime can be helpful.

this plant is almost unequalled in this genus of beautiful flowers.

The popularity of this variety has been in evidence for many years. The stems do not necessarily captivate the imagination of the collector seeking species with particularly intricate body and spine formations, and the plant's prostrate, almost creeping habit can quickly demand a large space. The flowers are adequate compensation – rich in colour, 4in (10cm) or so long, 3in (8cm) in diameter.

In common with the majority

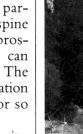

Echinocereus pentalophus 'Procumbens' (*above*) is native to northern Mexico and produces large cushion-type offsets.

of echinocereus species, this plant is free-growing and tolerant of cold weather, though it resents extreme cold. A sunny location is best, and throughout the growing and flowering season it tends to be a thirsty plant.

Echinopsis

This is a large genus of South American cacti. The title refers to the spination of the plants – 'echinus' means hedgehog, and 'opsis' appearance.

ECHINOPSIS		
Light and position  A sunny position is essential; shade is liable to cause etiolation.		**Feeding** Provide weak fertilizers with each watering during the growing season.
Temperature range Cool Intermediate Warm Keep plants very cool and dry in winter; this is essential for successful flowering. In summer temperatures can rise to over 86°F (30°C) without harm to plants.		**Seasonal care** Winter Spring Summer Autumn Pests tend to besiege plants during the rest period, so keep a sharp eye for pests during this time. Offsets can be removed and set early summer. Also repot at this time. Sow seeds in the early spring.
Watering Do not water at all from winter to early spring. Water regularly at other times.		**Soil** Use a mixture of peat, leaf-mould and sharp sand in even parts. Soil must be porous.

Encephalocarpus

Echinopsis aurea 'Aurantiaca' is a colourful species that remains somewhat uncommon in collections. It was originally described by the German authority Curt Backeberg as a member of the *Lobivia* genus, but after subsequent research it has usually been included under *Echinopsis*. Whatever its title, it is nevertheless a plant deservedly coveted because of its unusually coloured flowers.

Its actual origin remains uncertain, but records suggest that its habitat is in Argentina. In growth, the species is very variable, sometimes remaining solitary, but frequently off-setting quite freely. The body of the plant is a dull brownish-green, and has many ribs and somewhat twisted and untidy spination – some of the spines are as much as 2–3in (5–8cm) long. The handsome brownish-orange flowers appear from late June to August.

Encephalocarpus

This is a monotypic genus, and one that has excited the imagination of collectors for many years. A very distinguished species of peculiar charm and attraction, *E. strobiliformis* differs from any other

Encephalocarpus strobiliformis (*above*) is a distinctive species native to Mexico. Scale-like tubercles, compressed together in the form of a cone, distinguish this species from any other cacti. The large, delicately coloured flowers frequently open several at a time, and the flowering period can extend over several weeks.

Echinopsis aurea 'Aurantiaca' (*above*) has unpredictable spination and flowers an uncommon shade of brownish-orange.

cacti on account of the flattened tubercles or scales tightly enclosing the plant body. Its native habitat is Mexico, near the Nuevo León.

The plant has a very pronounced taproot, which indicates it may be related to the genus *Ariocarpus*. The greyish-green tubercles keel outwardly and are pointed at the tips, each having an areole bearing minute spines and wool. Many

flowers are usually produced; their vivid colouring provides a sharp contrast to the greyish tubercles.

Each flower is about 1in (3cm) long, borne from the tips of the young tubercles, and usually opens in late morning and lasts for one day.

This is a real connoisseur's plant, but for all its unique features, *Encephalocarpus strobiliformis* is not necessarily a difficult subject in cultivation. Really good light is necessary, or the tubercles tend to 'bronze' and lose their attractiveness.

ENCEPHALOCARPUS STROBILIFORMIS	
Light and position  Provide plants with very good light rather than full sun, as plants tend to discolour.	**Feeding**  Frequent applications of liquid feed will hasten and extend the flowering period. Feed only in the growth period.
Temperature range Cool　Intermediate　Warm Plants withstand low temperatures in winter but must be kept completely dry. The temperature should not fall below 45°-50°F (7°-10°C). High temperatures are fine as long as plants are shaded	**Seasonal care** 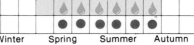 Winter　Spring　Summer　Autumn Keep plants dry and cool in winter. Carefully re-start into growth in spring with small amounts of water. Increase water as weather warms. Repot in summer if necessary. Sow seeds in a temperature about 70°F (21°C).
Watering Water from above or below but never in winter. Excessive water can cause rot.	**Soil** Plants need a typical cactus compost. It must be porous, preferably with good leaf-mould content.

Epicactus

Epicactus

The title 'Epicactus' refers to the numerous hybrids of *Epiphyllum* crossed with other closely related genera. For many years *Phyllocactus* was a name associated with such plants, but it was never botanically acceptable – it means 'leaf-like cactus', and a great number of the plants dubbed this were certainly not leaf-like.

Epicactus plants have been popular for over 100 years. Even in Victorian times many a cottage window was adorned with *Epiphyllum ackermannii,* hybrids which produced a succession of scarlet flowers during the early months of the year, and the plant still retains a place of consequence today. Hybridizers around the world, particularly those in Europe and America, have sought repeatedly to produce new and more exotic strains, resulting in numerous cultivars of almost every colour imaginable – from purest white through cream, yellow, orange, pink, scarlet to deepest purple, plus innumerable tones in between – as well as plants with multicoloured blooms. Really, only green or blue have to date eluded the hybridizers. In earlier times the red cultivar held pride of place, but with the introduction of new colour forms it now competes for popularity.

All epicactus are essentially houseplants. With isolated exceptions, all succeed in the home environment. Flowers last for up to five days, and they are forthcoming successively from March to late June or July.

All cultivars accept the same conditions in cultivation. Very good light, but not full sun, supports continuing good growth. Water regularly throughout the growing season, keeping the soil moist but never wet.

Epicactus 'Regency' is an im-

Epicactus 'Court Pink' (*top*) is a spreading plant with pink flowers. **Epicactus 'Impello'** (*left*) has fragrant flowers in pastel shades. **Epicactus 'Pegasus'** (*above*) is a tall plant that demands space but flowers for several weeks.

proved form of 'Cooperi', a direct product of *Epiphyllum crenatum,* a beautiful white flowering species, and *Selenicereus grandiflorus,* which is better known as Queen of the Night and has creamy-white, almost yellow flowers. Both parents are truly epiphytic and are responsible for the plant's beautiful scent. In flowering, *Epicactus* 'Regency' is very similar in habit to *Epiphyllum crenatum,* being day-flowering. In shape, it is also similar, with its trumpet-shaped bloom, 5in (13cm) in diameter. The colouring is obviously derived from both parents, the pale yellowish-cream being very much in evidence. Stems are flat, thick

and smooth, often 16in (40cm) or so in length.

Epicactus 'Queen Anne' has a more complicated parentage, the result of a hybrid being crossed with a hybrid in an attempt to create a yellow form. This dwarf yellow cultivar is one of the finest epicactus. Stems rarely exceed 12in (30cm) in length, are mainly flat but somewhat twisting, and give a wonderful succession of flowers, medium in size, from late March to June.

Epicactus 'Giant Empress' is an improved form of 'Deutsche Kaiserin', one of the earliest of hybrids. Here again the stems are slender and flattened.

This plant makes an excellent subject for a hanging basket, and as such will thrive in normal house conditions.

Epicactus 'Court Pink' is a spreading plant. The stems and branches rarely stand erect, but are certainly not pendent. The medium-sized blooms are produced freely along the branches, and while predominantly pink, there is just a suggestion of an orange suffusion in the colouring. This plant is of British origin, but little is known of the parentage, except that it is apparently not a direct hybrid between definite species. One interesting characteristic of the plant is that the buds are deep yellow before opening.

Epicactus 'Impello' is one of the author's hybrids, developed over a period of seven to eight years in Sussex. Some hybrids are planned; others 'just arrive'. Indeed there was planning in this particular instance – an attempt to produce a yellow epicactus. However, when this plant's unusual colouring made itself manifest, it was decided to cultivate the hybrid for its own sake. It is highly scented, and with its delicate shadings of pink, lilac and pale violet and the erect yet not over-tall growth, it has proved itself to be one of the best of the paler, multicoloured cultivars.

Epicactus 'Pegasus' is of American origin and is undoubtedly outstanding. Flowers are extra large, with reddish-orange petals. Sepals are edged brownish-violet and often have a ruffled appearance. The plants are generally rather tall, as high as 24in (61cm); the branches are flat and wide and very firm. This is one of the best of the darker-coloured varieties with multicoloured flowers. Flowers are readily and regularly produced, and in a large space this cultivar will be a rewarding showpiece.

Epicactus 'Giant Empress' (*top*) is a plant that makes an excellent subject for a hanging basket.
Epicactus 'Regency' (*above left*) is a sturdy, late-blooming plant.
Epicactus 'Queen Anne' (*above right*) is valued for its compact growth.

EPICACTUS	
Light and position	**Feeding**
Full sun is not good for epicacti — A bright but semi-shaded location is best.	Establish regular weak fertilizing directly flower buds appear. Thereafter, fertilize until September.
Temperature range	**Seasonal care**
Cool Intermediate Warm A temperature of 45°F (7°C) is the lowest epicactus can accept, and since plants should never dry out it's best to maintain a temperature of 50°F (10°C) for safety.	Winter Spring Summer Autumn After flowering, plants can be placed outdoors in shade until early autumn . Watch for pests and remember to water. Such treatment encourages branches to mature and to bear flowers the following season. Take cuttings in the summer.
Watering	**Soil**
Always keep plants just moist. Water freely in spring, but never let plants stand in water.	Epicacti will do well in a mixture of equal parts peat, leaf-mould and sharp sand, to which basic fertilizer has been added.

Epithelantha/Ferocactus/Gymnocactus

Epithelantha

Epithelantha micromeris is the sole member of the *Epithelantha* genus, for although there are supposedly a few varieties of the species, they are more likely to be just local forms.

The habitat of *Epithelantha micromeris*, sometimes called the Button Cactus, covers quite a widespread area, from West Texas in the USA to Coahuila in northern Mexico.

The body of the plant is basically spherical, although sometimes it elongates or even develops small groups. Numerous minute white spines cover the whole plant, and these are longer towards the crown. It is from the often woolly area of the crown that the flowers develop.

Flowers are mainly pink, rather small in size, but with several opening at once they make a most pleasing effect. The seed capsules that develop later are scarlet, somewhat club-shaped, and contain a few black seeds. If sown the following year, these should germinate successfully.

Care should be taken in cultivation. A sunny position is important, together with a very

open soil to which lime is added. Excellent drainage will avoid the possibility of root-rot – plants with taproots such as *Epithelantha micromeris* are susceptible to overwatering. Keep completely dry from late October to March. Flower buds appear soon after.

Ferocactus

The generic title refers to the rather fierce spination that is apparent on all species of this popular genus.

Ferocactus fordii is one of the lesser-known cacti, found in a rather limited area of Baja Cali-

Epithelantha micromeris (*above*) has pink flowers and is one of the neatest of miniature cacti. Use rich calcareous soil to maintain the distinctive colour of the tubercles.

fornia in Mexico. It is also one of the most beautiful cacti, particularly when in flower. The fact that it rarely grows too large makes it welcome in the greenhouse.

The dark greyish-green body is globular in shape, rarely exceeding 5in (13cm) in diameter. The horizontal ribs, usually 21 of them, carry areoles situated about 1in (3cm) apart, and with these are

EPITHELANTHA

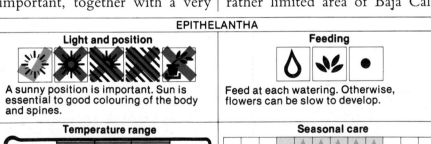

Light and position

A sunny position is important. Sun is essential to good colouring of the body and spines.

Feeding

Feed at each watering. Otherwise, flowers can be slow to develop.

Temperature range

Cool | Intermediate | Warm

Maintain the temperature around 50°F (10-12°C) during the coldest months, but let the temperature rise as the growing season approaches.

Seasonal care

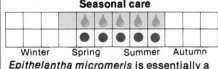

Winter | Spring | Summer | Autumn

Epithelantha micromeris is essentially a desert plant that can be 'forgotten' in winter, but in spring can be coerced into prime growth and flower development with a little extra care. Repot in summer, making sure the pot drains well Sow seeds in winter months.

Watering

Do not water from late autumn to early spring. Thereafter, water moderately and regularly as soon as plants are dry.

Soil

The epithelantha needs a typical cactus soil, 30 percent being sharp grit with leaf-mould and lime.

Ferocactus fordii (*above*) is smaller than most ferocactus species. It enjoys full sun in its native habitat and needs excellent light to flourish indoors.

associated about 15 stiff spines, white in colour and radiating around four larger central spines, one of which is hooked and thick, about 2in (5cm) long.

This is a plant that grows in full sun. In nature it is seldom found in scrub country, so place it in the sunniest spot available in your house or greenhouse. Without excellent light, the spines are liable to lose their lustre and flowering will be affected. Only with good light do blooms come readily and maintain their attractive colouring. The majority of ferocactus have yellow flowers, but *Ferocactus fordii* boasts of deep rose-red or pale violet blooms, all carried within the crown of the plant. Guard against overwatering – plants require no water at all from early November to late March – but when watering commences, be sure to add fertilizers regularly.

Gymnocactus

A small genus of plants created in quite recent years, *Gymnocactus* contains a number of plants originally included under *Thelocactus*. There is certainly a close affinity, but species of gymnocactus tend to have much smaller flowers.

FEROCACTUS	
Light and position Place plants in full sunshine, or spine colour will fade and flowers will be less readily produced.	**Feeding** 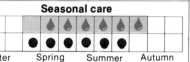 Feed with weak liquid fertilizer at each watering. Do not fertilize in winter.
Temperature range Cool　Intermediate　Warm Maintain a winter temperature of 45°F (8°C), keeping plants dry. During growth, temperatures can rise to 90°F (32°C).	**Seasonal care** Winter　Spring　Summer　Autumn Complete dryness during the rest season is essential and will prove invaluable when the new growing season commences. Plants in full growth need plenty of water and fertilizer
Watering Keep plants completely dry during the winter months. In summer, water either early morning or late afternoon.	**Soil** Most cactus composts are suitable, but be sure there is sufficient sharp sand added. A mixture of loam, peat, leaf-mould and sand in even parts is advised.

Gymnocactus viereckii (*above*) is a lesser-known Mexican cactus. The dense spination almost obscures the bluish-green body and is an outstanding feature of the plant.

These arise from the well-developed areole, which is elongated and resembles a short furrow.

Gymnocactus viereckii is one of the more uncommon species, but is gradually becoming more available as nurseries develop plants from seeds. Native to eastern Mexico, it has a globular stem densely covered with longish spines of silvery white, almost obliterating the ribs. The stem only grows to about 3in (8cm) in diameter, is deep bluish-green in colour and crowned with twisted white wool. Through this wool emerge the flowers, and their unusual colouring emphasizes the beauty of the species.

With care, *Gymnocactus viereckii* will produce its seed capsules quite readily – these are entirely spineless, as is the ovary. This is a particular feature of the genus and probably accounts for its generic title – 'gymno' means 'spineless'.

In cultivation, plants need good light. They succeed quite well on a window ledge, but not if the window faces north. Keep plants completely dry during winter, but water regularly while in active growth. Fertilize during the growing season to ensure flowering.

GYMNOCACTUS	
Light and position 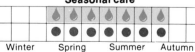 Plants will take full sunshine, but a position in good direct light is preferable.	**Feeding** Use weak liquid fertilizer with each watering, but withhold fertilizer in winter.
Temperature range Cool　Intermediate　Warm Try to maintain a temperature of 50°F (10°C) in winter. Thereafter, plants can receive higher temperatures without injury.	**Seasonal care** Winter　Spring　Summer　Autumn Repot immediately after the rest period. Be sure not to overpot; plants like to feel they 'belong'. Sow seeds in the early spring. Watch for pests at all times.
Watering Keep plants quite dry during dormancy. Water from April onwards. Never allow plants to stand in water.	**Soil** Use equal parts loam, peat and sharp sand, and add a basic fertilizer.

Heliocereus/Mammillaria

Heliocereus

This genus represents some of the most glamorous flowers within the Cactaceae. Without exception, each species carry blooms of outstanding beauty, but *Heliocereus speciosus* 'Superbus' is supreme in size, colour and elegance. This variety, together with other species of heliocereus, has been instrumental in introducing some of the original spectacular colourings apparent in early-day epicactus cultivars.

An erect-growing plant, the Sun Cactus is up to 24in (60cm) tall. The stem has six to seven angles or ribs and very prominent areoles, with many short brownish-yellow spines. Its habitat is in central Mexico, near to Mexico City, where in shady areas its habit can be that of a clambering plant. Occasionally it is an epiphyte, rooting in the shade and bearing flowers towards the tips of the stems in the sun.

The flowers are the plant's important feature. Their brilliant, dark, crimson-red blooms, frequently 6in (15cm) long, give this variety a place of consequence; in flowers of this colouring, it has no equal in the world of cactus.

Heliocereus speciocus 'Superbus' (*above*), commonly called the Sun Plant, is native to Mexico. The superb crimson-red blooms this plant produces make it a popular parent for epicactus cultivars. Despite its exotic appearance, this plant is not difficult to cultivate indoors.

Plants will take a shady place so long as their flowers can open in the sun. They are generally easy to cultivate and do not demand a high temperature. A compost including leaf-mould, peat and sand in even proportions is recommended.

Mammillaria

Mammillaria is one of the most important and justifiably popular genera of the large cactus family. To provide even a representative selection of these 400 or more species and varieties would prove a mammoth task. Cushion Cactus, the common name, is certainly applicable in many instances, but not in all. While a numerous species offset freely and develop 'cushions' – flat mounds of growth – others remain solitary plants, attaining quite sizeable dimensions. The majority are of North American origin, native to Mexico and to varying places in the USA. A very few particularly choice species have their natural home in the West Indies. It is perhaps significant that a specialist society exists just to encompass this and a few kindred genera – such is its importance to cactus enthusiasts.

In cultivation, mammillarias generally are among the least difficult plants to manage. Cushion-type plants seem to benefit from good light rather than full sun. In nature, the majority of species are found near, or even under, scrub. However, plants with a solitary

---

HELIOCEREUS

Light and position

Place pots in semi-shade. The tips of the stems will grow in the direction of the light and help flower production.

Feeding

Fertilize while watering. It's the easy way of obtaining flowers.

Temperature range

Cool	Intermediate	Warm

The Sun Cactus should be kept quite cool during overwintering, around 45°F (7°C). Beginning in spring, gradually raise the temperature a few degrees at a time.

Seasonal care

Winter	Spring	Summer	Autumn

After winter dormancy, trim or prune the plant if necessary. Cuttings can be taken in summer before flower buds appear; they will root readily once they have callused. Overwatering in very hot weather can prove dangerous, causing stem-rot.

Watering

Keep plants dry while temperatures are low. Then water freely once growth is underway.

Soil

Equal parts leaf-mould, peat and sharp, gritty sand suit this plant well.

habit prefer full sun. Careful watering is essential with all species, perhaps to a greater degree with the cushion type, for if water remains too long around the plant in inclement weather, when natural evaporation is less likely, rot can set in. All species require a really porous soil; good drainage must be a major concern.

Mammillaria oliviae is one of the species with the inclination to group, the offsets appearing towards the base of the plant. In current botanical opinion, this plant is represented as a variety of *Mammillaria microcarpa*, with

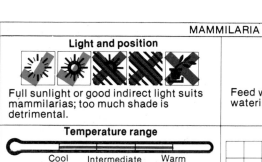

MAMMILARIA		
Light and position		**Feeding**
Full sunlight or good indirect light suits mammilarias; too much shade is detrimental.		Feed with weak liquid fertilizer at each watering.
Temperature range		**Seasonal care**
Cool Intermediate Warm		Winter Spring Summer Autumn
The temperature can be low — about 50°F (10°C) — if plants are kept completely dry in winter. When in growth, plants will tolerate high temperatures.		Keep plants out of draughts during the dry overwintering. Repot from mid to late spring but before flower buds appear. Offsets can be removed in the growth period and used for propagation. Sow seeds from late winter to early spring.
Watering		
In inclement weather, watering may have to be restricted. Keep plants completely dry in winter months ·		**Soil** Use a mixture of loam, peat, leaf-mould and sharp sand in even proportions.

Mammillaria mystax (*above*) is one of over 400 mammillaria species found in Mexico and the USA. The symmetrical arrangement of the spiny tubercles in conspicuous spirals is an outstanding feature. In *Mammillaria mystax*, reddish flowers form rings around the crown.
Mammillaria oliviae (*right*) has a clustering habit and produces large flowers that are variable in colour. The species is native to Mexico and the southwestern USA, where in habitat it enjoys the rather sparse protection of surrounding scrub.

which it obviously has a close affinity. It is native to Sonora in northern Mexico and also appears in southern Arizona in the USA.

A heavily spined plant, *Mammillaria oliviae* has 25–35 whitish spines to an areole, including up to three longer central spines. The flowers are the crowning feature, their pale to medium pink blooms are in evidence for a number of weeks in late spring and early summer. With individual flowers close to 1in (3cm) in diameter and occurring successively over a long

period, it is a very desirable plant. Flowers can be variable in colour. White and violet tones are frequently apparent.

Mammillaria mystax is one of the most well-known species originating in high ground in southern Mexico, at altitudes of around 6,000 feet (1800m). The stem is usually solitary, as much as 12in (30cm) tall, darkish green, sometimes reddish green, often woolly on the crown. The tubercles are symmetrically arranged, the areoles white and woolly, especially on young growth. Spines can be variable in number, size and colour, but are usually white. One of the most pleasing aspects of the plant is the arrangement of the flowers; these occur in a ring around the crown and are numerous. Each of these flowers is around 1in (3cm) or a little less in diameter and is reddish pink, sometimes carmine-red in colour. Flowering is during the early months of summer.

Mammillaria mystax needs more sun than *Mammillaria oliviae*. If this is provided, it makes an excellent houseplant, thriving quite as well on a window ledge as in a greenhouse.

Melocactus/Neogomesia/Notocactus

Melocactus

Turk's Cap Cactus were among the very earliest cactus species introduced into cultivation, and due to their exceptionally unusual body shape, they have fascinated collectors for years.

All known species are native to South America, and are also found in Central America, Mexico and several of the West Indian islands. Many specific titles are debatable, as it's very difficult to determine what species young plants are until they reach reasonable maturity.

Great understanding must be exercised in cultivation – melocacti are not easy plants to grow in either greenhouse or home. They need a considerably higher temperature than other kinds of cactus; a minimum of 59°F (15°C) is required to maintain the majority of melocacti successfully. Placing plants in good light with as much sun as possible is advantageous, for in their native habitat they are constantly exposed to the sun and receive little or no shade.

The plants depicted are *Melocactus bahiensis,* a Brazilian species. Note the cephalium, or crown, which develops as plants mature, and from which the pinkish-red flowers emerge.

Neogomesia

This is a controversial genus created for just one species. Its title commemorates a certain Marte Gomez, a governor of Tamaulipas, where *Neogomesia agavoides* was discovered.

Neogomesia agavoides is a mountain plant from limestone slopes near Tula (Tamaulipas) in eastern Mexico. The species name refers to the shape and formation of the elongated tubercles, which resemble a miniature agave's leaf structure. Plants are quite small, only 3in (8cm) or so above ground level, greyish-green in colour, and

rise from a large rootstock in the form of a somewhat round taproot. Flowers are somewhat bell-shaped, about 2in (5cm) long and pale to deep reddish-pink. They are produced from the newest, large woolly areoles found near the tips of the upper surfaces of the tubercles.

This is yet another plant for the 'specialist' collector. Although its existence has been known for a great number of years, it still remains uncommon.

Notocactus claviceps (*right*) has whitish-yellow spines and soft-textured flowers that bloom in summer.
Melocactus bahiensis (*below*) is a Brazilian species whose pinkish-red flowers emerge from the cephalium of the plant.

NEOGOMESIA

Light and position

Neogomesia agavoides benefits from full sunshine and an airy position.

Feeding

Apply weak liquid feed when watering, preferably around the base of the plant.

Temperature range

Cool   Intermediate   Warm

Keep a minimum temperature of 50°F (10°C) to avert any tendency to root damage. Throughout growing season, temperatures can rise considerably, to 80-90°F (27-32°C), without harm.

Seasonal care

Winter   Spring   Summer   Autumn

After winter dormancy, repot if necessary, but be careful of the large taproot — a deep container is advisable.

Watering

Keep plants very dry during dormancy; water only moderately thereafter. Never water when the soil is still moist.

Soil
A very porous soil is of paramount importance. Use one rich in humus that will not hold moisture for too long.

good sunny position with a winter temperature of around 50°F (10°C). During the growing and flowering season – spring and summer – plants must be watered freely and fertilized regularly. This encourages the plant to develop and flower. Flowers may last for several days. A rich compost is necessary – the introduction of leaf-mould will work wonders. This, with peat and gritty sand in even proportions, makes an ideal growing medium.

Notocactus claviceps would appear to be closely related to the popular *Notocactus leninghausii* species, but has certain distinctive differences. The spines of *N. leninghausii* are golden-yellow. Those of *N. claviceps* are whitish yellow, longer, and untidily arranged along the 26–30 ribs, which have deep furrows between them. Flowers have been described as whitish gold – they undoubtedly have a silvery sheen on their pale golden petals. This species has its habitat in Brazil, where it is found at altitudes of around 6,500ft (2,000m).

Neogomesia agavoides (*left*) has elongated tubercles and bell-shaped flowers. Native to eastern Mexico, the plant now faces extinction.

Notocactus

Notocactus is a very important, popular and colourful genus.

While the flower colour range is limited – primarily varying shades of yellow and reddish purple – the different shapes these plants assume are an eye-catching feature. All known species are of South American origin. Plants are mainly solitary, but with maturity several of the species sprout offsets at the base, thus developing attractive clusters.

Notocactus generally are considered excellent subjects for cultivation in the home and greenhouse. The main requirement is a

MELOCACTUS

Light and position

This plant needs full sun; very little shade can be tolerated.

Feeding

Feed regularly at each watering between late April and early October.

Temperature range

Cool   Intermediate   Warm

During winter, it is wise to maintain a 59°F (15°C) minimum temperature. This temperature can increase to 80-90°F (30°C plus) when melocactus are in growth

Seasonal care

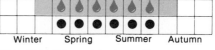

Winter   Spring   Summer   Autumn

The spreading root system offers problems if soil dries out too much and too often. Hence careful watering is essential at all times to avoid both dehydration and wet-rot; either can happen.

Watering

Melocactus easily dries off, so keep root system just moist in coolest weather. Water freely in the growing season.

Soil
Use leaf-mould, loam and sharp sand in even proportions. Make sure the mixture is completely lime-free.

Notocactus/Selenicereus/Weingartia

Notocactus uebelmannianus is a rather flattened, globular plant of glossy dark green, some 7in (18cm) in diameter and 5in (13cm) high. The 14 or more ribs are bedecked with greyish spines of unequal length – some directed upwards, others downwards, without any set pattern. The rich violet-red flowers caused a sensation when this species was discovered just a few years ago and became available to amateur collectors. Such colouring is not common in the genus.

The 2in (5cm) diameter flowers, produced several at a time in the crown of the plant, with the whitish style and yellow filaments adorning their centres, make this an outstanding species. It is found only in a very limited area near Cacapava in Rio Grande do Sul, Brazil.

NOTOCACTUS

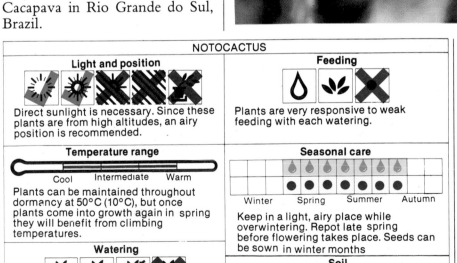

Light and position
Direct sunlight is necessary. Since these plants are from high altitudes, an airy position is recommended.

Temperature range
Cool — Intermediate — Warm

Plants can be maintained throughout dormancy at 50°C (10°C), but once plants come into growth again in spring they will benefit from climbing temperatures.

Watering
Keep plants dry in winter. Water from above or below, but not in the midday sun or scorching could ensue.

Feeding
Plants are very responsive to weak feeding with each watering.

Seasonal care
Winter — Spring — Summer — Autumn

Keep in a light, airy place while overwintering. Repot late spring before flowering takes place. Seeds can be sown in winter months

Soil
Notocactus thrive in a rich compost that includes good dehydrated leaf-mould, peat and sharp sand. Keep the mixture porous.

Notocactus uebelmannianus (*top left*) is remarkable for its violet-red flowers. **Selenicereus innesii** (*left*) is an epiphytic species native to the West Indies that bears fragrant flowers.

Selenicereus

All species of selenicereus are epiphytic or partially so. They are climbing or clambering plants, occasionally pendent in habit.

Selenicereus innesii, which this author discovered growing on a shoreline rock-face in the West Indian island of St Vincent, has proved to be unique in the world of cacti. While most cacti bear flowers with both male and female organs, some *Selenicereus innesii* plants produce flowers that have either only male organs or only female organs. The species may have been completely destroyed in habitat because of the volcanic disturbances in the 1970s that played havoc with the northerly parts of that beautiful island.

There are no special difficulties in growing *Selenicereus innesii* in cultivation. The plant with its flowers is here depicted – each trumpet-shaped bloom is slightly scented and provides a display for several weeks on end, particularly in late summer. It is an ideal subject for a hanging basket; most of the branches hang down, but some are occasionally semi-erect.

SELENICEREUS

Light and position

Plant *Selenicereus innesii* in the semi-shade near a window, so that plants can climb towards the light.

Temperature range

Cool   Intermediate   Warm

In winter, keep temperature reasonably cool at 55°F (13°C). Plants appreciate high temperature and high humidity during the growing season from spring to autumn.

Watering

Water freely during the growing and flowering period. Keep plants just moist during the resting period.

Feeding

Water and fertilize at the same time; spraying the stems and branches will enhance the appearance of the plant.

Seasonal care

Winter   Spring   Summer   Autumn

Pruning and general tidying of the plant should take place from early spring to the summer. Cuttings taken then will usually root quite readily.

Soil

A rich compost with a good deal of humus added is conducive to growth. Keep the mixture very porous.

Weingartia multispina (*left*) is one of the most densely spined cactus.

WEINGARTIA

Light and position

Weingartia multispina requires direct sunlight at all times. 'Good' sunlight is inadequate.

Temperature range

Cool   Intermediate   Warm

During winter dormancy, keep plants at a temperature of 50°F (10°C). Gradually increase this from spring onwards, when plants respond to the natural warmth of summer.

Watering

Do not water from late autumn to late spring. Thereafter, water freely, but be sure there is excellent drainage.

Feeding

Weak liquid fertilizer should be included with every watering, particularly during the warmest months of the year.

Seasonal care

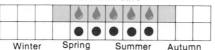

Winter   Spring   Summer   Autumn

Extreme care is essential in winter; moisture or draughts will cause plants to suffer. If required, repot in summer — this may prove to be an annual necessity. Seeds can be sown in winter months in a temperature of 70°F (21°C).

Soil

Use leaf-mould, loam and sharp sand in even parts. *Weingartia multispina* likes an acid substrate.

Weingartia

The genus *Weingartia* comprises a few very desirable species. One of the most unusual is *Weingartia multispina,* which is found in Bolivia near Aiquile, Cochabamba. The stem or body can attain 6in (15cm) or more in diameter and is bright green in colour. At first it is almost globular, but it often becomes somewhat cylindrical in maturity. Areoles are densely and evenly distributed, each bearing 25–30 thin, spreading spines, pale to deep brown in colour, about ½in (1cm) long, and 20 or more longer central spines of similar colour.

The symmetrical flowers are numerous. They are carried around the crown of the plant, and are yellow in colour with a greenish sheen, accentuated by the greenish yellow style.

By no means a common plant in cultivation, *Weingartia multispina* needs a position in good sunlight. Water and fertilize regularly during summer months, but keep very dry throughout the winter. Heavily spined plants are subject to wet-rot if incorrectly watered.

Aloe/Ceropegia

Aloe

One of the foremost genera of succulent plants, the *Aloe* genus comprises Old World plants originating from various parts of Africa, Arabia and Madagascar. These are indeed succulent lilies, possessing many of the same characteristics as the more familiar varieties of the lily family. With only a few exceptions, the foliage is thick and fleshy, exuding moisture if broken. Their succulence lies in their leaves; plants are able to store nourishment to withstand periods of drought in a countryside where little rainfall is registered for months at a time.

Aloe niebuhriana is quite a unique species, and, though discovered over two decades ago, it still remains uncommon in private collections. It is one of the comparatively few plants of the genus so far located in Arabia. It was found in South Yemen at altitudes up to 1,640 feet (500m), growing on hot, dry hillsides and low-lying valleys in semi-arid country. The first plants discovered had scarlet flowers. Later, when plants that had a yellowish green colour were found, it was thought that they constituted another new species. It is now an accepted fact that the flowers are variable, but

regardless of colour they have the peculiarity of being pubescent, which is not often characteristic of African species.

Leaves are thick and greyish green. The rosette is comprised of 15–25 leaves, their margins armed with dark brown teeth. Flowering occurs during the early weeks of the year, the stem developing from the side of the rosette, not the apex.

Aloe 'Sabra' is a hybrid, devel-

Aloe niebuhriana (*left*) is one of the few Arabian species grown indoors. Plants are fluffily pubescent and covered with short, fine hairs.
Aloe 'Sabra' is a floriferous hybrid that bears pink blooms in the autumn (*above*).

oped by the author several years ago. It derives from *Aloe bellatula*, a pinkish-flowered species, and *Aloe albiflora*, one of the few white-flowering plants of the genus. The latter is distinctive in having a wide bell-shaped bloom about ½in (1cm) in diameter. That of *Aloe bellatula* is more rounded and cylindrical. Both species are Madagascan plants in origin. The leaves indicate their very close affinity; in shape, length and colour there is little to distinguish one from the other. The resultant cultivar retains leaves similar to both parents; the flowers have the shape of *Aloe albiflora* but have the colouring of *Aloe bellatula*.

There are no untoward problems with cultivation. The flowers of *Aloe* 'Sabra' begin to show in mid-September and continue over a period of several weeks. They are borne on stems about 12in (30cm) tall; there are usually two or three inflorescences on each plant. Given a bright position, *Aloe* 'Sabra' makes an excellent flowering houseplant. *Aloe niebuhriana* flowers later and is considerably taller than *Aloe* 'Sabra', reaching a height of 35in (90cm) when in full spike.

ALOE

Light and position	Feeding
 Good light is essential since flowers occur late or early in the year. Shade will diminish flower potential.	 Provide weak liquid feed with most waterings.
Temperature range	**Seasonal care**
Cool Intermediate Warm Never let the temperature fall below 50°F (10°C), and try to secure even higher temperatures as flowering time nears.	Winter Spring Summer Autumn Remove offsets for propagation in the summer. Be careful when doing this, for some may have roots attached. Sow seeds in winter months in a temperature of 70°F (21°C), covering the seeds with sharp sand.
Watering	**Soil**
Water moderately throughout the year, but never let plants stand in water or get too wet.	Use a permeable mixture that includes humus.

Ceropegia

There are few groups of succulents that are as captivating to the eye as ceropegias. The rootstock of these consists of a globular or elongated fleshy tuber, producing long twining or trailing stems. Flowers are the most intriguing feature of ceropegias, more than compensating for the somewhat uninteresting stem and leaf growth. Flowers take the form of old-fashioned lanterns, and bloom in a combination of colours rarely encountered in the plant world. The plants are native to many parts of Africa, India and the Canary Islands, and almost all are adaptable to growing indoors. Many of these plants trail; narrow stakes, wires or slim trellis can afford stems a good anchorage and will help display the flowers to advantage.

Ceropegia adelaidae is quite possibly a variety of *Ceropegia devecchii,* a Somali plant that is itself a remarkable species. With its intricate markings and artistic shape, almost artificial in its contours, the flower is the outstanding feature. It is produced from attractive mottled stems, which are divided into long internodes. From the nodes small leaves sometimes appear but quickly fade. The flower is also produced from the nodes. The plant is native to northern areas of Kenya and the neighbouring Somalia border.

Ceropegia haygarthii is a fine trailing and twining species with elongated, slender green stems. Greenish, ivy-shaped leaves develop in pairs at intervals along the stems and are always set opposite one another. The flower is startling in shape and colouring – a purple-spotted trumpet-shaped bloom, with pinkish ground colour, is crowned by the incurved lobes that unite to produce the slender, pistil-like column. This

Ceropegia nilotica (*above*),
Ceropegia haygarthii (*above right*) and
Ceropegia adelaidae (*right*) produce lantern-shaped blooms in which pollinating insects are often trapped. Insects are released only after pollination is effected.

species is from South Africa.

Ceropegia nilotica is a tropical East African plant. The four-angled fleshy stems arise from a tuberous rootstock. Leaves, set opposite one another, are very succulent. They are oval in shape,

tapering to a point at the tip, and persist until after the flowers have faded. Flowers form from the axils of the upper leaves, usually blooming two together. They have an intricate shape and are dark brown with yellow markings.

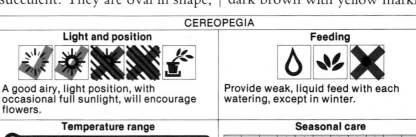

CEREOPEGIA		
Light and position		**Feeding**
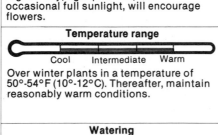		
A good airy, light position, with occasional full sunlight, will encourage flowers.		Provide weak, liquid feed with each watering, except in winter.
Temperature range		**Seasonal care**
Cool Intermediate Warm		Winter Spring Summer Autumn
Over winter plants in a temperature of 50°-54°F (10°-12°C). Thereafter, maintain reasonably warm conditions.		Trim shoots and stems in early summer; cuttings can be used for propagation. Sow seeds in winter in a temperature of 70°F (21°C) or a little higher. Cover seeds with sharp sand.
Watering		**Soil**
Water slightly in winter; complete drying-off is not recommended. Water moderately at other times.		Use peat, leaf-mould and gritty sand in equal parts. Add just a little loam; soil must be porous.

Crassula/Euphorbia/Hoya

Crassula

This is the largest genus of plants within the Crassulaceae family and has over 300 species. They are extremely varied. Some are large and shrub-like; others have densely compacted leaves in the form of a miniature column only 2in (5cm) or so high. In all instances, leaves are set opposite one another, and flowers are usually in panicles.

Crassula falcata is native to southeastern parts of Cape Province in South Africa, and can grow to a height of 3¼ft (1m) when in flower. While the flowers are very beautiful, the plant can be a little unwieldy for normal households.

A number of hybrids have resulted from *Crassula falcata,* and are probably the product of crosspollination with *Crassula perfoliata.* A rather miniaturized replica of the former, *Crassula falcata* hybrid, has become a most useful plant. It has the species' leaf shape and flower colour, but rarely grows taller than 12in (30cm). Being of hybrid origin, it can only be reproduced by vegetative means. Two methods are possible – sectional stem cuttings, or leaf cuttings. The latter method is slower, but more satisfactory.

Crassula falcata hybrid (*top*) bears long-lasting blooms. It is smaller and more suitable for indoor cultivation than its parent.
Euphorbia flanaganii (*above*) has a caudex whose head is crowned with spreading branches. Because of its shape, this species is said to have a 'Medusa' head.

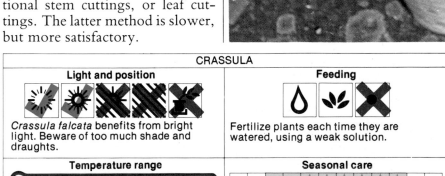

CRASSULA

Light and position	Feeding
Crassula falcata benefits from bright light. Beware of too much shade and draughts.	Fertilize plants each time they are watered, using a weak solution.

Temperature range	Seasonal care
Cool Intermediate Warm During winter months, maintain plants at about 55°F (13°C). As the growing season starts, increase temperatures accordingly.	Winter Spring Summer Autumn Trim plants into shape in spring . Cuttings can be taken early summer — keep them shaded during rooting. Seeds are best sown in the early autumn, keeping the temperature at 70°F (21°C) until germination is affected. Then give seedlings a good light, airy position.

Watering	Soil
Keep plants completely dry in winter, but if placed in temperatures above 55°F (13°C), water them at soil level.	Mix peat, leaf-mould and sharp sand in equal parts. The introduction of a little loam is helpful.

EUPHORBIA

Light and position
Full sun or partial shade will suit this species, which needs an airy position.

Feeding
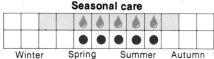
Apply weak fertilizer with each watering when plants are in full growth.

Temperature range
Cool   Intermediate   Warm

In winter, a minimum temperature of 55°F (13°C) is best for safety. At all other times, high temperatures are generally conducive to growth.

Seasonal care
	Winter		Spring		Summer		Autumn	

Watch for any root-rot should temperatures fall below those recommended for winter. Bring plants into growth in spring . Take cuttings in summer . Dip in tepid water to stop 'bleeding'; set when calloused. Sow seeds in the early spring

Watering

Keep plants fairly dry, scarcely moist in winter. Water abundantly during the growing period.

Soil
Use loam, peat and gritty sand in equal parts, adding a small quantity of humus.

Hoya multiflora (*above*) has only recently been grown as a houseplant. It is one of many succulent species in the *Hoya* genus.

Euphorbia

Euphorbia is one of the largest genera of plants and is said to include over 2,000 different species. A number of species are succulent, principally those found in Africa, Madagascar, Arabia, the Indian subcontinent and parts of Central and South America. Their weird, often almost grotesque shapes attract the attention of the plant enthusiast, but no less so than the many species with growth of perfect symmetry.

Euphorbia flanaganii grows in South Africa. It has a low, subcylindrical caudex at just above ground level, crowned with two to three rows of more or less erect 'branches' set around the tuberculate head of the caudex. The older branches tend to spread and help to create the attractive form depicted. The inflorescence, or cyathia, is a characteristic of the whole genus – some have male or female 'flowers' on the same plant, other are unisexual.

All euphorbia plants have a dangerous white sap or latex that will exude upon any injury to the plant. Care should be taken that this sap does not reach cuts or any sensitive part of the body.

Hoya

Fleshy, wax-like flowers are a generic characteristic of hoyas. A few species, like *Hoya carnosa* and *Hoya bella,* have held pride of place as houseplants for many years. *Hoya multiflora* is yet another species now adorning many homes. Its habitat is the Malacca Straits region – Sumatra, Borneo and Java.

There appears to be two forms of *Hoya multiflora*. One is of climbing habit; the other remains bushy, but leaf and flower are identical. The leaves are large, leathery, dark green, often with whitish blotches. Flowers are borne in terminal clusters, 25–30 individual flowers in each. The bloom is straw coloured, has a brown centre, is sweetly scented and proves to be long lasting.

Like *Hoya carnosa, Hoya multiflora* requires training. Otherwise the plant becomes untidy and loses its appeal. Prune carefully in late spring. Make certain that any flow of the white sap is staunched by inserting the cuts in water.

HOYA

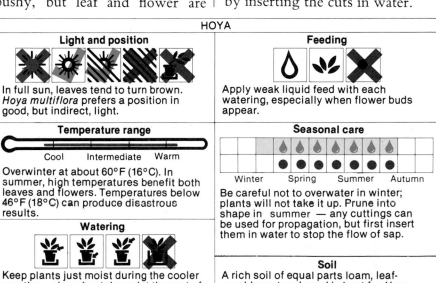

Light and position
In full sun, leaves tend to turn brown. *Hoya multiflora* prefers a position in good, but indirect, light.

Feeding
Apply weak liquid feed with each watering, especially when flower buds appear.

Temperature range
Cool   Intermediate   Warm

Overwinter at about 60°F (16°C). In summer, high temperatures benefit both leaves and flowers. Temperatures below 46°F (18°C) can produce disastrous results.

Seasonal care
	Winter		Spring		Summer		Autumn	

Be careful not to overwater in winter; plants will not take it up. Prune into shape in summer — any cuttings can be used for propagation, but first insert them in water to stop the flow of sap.

Watering
Keep plants just moist during the cooler months and moderately moist the rest of the year.

Soil
A rich soil of equal parts loam, leaf-mould, peat and sand is best for *Hoya multiflora*.

Huernia/Ipomoea/Lampranthus

Huernia

This is an important genus in the Asclepiadaceae family. There are a large number of species in this genus, and they are all found in an area stretching from South Africa to Ethiopia. They belong to the milkweed family, and in the main develop into cushion-like plants, the stems and side branches continually spreading and rooting, rarely growing more than 2in (5cm) high. While the stems of various species are usually quite similar, flowers vary and present an elaborate array of colours and shapes.

Huernia schneiderana was discovered many years ago by a Dutch missionary. His name was Justus Huernius, and the genus was subsequently named in his honour. The species was found on the northern side of Lake Malawi, and its habitat extends from Malawi through to Mozambique.

The stem growth of *Huernia schneiderana* is remarkably rapid. The slender green cylindrical stems quickly form a compacted grouping. Each stem is about 2in (6cm) long, though in cultivation stems may become considerably longer. Stems are five-to-seven-angled, with inconspicuous acute teeth.

The shallow bell-shaped flowers, about 1½in (3cm) in diameter, appear towards the base of the stem and bloom in late summer. Externally, the flowers are dull brown in colour; internally, they are velvety blackish-purple with reddish margins, the lobes recurving so as to display the rich colouring. Plants are equally suitable for home or greenhouse. They need good light and frequent watering during the growing season.

Huernia verekeri is from southern Zimbabwe, near the Mozambique border. Stems are always diminutive, only about 1½in

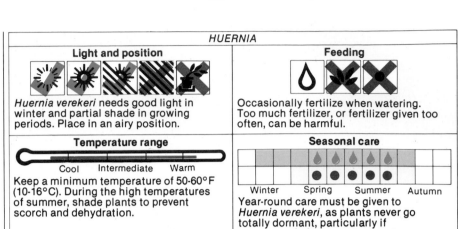

HUERNIA

Light and position

Huernia verekeri needs good light in winter and partial shade in growing periods. Place in an airy position.

Temperature range

Cool Intermediate Warm

Keep a minimum temperature of 50-60°F (10-16°C). During the high temperatures of summer, shade plants to prevent scorch and dehydration.

Watering

Watering at the roots is preferable to overhead watering. Keep soil barely moist in winter.

Feeding

Occasionally fertilize when watering. Too much fertilizer, or fertilizer given too often, can be harmful.

Seasonal care

Winter Spring Summer Autumn

Year-round care must be given to *Huernia verekeri*, as plants never go totally dormant, particularly if recommended temperatures are provided. Take cuttings of stems in summer . Seeds should be sown in the early spring .

Soil

A mixture of leaf-mould, peat and gritty sand in equal parts is advisable.

Huernia verekeri (*above*) has tapering flower lobes that are covered by minute purplish hairs.
Huernia schneiderana (*above right*) has fleshy stems and basally produced flowers. It exemplifies the general growth patterns of the huernia species.

(4cm) high, and have five to seven angles bearing triangular, pointed teeth. Flowering is from the base of the stem; there are usually one to three flowers to a stem. The rather small size of the flower is more than compensated for by the exotic patterning of the bloom.

Flowers develop and open during middle to late summer, occasionally a little earlier. It is essential to maintain good moisture around the root system during this period

of general growth when the absorption of water and nutrients is at its peak.

Ipomoea

This is a very large genus of about 400 species, many of them native to sub-tropical and tropical regions. Not all are succulents, and those that are must be termed 'root succulents' due to the often large, tuberous root-systems.

Ipomoea holubii is a South African root succulent that was, until recently, included under *Merremia,* a genus of exotic plants within the Convolvulaceae family. In the wild it grows in coarse gravel in open grasslands. The round caudex body is usually about 4in

(10cm) underground. Only the slender grasslike leaves, often lying flat on the ground, are visible. Due to the close resemblance to grass, plants avoid detection until they produce their bright blooms. Flowers may vary in colour from deep purple to much paler pastel shades.

This is not a difficult plant to cultivate. However, the caudex should not be buried but left exposed at ground level. This prevents any rot that might otherwise set in. With just the very base set

Ipomoea holubii (*above left*) bears large, showy flowers freely produced. **Lampranthus conspicuus** (*above*) is a thickly branching species remarkable for its vivid violet-red flowers.

in the ground, roots readily develop, followed by leaves and then flowers. By no means a common plant, it is something of an indoor floral 'novelty' – vivid flowers are followed by the rounded, leathery seed pods.

Lampranthus

This large genus of over 200 species has remarkably bright, shining flowers. The generic title registers this outstanding fact: 'lampros' means 'shining', 'anthos' means 'flowers'. With scarcely an exception, all species of *Lampranthus* are native to Cape Province in South Africa, where at certain times of the year the veldt is literally carpeted with these wonderful flowers.

Lampranthus conspicuus is thought to have originated in the area of Albany, but this is not certain. It is a densely branching species with thick stems and branches reaching 12in (30cm) or more in length. Leaves are thick and fleshy, somewhat cylindrical in shape and narrowing towards the tips. They appear in dense formation at the tips of the branches. Flowers are the central feature. The rich violet-red bloom, of an almost iridescent brightness, appears in early to quite late summer. As a rule, the plant blossoms singly, but sometimes two or three blooms appear together.

Given a position in full sun, plants will do well in either home or greenhouse. They may even be used as garden bedding plants when summer conditions are good.

IPOMOEA/LAMPRANTHUS	
Light and position 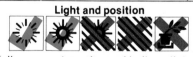 Full sun or extremely good indirect light is essential.	**Feeding** Use a very weak liquid feed when watering.
Temperature range Cool Intermediate Warm Overwinter at 50°F (10°C). Temperatures can soar from spring onwards without ill-effects.	**Seasonal care** Winter Spring Summer Autumn Prune into shape early spring — the cuttings can be used for propagation. Sow seeds in winter months in a temperature of 70°F (21°C) and in sandy soil.
Watering Keep plants dry in winter. Water moderately during the growing season, but beware of 'wet feet'.	**Soil** Use a mixture of loam, gritty sand and leaf-mould, with the gritty sand preponderant.

109

Luckhoffia/Pachypodium

Luckhoffia

The species *Luckhoffia beukmanii* is an uncommon plant and the only member of this monotypic genus. It is interesting to note that both the discoverer of the plant, C. Beukman, and the author of the genus, Dr. J. Luckhoff, are commemorated in the plant's title. It was first located in the Pakhuis Mountains in South Africa and considered to be a new species of stapelia, a title under which it was first described. While it is said to have an exceptionally long flowering season in habitat, in cultivation flowering occurs during a comparatively short period.

It is quite a tall plant; the stems are up to 30in (76cm) high and 1in (3cm) in diameter. The compressed tubercles, greyish-green in colour, give added prominence to the eight-angled formation of the stems. Flowers are variable, usually pale brown and densely yellow spotted but sometimes deep reddish-brown, on 1in (3cm) long pedicels.

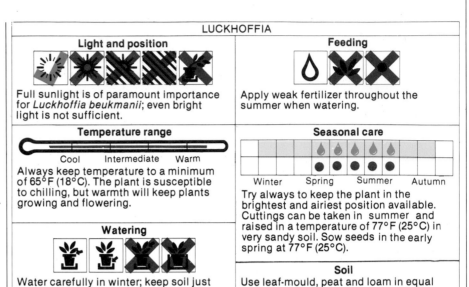

LUCKHOFFIA		
Light and position		**Feeding**
Full sunlight is of paramount importance for *Luckhoffia beukmanii*; even bright light is not sufficient.		Apply weak fertilizer throughout the summer when watering.
Temperature range		**Seasonal care**
Cool Intermediate Warm Always keep temperature to a minimum of 65°F (18°C). The plant is susceptible to chilling, but warmth will keep plants growing and flowering.		Winter Spring Summer Autumn Try always to keep the plant in the brightest and airiest position available. Cuttings can be taken in summer and raised in a temperature of 77°F (25°C) in very sandy soil. Sow seeds in the early spring at 77°F (25°C).
Watering		**Soil**
Water carefully in winter; keep soil just moist so that the roots do not dry out. Water plentifully in summer.		Use leaf-mould, peat and loam in equal parts, plus gritty sand equivalent to the bulk. Compost must be permeable.

This is closely akin to species of the genus *Hoodia,* another genus of cylindrical-shaped plants. Like hoodia, *Luckhoffia beukmanii* is not considered easy to grow but will nevertheless thrive in a dry atmosphere indoors. Excessive watering causes stem-rot; do not overwater.

Pachypodium

Pachypodium bispinosum is but one species of a genus renowned for plants of outstanding character, their habitat extending through the dry regions of South Africa, Namibia, Angola and Madagascar. They are erect plants that have spirally arranged leaves and re-

Luckhoffia beukmanii (*above*) is an unusual species demanding careful attention. It needs full sun and *plenty* of water during the growing season.
Pachypodium bispinosum (*right*) is a plant easily grown indoors. Pink, bell-shaped flowers appear in summer.

Pelargonium

semble shrubby trees. All species have fleshy stems and some are caudiciforms – that is to say, plants with a caudex root system.

Pachypodium bispinosum from Namaqualand in southern Africa is one of the species with a caudex. The caudex is mainly subterranean, often completely below ground level. A tangle of dark green branches, well armed with prickles, develops at the crown of the plant, which produces leaves from between the spines and, later, small, bell-shaped pink flowers. There is a similar plant from the same locality, *Pachypodium saundersii,* which has white flowers and is inclined to be variable in its growth.

Pachypodium bispinosum responds exceedingly well to cultivation conditions. Given satisfactory care, it can become a most floriferous houseplant. Knowing when to water and, just as important, when not to water is important to whether this plant succeeds indoors.

PELARGONIUM		
Light and position		**Feeding**
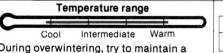		
Full sun or a very bright position is best for *Pelargonium violareum*.		During the growing season only, apply weak fertilizer when watering.
Temperature range		**Seasonal care**

Cool Intermediate Warm		Winter Spring Summer Autumn
During overwintering, try to maintain a temperature of 50°F (10°C). During summer, temperatures can rise naturally without harm to the leaves or flowers.		It is unwise to allow roots to dry out, for they dehydrate easily. Trim plants into shape in early spring when cuttings of ripe growth can be used for propagation. Seeds should be sown early in the year in a sandy soil and in a temperature of 70°F (21°C).
Watering		**Soil**
Keep plants just moist at the roots in winter. Water regularly from spring to late autumn .		Use a porous mixture composed in equal parts of leaf-mould, loam and sand.

Pelargonium violareum (*below*) is very much a feature plant, whether grown in a sunny spot indoors or bedded out in the garden during the warmer months. This South African plant bears flowers of exceptional beauty, which bloom during the summer months.

Pelargonium

It may be surprising to some that pelargonium species are considered succulents. A large number of plants in this genus are extremely succulent, others not at all and some fall within a 'border-line' category. *Pelargonium violareum,* the viola geranium, is such a plant. It is included principally on account of its pleasing flowers and because it is seldom mentioned in botanical books.

Pelargonium violareum is native to the southern part of Cape Province in South Africa, where it grows about 14in (35cm) high on stony, sandy hillsides. The plant is small and bushy in appearance; the stems and branches are quite densely covered with fine, hairy grey-green leaves with indented margins. Without question, flowers are the distinguishing feature – the pedicels bear two to four blooms of decidedly unusual colouring. The lower three petals are almost pure white, sometimes slightly suffused pink, while the upper two are ruby-red.

In habitat, plants bloom in autumn, but in cultivation plants provide their flowers for several weeks in the summer.

Pelargonium/Plumeria/Pterodiscus

Pelargonium oblongatum, which may soon be renamed *Pelargonium ensatum,* is found in Namaqualand in South Africa, where it grows at altitudes from 1,000 to 3,000ft (300 to 900m) on the slopes of the Langehoof Mountains.

This is an excellent representative of 'stem succulents'. It possesses a roundish, tuberous base, just above ground level, which is covered with thin layers of brownish skin. The few leaves, somewhat oval-oblong in shape and tapering towards the tips, are borne on hairy stalks and precede the flowers.

Flowers appear in umbels on stems about 12in (30cm) long. The broad, rounded, pale yellow petals – the two upper ones bearing pale red stripes – present an unusual flower. In cultivation it is likely that the leaves will fall before the flowers show themselves.

This plant is recommended for pot culture, but do not overpot – it seems to prefer a compacted rooting area to being able to spread roots around. Follow this suggestion for other species of pelargoniums that have comparable stem growth. Flowering is from late summer to autumn.

Pelargonium oblongatum (*left*) is a 'stem succulent'. The leaves invariably wither before the flower buds appear. **Plumiera acutifolia** (*above*) produces flowers with exquisite perfume.

Plumeria

The genus *Plumeria* comprises only a few species, all of which are shrubby or tree-like in their growth. The main stem or trunk is very succulent, thick and fleshy and frequently branches, and can attain a height of 8ft (2.4m) or more. However, careful pruning will restrain this growth to a size more convenient for indoor decor.

Plumeria acutifolia is a well-known plant familiar to anyone who has travelled in sub-tropical and tropical countries. While it is native to Mexico and some of the West Indian islands, frangipani, also called West Indian jasmine, has become an important cultivated plant in many parts of the Far East. In India it is referred to as the 'Temple Tree of India'. It was first described as *Plumeria acuminata,* and even now some doubt remains as to which is valid.

Flowers develop readily on comparatively young, sparsely leaved plants three to four years old. The fragrant, funnel-shaped flowers are waxy white suffused

PELARGONIUM		
Light and position		**Feeding**

Good light is necessary for *Pelargonium oblongatum*; shade will affect the habit of the plant.		Apply weak liquid feed with each watering between spring and autumn.
Temperature range		**Seasonal care**
Cool · Intermediate · Warm		
During overwintering, maintain a temperature of 55°F (13°C). Beginning in late spring gradually increase temperature. Give light shading *only* if temperature rises too high–over 85°F (30°C).		Winter · Spring · Summer · Autumn. Make sure there is not dehydration or rotting of roots in winter due to failure to follow the treatment prescribed above. Seeds may be sown in the early spring or immediately after ripening. The temperature should be 72-77°F (22-25°C).
Watering		
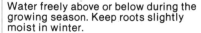		**Soil**
Water freely above or below during the growing season. Keep roots slightly moist in winter.		Use equal parts of leaf-mould and loam to equal the bulk in sharp sand.

with yellow. In many parts of the world these beautiful flowers are used at marriage feasts.

Frangipani is becoming increasingly available. There are other species of the genus bearing red, cream and totally yellow blooms.

Pterodiscus

This is a very small genus of African plants, none of which tends to grow more than about 12in (30cm) high. The more succulent species usually have a fleshy rootstock, and this feature is true of *Pterodiscus speciosus*. This is one of only two or three species native to South Africa – the others are mainly East African, found as far north as Ethiopia.

Pterodiscus speciosus has quite a widespread habitat, extending from Griqualand West in Cape Province through to Transvaal. The rather rounded, often misshapen stem, is a development from the subterranean taproot and will grow about 6in (15cm) high, developing many leaves. These leaves are usually rather narrow and elongated, dentate on the margins and are from 1 to 2in (3–5cm) long. Flowers appear in

PLUMIERA		
Light and position		**Feeding**
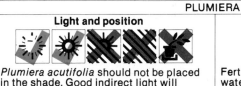		
Plumiera acutifolia should not be placed in the shade. Good indirect light will suffice, but sun will produce flowers.		Fertilize regularly with a liquid feed when watering.
Temperature range		**Seasonal care**
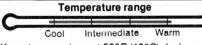		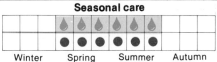
Cool Intermediate Warm		Winter Spring Summer Autumn
Keep temperature at 50°F (10°C) during winter; anything much lower will result in leaf loss. From early spring, increase temperature, keeping it high throughout summer.		Any trimming of plants should be undertaken no later than spring. Cuttings can be taken in summer. Seeds sown in winter months in a temperature of 70°F (21°C) quickly germinate.
Watering		**Soil**
		Use leaf-mould, peat and sharp sand in equal parts.
Keep soil slightly moist during overwintering. Freely water throughout the growth period.		

Pterodiscus speciosus (*above*) is one of the more uncommon species in cultivation. This South African plant produces purplish-red flowers.

early summer, and the flowering period can last for a number of weeks. The purplish-red blooms are produced from near the tips of the stems.

This is very much a deciduous plant. The leaves dry off in late summer, and the plant becomes almost totally dormant in October. There are two closely related species with almost identical characteristics – *Pterodiscus luridus,* with reddish-yellowish flowers, and *Pterodiscus aurantiacus,* with blooms of intense yellow.

PTERODISCUS		
Light and position		**Feeding**

Full sun or a position in bright light is essential.		Once leaves start to appear, feed plants with weak liquid fertilizer when watering.
Temperature range		**Seasonal care**
Cool Intermediate Warm		Winter Spring Summer Autumn
Maintain a temperature of 50°F (10°C) even when plants are dormant. During the growing season, give plants very high temperatures to accelerate the growth of leaves and flowers.		Every care should be taken to prevent the taproot shrivelling in winer. Remove dead leaves and flowers in late summer. Seeds are rarely available, but when they are, it is best to sow them in the early spring in a 70-77°F (21-25°C) temperature.
Watering		**Soil**
		Use a loamy-sandy mixture. The addition of humus is advantageous.
The roots should be dry, but not dust-dry in winter. From spring onwards, increase water. Do not water lavishly, however.		

Stapelia/Stultitia/Tacitus

Stapelia

There are a great number of species in *Stapelia,* one of the larger genera in the Asclepiadaceae family of plants. Many species are similar both in stem appearance and in flower.

Though it is slow growing, *Stapelia erectiflora* has outstanding merits. Stems often reach 6in (15cm) in length and ⅓in (1cm) in diameter. Flowers are borne on a pedicel or stalk 2–4in (5–10cm) in length. The corolla lobes of the flower are tightly recurved, creating a cap-like effect. The lobes are mainly purple and the densely set white hairs completely covering them give the plant a glamour all of its own. However, the flower is not large – in its recurved state only about ½in (1cm) in diameter.

This plant, like the majority of stapelia species, is native to South Africa. Cultivation requirements are much the same as those for huernias, a warm situation is better than a cool one, and it thrives better in an airy position. Complete dormancy is not advisable, as roots can quickly dehydrate and the plant may take a long time to recover from damage and shrivelling of the stems. Nevertheless, it

STAPELIA		
Light and position		**Feeding**
 In winter, provide *Stapelia erectiflora* with good light and an airy position. Plants need semi-shade in the summer.		 Apply weak liquid fertilizer periodically when watering.
Temperature range		**Seasonal care**
Cool Intermediate Warm Keep a minimum temperature of 50°F (10°C) in winter, slightly higher if possible. High temperatures encourage growth in summer, but give plants shade. Try to increase temperature in the spring		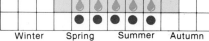 Winter Spring Summer Autumn Watch for any signs of rot — root or stem. Rot develops if treatment is incorrect. Take cuttings in summer. Sow seeds in early spring in a temperature of 70-77°F (21-25°C) and in very sandy soil. Seeds germinate quickly.
Watering		**Soil**
Keep soil just moist in winter. Beginning in spring, gradually increase water, but do not overdo; waterlogging is fatal.		Use peat, leaf-mould and loam in equal parts to an equal quantity of sharp sand. Add charcoal to prevent souring of the soil.

Tacitus bellus (*left*) is a recently discovered species native to Mexico. Compacted leaves and brilliant flowers combine to make this dwarf succulent exceptionally appealing to the eye. Clusters of flowers appear in spring and late summer; there may be as many as 10 blooms to a stem.

Stultitia cooperi (*above*) is a miniature species that bears purplish star-shaped blooms and is ideal for indoor cultivation.

can be recommended as a houseplant since it does better in the dry conditions that prevail indoors than in the greenhouse.

Stultitia

This is a very small genus of South African plants that is closely related to the *Stapelia* genus. The main difference between stultitias and stapelias is that the former have a pronounced ring around the mouth of the flower tube.

Stultitia cooperi is one of the more dwarf plants in the genus. Stems are erect and only 1in (3cm) high. The four-angled stems are most pronounced, and they are emphasized by the stems' round and pointed protuberances. Flowers arise from low on the stem. Several buds may appear almost together, but usually buds open only one or two at a time. The complex bloom is borne on a pedicel, and when fully open presents a star-like flower 1½in (3–4cm) in diameter. The flower is basically purplish but has lines and dots of other colouring; the margins of the lobes are decidedly hairy.

Stultitia cooperi bears a seed pod shaped like a horn. Within this horn are numerous flat seeds, each with a little 'parachute' attached. The parachutes contribute to the dispersal of seeds from the ripe horn. Plants are native to South Africa.

Tacitus

Tacitus bellus has become a very sought-after plant. It is the only species in the *Tacitus* genus and is currently considered so close to those in *Graptopetalum,* another genus of succulent rosette plants, as to be inseparable. *Tacitus,* however, is still the most common generic name.

The plant was discovered at altitudes of around 5,400ft (1,600m) on the slopes of Sierra Obscura in Mexico. The plant develops a rosette of darkish grey-green leaves, exceptionally compact and with an almost flattened surface. Flowers are produced in small clusters on stems only 1–2in (3–5cm) long. As many as 10 or more may adorn each stem. They appear

in spring and early summer; flowers bloom successively. The vivid reddish-pink petals, widely spreading, surmounted by white, equally spreading stamens makes this one of the most beautiful of dwarf succulents.

The popularity of *Tacitus bellus* has been phenomenal. No other new species has created such enthusiasm on the part of the collector. There is no difficulty in its cultivation. Being from high altitudes, it is able to withstand cold, dry winters.

STULTITIA	
Light and position  *Stultitia cooperi* needs full sun during the coolest months. At other times keep in a slightly shaded position.	**Feeding** During the growing season, fertilize when watering, but use only a weak solution.
Temperature range  Cool　Intermediate　Warm In winter, keep plants at about 50°F (10°C). With increased temperatures, give plants a little protection from full sun.	**Seasonal care** 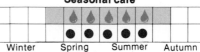 Winter　Spring　Summer　Autumn Keep an eye out for stem or root rot at all times, and especially during cooler weather when plants need to be kept on the dry side. Cuttings can be taken in the summer. Sow seeds as soon after ripening as possible. A very sandy compost is required.
Watering  Keep soil barely moist in winter, but from spring to autumn, water moderately, reducing quantities toward the end of the year.	**Soil** Use equal parts humus, peat and sharp sand.

Stapelia erectiflora (*above*) produces very unusual flowers. The corolla lobes are densely covered with white hairs, obliterating the purple colouring of the lobes.

TACITUS	
Light and position Place *Tacitus bellus* in full sunlight or very bright light.	**Feeding** 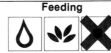 During the growing season, apply weak liquid fertilizer with each watering.
Temperature range Cool　Intermediate　Warm In winter a temperature of 45°F (7°C) is sufficient, but as spring and summer arrive, increase temperature to encourage growth and flowering.	**Seasonal care** 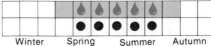 Winter　Spring　Summer　Autumn Protect from frost or extreme cold. Leaf cuttings can be made after flowering — they will quickly root and establish new roots. Seed is seldom available, but if it is, sow in early spring at a temperature of 70°F (21°C).
Watering  Keep plants almost completely dry in winter. Water freely in the summer either early or late in the day.	**Soil** A very porous compost that includes humus is necessary. Use leaf-mould, peat and sharp gritty sand in equal parts.

Caladium

The caladiums have large heart-shaped leaves which are supported on petioles 12 or 18in (30–51cm) in length that sprout from soil level. There are many different species, and their foliage ranges in colour from white to very deep red with many mottled shades in between.

Few plants in nature can compete with the caladiums when it comes to foliage colour, and an added attraction is that leaves are so thin they are translucent in some species, notably *C. candidum*. The latter is the most popular plant and one that is readily available during the summer months of the year, when caladiums are in their prime. Caladiums have the common name of Angel's Wings, which suits *C. candidum* in particular, with its white colouring and prominent green venation.

To succeed, these plants need a light but not sunny location in a temperature not less than 65°F (18°C). Humidity helps caladiums flourish. Plants are normally available in the spring and early summer and are sold in 5in (13cm) pots, in which they can remain if a regular weekly feed is given. Towards the end of the summer, plants will die down naturally and should then be gradually dried off until such time as the soil is completely dry. After the plant is completely defoliated and the soil is dried out, the plant should be stored in a warm, dry place until early spring, when it should be watered and brought into the light to start the new season.

Caladiums are decorative plants with extremely delicate-looking foliage. The large heart-shaped leaves are papery thin and vary widely in colour, from pale creamy white to pink and deep red. *C.* 'Silver Leaves' (**right**) is one of many hybrids. As in most plants of this genus, the pattern on the leaves largely follows the leaf veining.

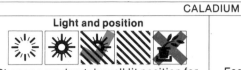

CALADIUM

Light and position

Choose a moderately well-lit position for these plants, away from direct sun.

Temperature range

Cool   Intermediate   Warm

Protect caladiums from cold at all times. Never let the temperature fall below 60°F (16°C) and, if possible, maintain the plant in temperatures of 70°F (21°C) and above.

Watering

Water these plants freely during the summer period. Stop watering when the foliage dies down in autumn.

Feeding

Feed generously with standard liquid fertilizer every two weeks during the period of active growth.

Seasonal care

Winter   Spring   Summer   Autumn

In the autumn keep dormant tubers in potting compost at 60°F (18°C). Pot in fresh mixture in the spring and maintain a temperature of 70°F (21°C). To propagate, detach small tubers from parent growth and repot to produce a new plant.

Soil

Pot tubers in fresh peaty soil that is rich in nourishment.

Calathea

Most calatheas are grown for their colourful foliage, and all are tender plants needing a minimum temperature of 60°F (16°C) and light shade in which to grow.

With upright leaves that are colourfully patterned on their upper surface and maroon in colour underneath, *C. insignis* is a bold and striking plant that will require all the experienced gardener's skill to do well.

The Peacock Plant, *C. makoyana,* has crowded leaves that are paper thin and carried erect on long petioles. Its bronze-coloured leaves are heavily patterned with many contrasting shades of colour, which makes this plant especially desirable.

C. ornata has upright but more elongated leaves. Close-set, colourful stripes extend from the midrib of the leaf to its outer edges – stripes become paler in colour as the plant ages.

C. roseo-picta is one of the finest of the more compact calatheas. The background colouring of olive-green has a metallic sheen that sets off perfectly the rosy-red lateral stripes.

Calathea crocata is one of the few calathea species that have attractive flowers. The foliage, however, is less appealing than other calatheas'. The bracts are bright orange; leaves are dark green and ovate in shape.

Calatheas are challenging houseplants, grown for their strikingly patterned foliage, *C. makoyana* (**above left**) and *C. roseo-picta* (**above right**) show the variety of leaf colour and patterning.

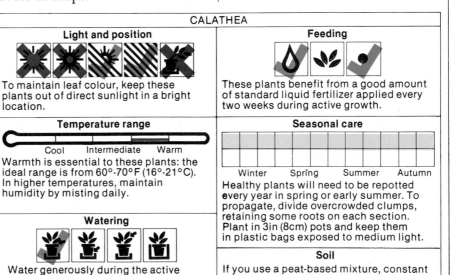

CALATHEA	
Light and position To maintain leaf colour, keep these plants out of direct sunlight in a bright location.	**Feeding** These plants benefit from a good amount of standard liquid fertilizer applied every two weeks during active growth.
Temperature range Cool Intermediate Warm Warmth is essential to these plants: the ideal range is from 60°-70°F (16°-21°C). In higher temperatures, maintain humidity by misting daily.	**Seasonal care** Winter Spring Summer Autumn Healthy plants will need to be repotted every year in spring or early summer. To propagate, divide overcrowded clumps, retaining some roots on each section. Plant in 3in (8cm) pots and keep them in plastic bags exposed to medium light.
Watering Water generously during the active growth period to keep the potting mixture thoroughly moist.	**Soil** If you use a peat-based mixture, constant feeding is essential while plants are in active growth.

Callistemon

Only one species of the genus *Callistemon* is grown indoors. Indigenous to Australia, *C. citrinus* is a strong-growing plant. Its common name of Bottlebrush refers to the cylindrical flowers that are formed in the shape of a bottle brush and are bright red in colour. Leaves are narrow and bright green; stems are woody and plants are evergreen, with flowers developing at the apex of the many branches during the summer months. *C. citrinus* reaches a maximum height of 5ft (1.5m).

During the summer months, plants will benefit if placed out of doors in a sunny, sheltered position. Pruning is seldom necessary, but removing the growing tips of young plants will encourage plants to branch as they age. New plants may be raised from seed, and by rooting cuttings about 4in (10cm) in length. Cuttings should be prepared from firm stems and taken after plants have flowered. These plants should be potted on in early spring into only slightly larger containers. A soil-less mixture will be suitable if plants are adequately fed, but a loam-based potting medium is preferable.

CALLISTEMON

Light and position

Callistemons need several hours of direct sunlight daily in order to flower well.

Temperature range

Cool   Intermediate   Warm

Normal room temperature is fine while plants are in active growth. Keep plants cooler during the resting period, at a temperature of 45 to 50°F (7°-10°C).

Watering

Water plentifully while plants are in active growth, keeping them just moist during the dormant period.

Feeding

Feed with liquid fertilizer once every two weeks while plants are in active growth.

Seasonal care

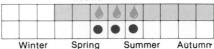

Winter   Spring   Summer   Autumn

Take cuttings in early summer. Cut back plants as soon as flowering is over. During the growing season, water plants well, but do not allow pots to stand in water.

Soil

Use a soil-based mixture composed of equal parts soil, sand and either peat moss or leaf-mould.

Callistemon citrinus (*above top*) is the only species of this genus of Australian evergreen shrub to be grown indoors, although the taller *C. speciosus* (*above*) may occasionally find its way into larger conservatories. The bright red cylindrical flower spikes consist largely of stamens and so give rise to the common name of Bottlebrush.

CAMPANULACEAE

Campanula isophylla

Italian Bellflower
Star of Bethlehem
Falling Stars

The foliage of the campanula is insignificant, but its trailing bell-shaped flowers will cascade naturally for many months from spring into late summer. The white campanula is by far the best, but there are also attractive blue and lilac shades. The white form is much the easiest to manage, and is a fine plant for growing in a small hanging basket or a hanging pot. New plants can be raised from cuttings, but the stock should first be checked thoroughly to ensure that it is free from any pests or diseases.

VARIETIES AND PURCHASING

Choose a plant or plants for colour and ease of care, or mix all three colours in a hanging pot. Buy young plants in the spring with many buds and some open flowers.
C. isophylla This will produce blue flowers between summer and autumn.
C. isophylla 'Alba' This white variety is the most prolific and the easiest to care for.
C. isophylla 'Mayi' This variety has mauve flowers.

PESTS AND DISEASES

These plants are easy to care for but may suffer from red spider and fungus.
Red spider mite If these appear, spray immediately with insecticide or immerse the pot in a dilute solution. Repeat after 10 days. Systemic insecticides will not be very effective.
Botrytis This may affect the plants if they get too wet.

Treat with fungicide, clean off the dead foliage and give the plants more air and space.
Healthy plant Seen at its best *C. isophylla* 'Alba' presents a mass of star-shaped white flowers and bright green leaves on trailing stems ideal for display in a hanging basket.

AVOIDING PROBLEMS

Light and position

Campanulas prefer bright light, with or without direct sunlight at all times although they can thrive in a sunless window if they are placed on the sill. Remember, however, that too much heat will dry the plants out. Spray the plant or move it if necessary.

Temperature range

Cool   Intermediate   Warm

Campanula plants prefer cooler temperatures: 45°-65°F (7°-18°C) in summer and around 40°F (5°C) and not above 50°F (10°C) in winter. If the temperature rises above 65°F (18°C) in summer, spray the leaves and stand the pot in a plant tray on wet pebbles.

Watering

These plants may be watered in any way but do not let the roots get too damp. Water well in the flowering period, keeping the soil moist, but do not allow the pot to stand in a pool of water. In the rest period moisten the soil lightly every two weeks.

Feeding

Campanulas will not need a lot of feeding but it is best to give them some liquid fertilizer once every two weeks after the roots have filled out the pots and until the flowers have fallen.

Seasonal care

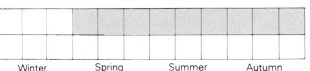

Winter   Spring   Summer   Autumn

To give a campanula the best care possible, spray the plant if the temperature rises above 65°F (18°C) and move it to a warmer spot if it drops below 45°F (7°C). Feed until the flowers fall and water less from that point onwards. To propagate new plants take 2in (5cm) long tip cuttings with three or four pairs of leaves each from old plants just as the growing period begins. Culture gently with the help of hormone rooting powder and potting mixture until they take root.

Soil

Take rooted cuttings and place three or four in a small pot in early spring. Move them to larger pots once the roots appear above the surface of the mixture. The largest pot size needed will probably be a 5in (12.5cm) one.

Carnivorous Plants

There are many odd plants in nature, but few as unusual as the carnivorous plants. These plants have various ways of trapping within their foliage flies and other creatures, which they digest and use as nourishment.

The Venus's flytrap, *Dionaea muscipula*, is the plant that is most commonly offered for sale as a subject for indoor decoration. The leaves of the Venus's flytrap are equipped with teeth along their margins and a trigger mechanism that is activated by any insect that chances to land on the upper surface of the leaf. The leaf folds together with the teeth interlocking, making it impossible for the prisoner within to escape. When flies are less plentiful, plants may be fed by placing on the leaves minute pieces of meat or fish. The plant will digest them in the same way it would a fly.

The Venus's flytrap must have a close, humid atmosphere if it is to succeed. It may be necessary, then, to provide a microclimate within a Wardian case of some kind. This could easily be a box filled with damp moss topped by a sheet of glass. To make a box, choose fresh, clean sphagnum moss. Wet it before making a bed

Dionaea muscipula, the Venus's Flytrap (*above*), is the most popular of the carnivorous plants.
The Venus's Flytrap has pairs of hinged lobes with toothed edges at the end of its leaves which snap shut around visiting insects.

PROPAGATION

The diminutive Venus's flytrap is not an easy plant to cultivate even when mature, and as such it can often be rather difficult to propagate. However, success achieved with this fascinating plant will be most rewarding.

With great care it is possible to separate the root gently from late spring to early summer. Ensure that the compost is moist and pot the root pieces in a 3½in (9cm) pot in a specialized mixture of sphagnum moss peat, sphagnum moss and, if possible, leaf-mould. Maintain a temperature of around 65–68°F (18–20°C) in moderate light. Covering the plant with a clear plastic bag or a glass bell jar may help it to propagate and develop more readily.

Alternatively, Venus fly trap may also be raised from seed sown in a similar material mixed in equal parts with sharp sand. The seed should be lightly covered, kept evenly moist and maintained at a temperature of about 70°F (21°C) until germination has taken place. Covering the seed tray or pan with a piece of clear plastic or glass will help to encourage germination.

When large enough to handle, prick out the seedlings and pot up singly, using the potting formulation, in 2½–3½in (6–9cm) pots.

about 5in (13cm) deep in the bottom of the box. Bury the pot in the moss up to its rim, so that the plant derives the maximum benefit from the surrounding moisture. (It goes without saying that while the plant is in the box the moss should at no time dry out.) The atmosphere must be moist, and the temperature should be 65°F (18°C) and above – the higher the temperature the better, if the air is moist.

Perhaps the most spectacular of the carnivorous plants are the nepenthes, which are commonly named Pitcher Plants. Green leathery leaves are not especially attractive, but from their extremities they produce strands of growth to which pitcher-like vases are attached. The bottom of the pitcher contains pepsin liquid in which insects drown when they are attracted inside; the cover of the pitcher enables the plant to shed rainwater and keeps the water from spilling into the bottom. There are numerous varieties of this plant, and all of them need the same humid and warm conditions.

In their natural habitat, almost all of the nepenthes are natural climbers, and in greenhouses they can be very exotic when suspended in baskets from the ceiling so that the pitchers hang freely away from the main part of the plant. It is not possible to confine these large plants to propagating cases, so a greenhouse or conservatory heated to a minimum of 65°F (18°C) is necessary.

Nepenthes, the Pitcher Plants, have a very unusual appearance with pitcher-like vases hanging from the ends of leaves. *N. hookeriana* (**above**) shows the special pitchers, which contain liquid in which insects drown and are digested.

CARNIVOROUS PLANTS

Light and position
Carnivorous plants like a sunny position, although they should be kept away from direct sunlight.

Temperature range
Cool   Intermediate   Warm

Try to keep the atmosphere warm and humid at all times. In winter the temperature should not drop below 50°F (10°C).

Watering
These plants come from marshy ground and should therefore be kept moist. You can stand them in a saucer of water.

Feeding
Feed plants occasionally with liquid fertilizer.

Seasonal care
Winter   Spring   Summer   Autumn

The majority of carnivorous plants will need potting on from time to time, during the spring or early summer.

Soil
Fresh sphagnum moss and peat mixture is best. Good drainage is essential.

121

Chlorophytum comosum

The green and cream grassy foliage of the Spider Plant is extremely popular. This is largely because it grows so well, and the fact that new plants are so easy to raise from the natural plantlets that are produced on long stalks as the plants mature. When they have grown to a reasonable size, the plantlets begin to form roots at their base even though they are only suspended in the atmosphere. After these roots have developed, the plantlets can be removed from the parent and simply pushed directly into small pots filled with houseplant potting mixture. It is better to peg the small plantlets down in the potting soil while they are still attached to the parent plant and to cut them away when they have obviously rooted.

VARIETIES AND PURCHASING

Spider Plants are usually sold in small pots and they are cheap, cheerful and easy to grow. It is sensible to check among the leaves for pests, such as aphids, which have a particular fondness for the Spider Plant. The plant looks especially attractive in a hanging basket as the bright green and cream foliage spills over on all sides. For a really good display, put no less than three plants into the basket. They will grow quickly and beautifully in good light, although strong sunlight can be damaging. *C. comosum* 'Variegatum is the only variety worth keeping. It is sometimes given the common name St Bernard's Lily as well as Spider Plant.

PESTS AND DISEASES

Aphids These are the main pests that bother the Spider Plant. Leaves that are attacked bear pit marks produced by the probing creatures (*see illustration*). Inspect the central leaves regularly and spray them with diazinon or malathion when aphids are found. Alternatively use a systemic insecticide such as disulfoton in granule form in the soil.
Symphalids Commonly named springtails, on account of their dancing motions on the surface of the soil when the plant is watered, symphalids are not harmful to the plant. They are often present on plants when the soil is musty and very wet. They can be killed if necessary by drenching the soil with malathion.
Mealy bug Spider Plants can suffer from these common little white pests. They are destructive and can cause the plant to wilt, shed leaves and eventually die if left untreated. The bugs are easy to recognize, as tiny pale lumps with a cottony casing, sitting on the leaves (*see illustration*). Spraying is an effective treatment provided all the leaves are saturated with insecticide by this method. An even better remedy is to sponge the leaves with malathion, firmly enough to remove all the bugs, but not so heavily as tc bruise the leaves.
Sciarid fly These pests, better known as fungus gnats, are found in the soil if it is very wet. Again, they are not at all harmful, though they may be irritating and unsightly. If you wish to get rid of them, this is easily done by soaking malathion into the soil.

AVOIDING PROBLEMS

Light and position

Good light is required if these plants are to retain their colouring and not become thin and wispy, but very strong light can damage the leaves. Protect the plants, too, from cold draughts, especially if they are placed on a windowsill.

Temperature range

Cool   Intermediate   Warm

These plants thrive at normal room temperatures in the range 50°-65°F (10°-18°C). They will not do well if the temperature is allowed to drop below 45°F (7°C). In winter, therefore, you may need to move them to a room which is always heated.

Watering

The Spider Plant is easy to water by any method and likes a lot of water in the growing period. In the rest period, water more moderately, allowing the top layer of soil to dry out between waterings.

Feeding

Feed fortnightly throughout the year with a good liquid fertilizer, especially once the plant has started to produce plantlets. Without feeding, the tops of the leaves will quickly turn brown, marring the appearance of the plant and retarding its growth.

Seasonal care

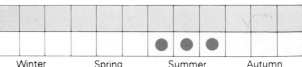

Winter   Spring   Summer   Autumn

In general this is an easy plant to care for but remember to water it less in the rest period and to protect it from direct sunlight and sudden drops in temperature. New plants can be grown at any time in one of two ways. Either cut off the plantlets when their leaves are 2-3in (5-7.5cm) long place them in a jar of water until the roots are 1in (2.5cm) long and then pot them. Alternatively, put the plantlets into soil and leave them attached to the mother plant until they take root.

Soil

Use a loam-based mixture for potting and make sure there is enough space around the plant for the growth of its thick fleshy roots. Place the root ball about 1in (2.5cm) below the rim of the pot. Repot in a larger pot whenever the roots force the soil to the rim.

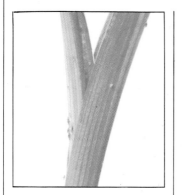
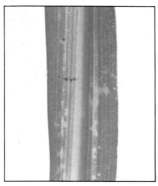

Problems *Aphids (far left)* often attack the young leaves and leave scars, which expand as the plant grows. This is why it is important to check the plant when you buy it. Mealy bugs (*centre*) are another common pest which can do a great deal of damage. Underwatering or insufficient nourishment cause the leaf tips to brown (*left*). This damage in the tips of young plants may indicate that they need potting on.

Healthy plant A Spider Plant grows well on its own, but also enjoys the company of many other plants and can be an attractive addition to a mixed display.

Cineraria

The cineraria is one of the many annual pot plants that are purchased in countless thousands each year. There are many other annual greenhouse plants that are sold for room decoration and most of them will respond to treatment similar to that required by the cineraria. The coarse green leaves of this plant radiate from a short central stem, and in season they are covered with a mass of brightly coloured daisy-like flowers. There are both compact and large-flowered types, the latter developing into impressive plants that will need plenty of space around them.

VARIETIES

The cineraria is really a member of the *Senecio* family – its full name is *Senecio cruentus cineraria*. They are peculiarly susceptible to almost every known pest, so it is extremely important to examine the leaves carefully for any signs of their presence.

S.c. cineraria **'Grandiflora'** As its name suggests, this plant has large flowers, which come in a variety of vibrant colours.
S.c. cineraria **'Nana'** This plant is much more compact and so is suitable for a windowsill where space is limited.

Healthy plants (*above*) Cinerarias come in a variety of brilliant colours – blue, purple, white, red and pink. It is important to choose a plant with bright green foliage – hard yellow leaves indicate that the plant has been neglected.

Unhealthy plant If the cineraria is attacked by botrytis (*right*) the results can be disastrous – the plant can be reduced to a pulpy mass of rot. The fungus attacks when the air is too humid. First signs are usually wet brown patches on the lower leaves. Treat with fungicide immediately and remove and burn the worst affected leaves. This plant (*left*) has both botrytis and leaf miner and is a classic example of bad culture.

PESTS AND DISEASES

Cinerarias, like other soft-leaved houseplants, are vulnerable to sap-sucking insects, and a careful look-out should be kept for aphids. Use a reliable insecticide.

White fly These are easily detected on the undersides of the leaves, but they are difficult to eradicate. Spray the undersides of the leaves with an insecticide such as pyrethrum or diazinon and repeat this treatment at least four times at four-day intervals.

Leaf miner and **botrytis** (*see illustration left below*) may also attack this plant.

Leaf miner (*left*) This is fairly easily detected. The grub leaves a white trail as it burrows between the upper and lower tissue of the leaf. When the pest is found, pierce its body with a pin. Badly affected leaves can be removed, but regular inspection will prevent a severe outbreak.

Unhealthy leaves
Sometimes the foliage of a cineraria will turn brown at the edges (*right*). Possible causes are overwatering or an attack of root fungus gnats. Slugs can cause great damage to the soft, delicate leaves of the cineraria (*below*).

AVOIDING PROBLEMS

Light and position

A cineraria appreciates a bright position but must be protected from the glare of direct sun. A light window is the best place providing the conditions are fairly cool and the plant should be placed well away from heating appliances of any kind.

Temperature range

Cool   Intermediate   Warm

It is essential that the plant should be given cool, airy conditions, with a temperature range of 50°-60°F (10°-15°C). As is commonly the rule with houseplants, the cineraria abhors draughts and should not be subject to sudden dramatic changes in temperature, at either end of the scale.

Watering

Regular watering is needed but the plant must never be overwatered or the roots will rot, causing yellowing of the leaves. If this persists the plant will die.

Immersion of the pot is a quite unsuitable method of watering and the cineraria dislikes foliar feeds.

Feeding

The cineraria often fails through lack of food. The plant has many roots when first bought and must be fed right away. A few drops of feed are not enough and the amount recommended by the manufacturer of the feed can easily be doubled without harming the plant.

Seasonal care

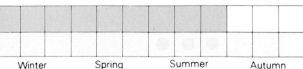

Winter   Spring   Summer   Autumn

The plant flowers in spring and, being treated as an annual, is thrown away when it has flowered. If it is properly fed and watered, and kept in a cool, bright position it should remain fresh and attractive. It is, however, a prey to many pests so it is as well to watch out for any signs of infestation or disease. Less water can be given in the autumn, before the active period leading up to flowering.

Soil

Since the plant has a brief pot life, repotting is not a problem, but a young plant may thrive for being potted on soon after it is acquired. Use a loam-based potting mixture and water the plant after potting.

Cissus

C. antarctica, which is better known as the Kangaroo Vine, has glossy green leaves with toothed edges. Recently it has lost much of its popularity, even though it is easy to grow. By contrast, *C. discolor,* the Begonia Vine, is quite tricky to grow; it is a delicate, much more colourful plant, with a similar climbing habit to the Kangaroo Vine.

Both these plants can be propagated from cuttings that are not too difficult to root in a peaty mixture in a temperature of around 70°F (21°C).

Healthy plant *C. discolor* (**right**) is quite difficult to care for but will repay the effort it demands many times. A natural climber, it has large heart-shaped leaves decorated with a profusion of coloured markings – metallic green, crimson, peach, white and even purple among them.

VARIETIES AND PURCHASING

Most varieties of cissus are easy to grow and will create a pleasant splash of green in a well-lit room. The most spectacular, however, is the Begonia Vine.
C. antarctica The Kangaroo Vine will reach a height of 10ft (3m) indoors. To grow well it will need some support, such as bamboo canes, and will provide a feature in a plant group or serve as a screen of bright, shiny leaves. It is quite an easy plant to grow.
C. discolor This plant has the common name of the Begonia Vine and it looks quite like *Begonia rex* varieties. The long heart-shaped leaves are patterned with silver and light purple on the upper surface and are a deep red colour on the underside. Ideally, this plant should be grown in a window where the temperature and humidity are closely controlled. This plant is a challenge, but one well worth taking on.
C. rhombifolia This is still called *Rhoicissus rhomboidea* by many growers. It has shiny green leaves growing in triplets. It too can reach 10ft (3m) if it is not pruned too harshly.

PESTS AND DISEASES

Although cissus plants, with the exception of *C. discolor,* do not require attention, it is important to check them for red spider, mealy bugs and root mealy bugs.
Red spider mite This may attack all types but especially *C. discolor.* It is very difficult to detect on this plant, so make periodic inspections, since once the pest has taken a grip it is difficult to shake off. Saturation spray with recommended insecticide. Treat immediately the mites are noticed. Repeat at 10- day intervals until clean.
Mealy bug These powdery white pests are more easily detected than the red spider. The young are encased in a waxy substance like cotton wool that protects them from insecticide. For this reason spray repeatedly.
Root mealy bug This pest will attach itself to the roots of these plants. Smaller than mealy bugs, they can only be seen by knocking the rootball from the pot. Spray the rootball with insecticide or immerse the whole pot in an insecticide solution.

AVOIDING PROBLEMS

Light and position

The cissus varieties in general need a good light without direct sunlight but the Begonia Vine is more delicate and needs the controlled conditions often found only in a plant window. Protect all varieties from direct sun and from draughts.

Temperature range

Cool   Intermediate   Warm

All these plants like a moderate atmosphere. The Kangaroo Vine needs 50°-60°F (10°-15°C). The Begonia Vine needs temperatures between 60°-70°F (15°-21°C) and will shed many of its leaves if the temperature drops below 65°F (18°C) in its growing period. It also needs a humid atmosphere. All types like a short rest period with the temperature at about 55°F (13°C).

Watering

Water most varieties well during the growing period so that the whole pot is moist but allow the top layer of soil to dry out between waterings. For the Begonia Vine wait until the top half of the pot is dry before rewatering and mist-spray to keep it moist.

Feeding

Once they are established all varieties should be fed regularly while in active growth. Feed at every watering with weak liquid fertilizer from early spring to early autumn.

Seasonal care

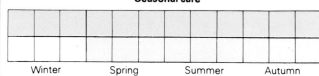

Winter   Spring   Summer   Autumn

All cissus plants should be given a cool rest period, with only just enough water to prevent the mixture from drying out. The Begonia Vine may well lose all its leaves in winter. To grow new plants, root tip cuttings, shorn of their lower leaves and dipped in hormone rooting powder, in a potting mixture. Enclose the pots in plastic bags in a warm, not too light place until the cuttings take root. It is also possible to root trailing stems by pegging them in small pots until they take root.

Soil

Small plants will do well in a soil-less mixture but when the plants take up 5in (12·5cm) pots use a loam-based mixture. Pot on in spring or summer. Plants of a height of 6 ft (2m) will need a pot of 8-10in (20-25cm). At this size they may be top-dressed with fresh potting mixture instead of being repotted.

Leaves Brown marks appear on an otherwise healthy leaf as a result of a sudden chill or too much light (*top*). When whole leaves start to wither and turn brown at the edges overwatering or lack of humidity may be the cause (*bottom*).

127

Citrus mitis

The citrus is one of the most fascinating of all the many houseplants that may be grown in a pot indoors or in the conservatory, and when in fruit one of the most admired. The plants are compact with many branches carrying shiny dark green oval-shaped leaves. Its heavily scented white flowers usually appear in late summer and a percentage of them become small green fruits that, given careful culture, will eventually develop into miniature oranges. When ripe these taste bitter, but they are ideal for making marmalade if there are enough of them.

Healthy plant The Calamondin Orange is an expensive plant and should be chosen with care. The mature plant has an abundance of glossy, unblemished leaves and will grow in a bushy and pleasing shape, whether straight and tall or slightly branching.

PROPAGATION

The *Citrus mitis* or Calamondin Orange is probably the most popular variety of citrus grown as a houseplant due to its compact habit and ability to bear fruit at a relatively diminutive height.

Propagation is not easy due to the prolonged warm temperatures and environmental control necessary, but this is a rewarding plant to grow.

From cuttings the procedure is relatively straightforward from mid-spring to early summer, when conditions are more opportune. Stem cuttings measuring 4–6in (10–15cm) should be removed with secateurs or pruning shears and dipped into hormone rooting powder before being dibbled one per pot into a 3½in (9cm) pot of seed and cutting compost. The cutting should then be covered with a clear plastic bag and positioned out of direct sunlight at a constant 70°F (21°C) for up to two months, or slightly longer, for roots to establish. Remove cover and grow on.

Seeds of citrus may also be germinated at a similar temperature when sown in a shallow pot or pan of seed and cutting compost. Germination may take just over a month, after which the clear plastic or glass cover may be removed and the seedlings carefully grown on. They should then be gently pricked out and potted up in 3½in (9cm) pots of potting compost.

AVOIDING PROBLEMS

Light and position

Full light is essential to this plant, and it will benefit from a period out-of-doors in the summer months. Place it in a sunny, sheltered corner, preferably on a stone base, and remember to keep up the necessary watering and feeding. Indoors or out, it will not stand draughts or too much shade.

Temperature range

Cool   Intermediate   Warm

The Calamondin Orange prefers cool temperatures and will survive comfortably in temperatures of 50°-60°F (10°-15°C). However, if it becomes too cold, this may contribute to browning of leaf tips which can spread across the whole leaf, and this is aggravated if the plant is overwatered.

Watering

This plant requires ample watering, especially in summer and if it is outdoors. Less water is required in winter, but the soil must never be allowed to dry out completely. If the plant is watered too lavishly in cold conditions, this may cause discoloration of leaves and root failure.

Feeding

It is recommended that the Calamondin Orange is fed at each watering, but it will require less food in winter. Soil deficiency will result in yellowing of the leaves, which can be rectified by watering with a solution containing iron, as directed by the manufacturer.

Seasonal care

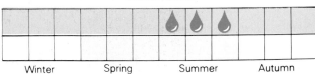

Winter   Spring   Summer   Autumn

The plant requires plenty of water all year round, through rather less in winter than in summer. The plant may be placed out-of-doors in late spring and can remain there until the nights become too chilly.

Regular feeding during spring and summer will be beneficial and the plant does require food through the winter, although rather less than needed in the growing season.

Soil

Pot the plant in loam-based mixture, preferably in a clay pot, which is crocked at the bottom before the soil is put in. The soil should be free-draining and a properly fed plant should not need frequent potting on unless the growth is extremely vigorous.

PESTS AND DISEASES

Aphids These small insects are also known as greenfly, but may in fact be grey, black or yellow as well as green. They suck the sap of the plant, preferring new growth such as small top shoots and flower buds. The plant gradually becomes stunted, with distortion of stems, leaves and flowers. In addition, the aphids deposit a sticky honeydew on the plant which causes it further damage and makes it very susceptible to sooty mould. Thorough and repeated spraying with malathion will get rid of aphids, or a systemic insecticide can be used as granules in the soil.

Mealy bug This pest may be a nuisance to older plants but fortunately it is easily spotted and treated.

Scale insect This could be the worst problem for a citrus mitis. The young flesh-coloured insects and dark brown adults attach themselves to the stems of the plant and the undersides of the leaves. Spray with malathion or soak a sponge in insecticide and firmly wipe the pests away. It is a wise precaution to clean the upper side of the leaves as well.

Red spider mite If the signs of infestation by red spider mites occur in the plant (*see illustration left*), prompt action must be taken. A steady stream of lukewarm water run over the foliage may dislodge the mites and their webs, as may a thorough spraying with malathion. However, if the problem is widespread, treatment with insecticide is unlikely to be effective and the insects will move to other plants if left. In this case, there is nothing to be done but to remove and burn the infected areas, or burn the entire plant.

Sooty mould This is a mould which lives on the excreta of the above pests. It is not harmful, but is very unsightly. A sponge soaked in malathion will clean away the mould.

VARIETIES

C. mitis This compact and decorative variety is the only one which reliably fruits indoors and retains a good shape.

Mealy bug (*top*) The white, cottony bugs show up clearly on the plant and can be easily treated. Wipe them away with a swab soaked in malathion or methylated spirits.

Red spider mite (*above*) It is difficult to detect this tiny pest but the plant will become stunted, the leaves brown and discoloured and minute webs can be seen on growing tips.

Clerodendrum

The only species in the *Clerodendrum* genus that is grown as a houseplant is *Clerodendrum thomsoniae*. Leaves are mid-green in colour; clustered flowering bracts are bright red and white.

Clerodendrum thomsoniae is best seen to advantage placed against a wall. But although the stems are stout and woody, the plant is not a natural climber and will have to be trained. It will attain a height of 8ft (2.4m) in time, but this vigorous plant can be easily contained by pruning.

To do well, plants need a minimum temperature of 60°F (16°C) and a light but not sunny position. Take cuttings following flowering in the autumn. They should be 6in (15cm) in length with two pairs of leaves. A temperature of not less than 60°F (16°C) and a close, moist atmosphere are necessary to root this difficult subject.

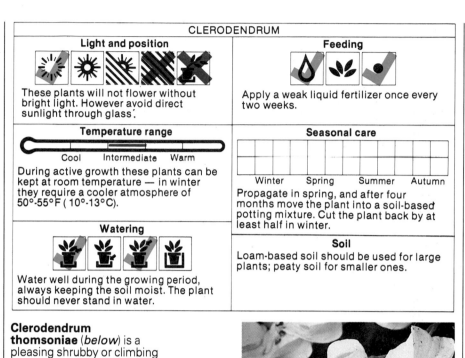

CLERODENDRUM	
Light and position	**Feeding**
These plants will not flower without bright light. However avoid direct sunlight through glass.	Apply a weak liquid fertilizer once every two weeks.
Temperature range	**Seasonal care**
Cool Intermediate Warm	Winter Spring Summer Autumn
During active growth these plants can be kept at room temperature — in winter they require a cooler atmosphere of 50°-55°F (10°-13°C).	Propagate in spring, and after four months move the plant into a soil-based potting mixture. Cut the plant back by at least half in winter.
Watering	**Soil**
Water well during the growing period, always keeping the soil moist. The plant should never stand in water.	Loam-based soil should be used for large plants; peaty soil for smaller ones.

Clerodendrum thomsoniae (*below*) is a pleasing shrubby or climbing plant that needs to be either pruned vigorously or trained to a support. The attractive flowers (***detail right***) appear in spring.

Clivia miniata

As its common name suggests, the clivia is indigenous to South Africa, where its native state is Natal. The clivia's rich green glossy leaves are broad and strap-like, sprouting from the thick bulbous base of the plant. Although a reasonably attractive plant when simply in leaf, it is at its best when clusters of bell-shaped flowers appear on strong stems. By far the greatest number of plants that are offered for sale are bright orange, but there are yellow and apricot-coloured varieties as well. Clivias not only have stocky leaf growth, they also develop an incredible amount of root that quickly fills the pots in which they are growing.

When propagating new plants the clumps of growth are divided into individual sections and potted separately. However, due to the thick intertwining roots, which can become difficult to divide, it is best to consider propagation before the plants become too large and unwieldy.

VARIETIES AND PURCHASING

Clivias, which make splendid free-standing showpieces when in flower, now come in a range of colours from pale yellow to deep orange. Although plants are seen at their best in flower they can be bought more cheaply when only in leaf.

C. miniata This is most commonly available and has dark green leaves.

C. miniata 'Variegata' This has a cream stripe along the length of the leaves.

Healthy plant The wealth of crocus- or trumpet-shaped flowers usually have a lighter centre. Here a cluster of brilliant red-orange blooms with yellow centres stand out from a mass of glossy leaves. Plants bloom in spring every one to four years.

AVOIDING PROBLEMS

Light and position

Clivias require good light if they are to flower successfully but they should be protected from bright sunlight. A shaded window is ideal but remember that these plants are also vulnerable to draughts.

Temperature range

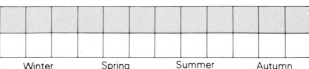

Cool   Intermediate   Warm

When the flower buds appear clivias need a temperature of 60°-70°F (15°-21°C) and should be kept within this range throughout the growing period. In winter they need to be kept cool while the plant is resting. Choose a place with a temperature of 45°-50°F (7°-10°C).

Watering

Water these plants well in the growing period. This will probably mean once a week. In the rest period water less so that the soil remains almost dry. Increase again gradually once the flower stalks appear.

Feeding

Clivias develop very sturdy root systems and for this reason require regular weekly feeding once the flower stalks are well established. Use liquid fertilizer but reduce the feeding in the rest period to one feed every two weeks or even less.

Seasonal care

Winter   Spring   Summer   Autumn

Water and feed well in the flowering and growing period and keep in a warm position. Reduce watering, feeding and temperature in the rest period. Keep in a good but not too strong light and protect from draughts. Remove the flower stalks once they wither and cut off the fruits that develop with a sharp knife. To grow new plants separate the young groups of new shoots from the main plant after flowering has ended and pot in small pots. Left on the plants these offsets will ensure several heads of flowers.

Soil

Use a loam-based mixture and firm the plants into position with your hands to avoid damaging the fleshy roots. Well-established plants are best top-dressed for two or three years. Then repot just before the flower stalks appear.

PESTS AND DISEASES

Few pests attack clivias but it is important to guard against leaf rot caused by too wet roots. If the leaf margins turn brown check that the pot is well drained and that the drainage holes are not blocked by earthworm casts.
Earthworms These can be cleared by inverting the pot and holding the rootball in your hand to clear the drainage holes and remove the worms.
Mealy bug These may also attack this plant. Remove the white patches they cause with a piece of cotton wool dipped in methylated spirits or spray with an insecticide.

An unhealthy plant A good specimen of this plant will have glossy dark green or striped leaves. If the leaves turn brown or look scorched this may be the result of direct sunlight on wet leaves. It is important to avoid watering this plant while in sunlight. If the leaves start to wither, give the plant more water and spray immediately. If new shoots are fragile and there are no flowers move the plant to a cooler position. If there is no new growth at all in spring, however, the plant needs more warmth. Discoloured yellow foliage means that the plant needs more feeding, particularly in the summer months. The most common cause of rot at the base of the plant is overwatering.

Codiaeum

One common name of the codiaeum refers to Joseph's coat of many colours, for the plant's leaves are also many coloured – yellow, orange, red and green. Mottled and general mixtures of these colours make the Croton the most brilliant of all the foliage plants that are grown indoors. Indigenous to Ceylon, codiaeums are temperamental and require a degree of skill if they are to survive in room conditions.

Almost all these plants are raised from cuttings about 4in (10cm) long taken from the top section of main stems. The cuttings should be put in a peat and sand mixture and kept humid in a temperature of not less than 70°F (21°C).

VARIETIES

Whichever of the numerous varieties you choose, inspect it carefully for browning or dull leaves, which may be a sign of root rot or the invasion of red spider mite. The following are popular among the many codiaeums.
C. reidii This has broad leaves, mottled in rich pink and orange and with proper care may grow to 6ft (2m).
C. 'Eugene Drapps' This plant has predominantly yellow foliage and is the best variety with this colouring.
C. holufiana This is a variety that is easy to manage and is one of the most commonly available.

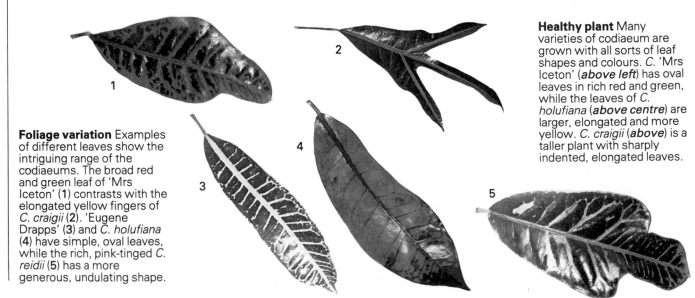

Foliage variation Examples of different leaves show the intriguing range of the codiaeums. The broad red and green leaf of 'Mrs Iceton' (**1**) contrasts with the elongated yellow fingers of *C. craigii* (**2**). 'Eugene Drapps' (**3**) and *C. holufiana* (**4**) have simple, oval leaves, while the rich, pink-tinged *C. reidii* (**5**) has a more generous, undulating shape.

Healthy plant Many varieties of codiaeum are grown with all sorts of leaf shapes and colours. *C.* 'Mrs Iceton' (**above left**) has oval leaves in rich red and green, while the leaves of *C. holufiana* (**above centre**) are larger, elongated and more yellow. *C. craigii* (**above**) is a taller plant with sharply indented, elongated leaves.

PESTS AND DISEASES

Red spider mite These share the codiaeums' preference for warmth and are likely to be found (*see illustration below*). They are difficult to detect on the bright foliage. Spray the plants with malathion once a month as a precaution. If the mites get a firm hold, the plant must be destroyed.
Scale insect This is a less common pest but it may attack older plants. Spraying with malathion should get rid of it.
Botrytis This is a disease that is not usually found in sturdy plants, but may attack soft, damp foliage. Remove the damaged leaves and spray the plant with dichloran.

Damaged leaves
Codiaeums like warm temperatures and some humidity, but excessive moisture in a cold position discolours and shrivels the leaf (*above*). Damage from red spider mites (*below*) is clearly seen in the starved, curling leaf of the weakened plant.

AVOIDING PROBLEMS

Light and position

The codiaeum requires good light and plenty of sun to retain the beauty of its multi-coloured leaves, but take care that it is not scorched or parched during a hot summer. In poor light, the leaves will revert to green and the plant cannot flourish as it should.

Temperature range

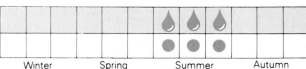

Cool   Intermediate   Warm

Warm, moist conditions are essential to this plant and the minimum temperature at which it is kept should be 60°F (15°C) but it will benefit from more warmth and may prefer a temperature nearer 70°F (21°C). These are the conditions which would prevail in its native country of Sri Lanka.

Watering

The codiaeum requires plenty of water in summer and regular watering during mild weather and the winter months. Water should be supplied to the soil from the top of the pot and the plant may prefer that the water is tepid. Do not spray the leaves of a codiaeum.

Feeding

Established plants are rather greedy, requiring nourishment with every watering, except possibly during the winter months. The food may be introduced through the soil as a liquid, but never try to use a foliar feed.

Seasonal care

Winter	Spring	Summer	Autumn

The plant requires a good deal of attention throughout the year and will need more water the better its health and growing conditions. In winter it will require slightly less water, but overwatering at any time may encourage disease which will damage the leaves, especially in older plants. Periodic cleaning of the foliage will improve the appearance of the plant, but cleaning chemicals should not be used too frequently.

Soil

Loam-based soil must be used and the plant should be potted with reasonable firmness. Regular repotting is advisable, annually in summer, until the plant is in a 10in (25cm) pot. Thereafter it can be sustained by careful attention and regular feeding.

Columnea

The strange common name of the columnea must surely relate to the open flower, which could be compared to the open mouth of a goldfish. The flowers are spectacular with glorious orange, red or yellow colouring. The plant's leaves are oval and small, attached to wiry stems that in all varieties other than *C. crassifolia* have a natural drooping habit, so they are good for hanging baskets and pots. By far the best variety is *C. banksii*, which produces masses of orange flowers from early spring onwards. The secret of successful flowering is to keep the soil as dry as possible during late winter without causing defoliation. Many columneas are much tougher plants than they are usually thought to be.

The flowers of the Goldfish Plant are highly coloured and exotic. The common name of the plant probably derives from the open, fluted shape, resembling the mouth of a fish. The flowers grow separately from the stems but hang in rich clusters on the whole plant.

Healthy plant The Goldfish Plant is extremely striking, with its dark foliage and very bright flowers. It hangs in a luxuriant mass of straight heavily laden stems.

PROPAGATION

Columnea may be propagated at almost any time from mid-spring to late summer.

As the plant naturally produces long trailing stems that occasionally need a trim to keep in check, it is worth taking advantage of this to generate cutting material for propagation.

Using a sharp knife, or a pair of secateurs or pruning shears, trim as required and select healthy tip cuttings measuring 3–4in (7.5–10cm). If necessary, pull off any lower leaves that may not be required and dip the cutting into a hormone rooting powder before sticking three cuttings directly into a 3½in (9cm) pot, or five cuttings to a 4¼in (11cm) pot, filled with a peat-based seed and cutting compost.

Keeping the compost hardly moist, the cuttings should root without needing to be covered at a temperature of 68°F (20°C), but if the atmosphere is dry it may be worth covering the cuttings with a clear plastic bag. After a month to six weeks of being kept warm and out of direct sunlight, the cuttings should have rooted sufficiently to allow the cover, if used, to be dispensed with and to be grown on accordingly.

As the cuttings start to grow it is important to start feeding as soon as possible after rooting to help build up a healthy, well-formed plant before winter conditions put the plant under stress.

AVOIDING PROBLEMS

Light and position

The columnea requires a position with good light, to encourage flowering, but shaded from direct sunlight. It is best seen as a hanging plant, so it could be placed near the window in a bright room. However, it will not tolerate draughts.

Temperature range

Cool   Intermediate   Warm

Few plants care for a large temperature range or periods of excessive heat or cold. A suitable range for the columnea is 60°-70°F (15°-21°C) and it may not do well in a centrally heated house as it does not like dry air. If, however, it is possible to keep up a good level of humidity, the plant may exist comfortably, but it will prefer a slight coolness around the winter flowering period.

Watering

Water the plant regularly during the summer growth period, giving slightly less in winter. Water the soil from the top of the pot or pour it into the saucer, always avoiding the foliage. Keeping the soil almost dry during mid-winter will encourage better flowering.

Feeding

The plant is not too fussy in its feeding habits, but established plants should be fed about once a week in summer when they are active, once a month during winter. Cease feeding towards the end of winter when the watering is cut to a minimum. Introduce the food through the soil.

Seasonal care

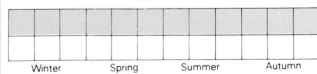

Winter   Spring   Summer   Autumn

The columnea is quite easy to care for and if the period of near starvation is adhered to in winter, the plant will flower more freely. The foliage can be trimmed to shape at any time when the plant is not in flower, but this is not essential to its health. The autumn is the time to tidy the plant and cut out any dead material. Beware of overwatering at all times, as this can ruin the leaves and ultimately whole branches.

Soil

Cuttings from the plant will root quite well in moist conditions and a temperature of 70°F (21°C). When transferring them to a hanging basket, use a loam-based potting mixture and include at least five cuttings, to ensure full and impressive growth.

VARIETIES

Finding a Goldfish Plant to buy can be a problem as they are grown in limited numbers. On finding a supplier, choose a plant with several cuttings in the pot so that it has a full appearance and is firm and healthy. The plant may be bought already in flower, but this need not be a condition of purchase.
C. banksii This is the finest variety and forms a full hanging plant with evergreen foliage and bright orange flowers. It is easily propagated from cuttings.
C. gloriosa The slender, less rigid stems of this variety carry soft, hairy leaves and can grow to 3ft (1m). The tubular flowers are a vivid red with yellow throats.
C. microphylla The leaves of this plant are very small and abundant, but the orange flowers are produced rather spasmodically and this variety may be rather less attractive than the others.

White fly This common pest is noticeable when the plant is disturbed as the flies rise up in a cloud. Persistent spraying with dichloran, at four-day intervals over about two weeks, should kill both adult insects and young flies. If they should seem to become immune to the spray, change to a different type of insecticide.

PESTS AND DISEASES

Columneas seem generally to have a natural resistance to many common pests, but they are sometimes affected.
Mealy bug This small, white pest will be found only on older plants and can be removed with cotton wool soaked in methylated spirits.
White fly These suck sap from the undersides of the leaves (*see illustration above*).
Botrytis This is rarely seen but may attack a plant that is cramped and overwatered.

ACANTHACEAE

Crossandra

Crossandra infundibuliformis (*above*) is the only species of this genus that is grown as a houseplant. It is a shrubby plant with glossy leaves, but tends to grow straggly with age. The cultivar 'Mona Walhed' (*left*) has attractive flowering bracts.

The only crossandra grown indoors is *Crossandra infundibuliformis*. It is generally sold as a compact little plant, with its orange-coloured bracts just coming into flower over the glossy green leaves, but it will eventually attain a height of some 6ft (1.8m), by which time it will be very straggly and much less attractive. Cutting it back will help to retain its attractiveness, but once plants have shown the tendency towards legginess they never regain their early appearance. The best solution is to take cuttings from growth ends and to start afresh. Give plants good light but not bright sun.

CROSSANDRA	
Light and position 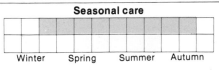 During the growing period, this plant needs plenty of light — it will benefit from direct sunlight in the colder months.	**Feeding** When in active growth, apply fertilizer once a fortnight.
Temperature range Cool Intermediate Warm These plants are best in a warm temperature — it should not go below 65°F (19°C) in the growing period, 55°F (13°C) in the winter.	**Seasonal care** Winter Spring Summer Autumn Only repot the plant if necessary, and do so in early spring, before flowering.
Watering Water moderately during the growing period and just enough to keep the soil moist in winter.	**Soil** Rich, peaty soil that is free-draining.

138

Cyclamen persicum

Cyclamen are among the most beautiful of all flowering plants, whether they are grown in pots or not, but they are no longer simply seasonal flowers that only appear in the autumn. Hybridists have made it possible for plants to be in flower throughout the year, although the plants still tend to be more popular during the winter months. Over the years, however, the development of *C. persicum* has been quite an achievement, as the plants today bear little resemblance to those initially collected in the eastern Mediterranean. The commercial grower raises fresh plants from seed each year, and for the main crop these are sown in mid-autumn in a temperature of around 70°F (21°C). The only time that plants need to be so warm is when they are germinating.

VARIETIES AND PURCHASING

The main quality to look out for when buying a cyclamen is that the stems, leaves and flowers are all fresh and upright. Avoid a plant with leaves drooping over the side of the pot. Look among the leaves to make sure there are plenty of healthy flower buds and inspect the whole plant for signs of botrytis, which will only become more and more troublesome. If the ends of leaves and flower stalks seem to be rotting, choose another plant. There are numerous strains and types among the many varieties of cyclamen. They are also available in many beautiful colours, so it is largely a matter of personal preference as to which should be bought, provided all the plants are equally healthy.

Healthy plant A plant that is kept in the right cool, airy conditions will thrive and flower longer than one that is in too stuffy or hot a place. Cyclamen with rich, pink flowers (*left*) are often favoured for their decorative appearance. The cyclamen originally came from the Mediterranean area. Modern varieties have been developed which bear flowers in all shades of pink, red and purple and, although the original plants had plain green leaves, the newer strains have attractive borders of pale green, delicately drawn into the centre of the leaf by the light-coloured veins (*right*). Cyclamen are very popular as gift plants, and in this case it is even more vital to ensure the plant is absolutely healthy when it is bought, as no-one will be pleased to be left with a present that rots or grows mould.

AVOIDING PROBLEMS

Light and position

Given cool, light and airy conditions, these plants remain in flower for a longer period and have a bright, healthy appearance. A kitchen windowsill might be a suitable location, but avoid subjecting them to hot sunshine through the glass on very sunny days.

Temperature range

Cool   Intermediate   Warm

A temperature range between 55°-65°F (13°-18°C) suits a cyclamen very well and it will not live happily in warmer temperatures or in a stuffy atmosphere. If the surrounding environment is too hot and dry the leaves of the plant will yellow. In common with many other plants, the cyclamen abhors cold draughts or sudden changes of temperature.

Watering

A cyclamen will be damaged if the soil becomes sodden. Water from below to moisten the compost, but never leave the plant standing in water. The plant will come to no harm if it gets to a stage where the leaves droop slightly before watering is repeated.

Feeding

A weak liquid feed given through the soil with each watering is required while the plant is in leaf. As with the watering, any excess should be avoided. The plant must be given the most attention during winter and spring.

Seasonal care

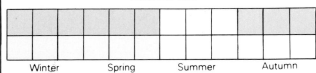

Winter   Spring   Summer   Autumn

The flowering season of the cyclamen is autumn to spring and the growth dies down after the flowering. The plant can then be allowed to dry out slightly and rest in a cool, but frost-free position until new growth starts in the summer. At this stage the corm can be divided and the sections repotted for propagation of the plant.

Soil

A good loam-based compost mixture is suitable for potting at any stage and can also be used to raise plants from seed. Cyclamen flower well if slightly pot bound so a pot of 5in (12.5cm) is the largest needed. Crock the pot and pot the plant firmly.

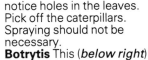

Aphids These (*above*) are damaging and unsightly but not particularly troublesome to cyclamen. Spray the plant with diazinon and repeat the treatment as necessary.
Caterpillars These (*below left*) are not often found on plants kept indoors, but may find their way in, especially to a conservatory. You will notice holes in the leaves. Pick off the caterpillars. Spraying should not be necessary.
Botrytis This (*below right*) is a dangerous and difficult condition. Cut away badly affected leaves and stems, move the plant to dryer conditions and spray it thoroughly with dichloran.

PESTS AND DISEASES

Cyclamen mite These tiny insects appear almost as dust on the reverse sides of leaves, which become stunted and very hard. Unfortunately there is no cure and the plant must be destroyed.
Red spider mite Check the leaves regularly if you have any suspicion that the plant has red spider. It is difficult to see and almost impossible to control. Spray the plant repeatedly with malathion.

Aphids These flies (*see illustration above top*) do occur on the cyclamen but are quite easily controlled.
Botrytis This disease (*see illustration above*) can quickly kill a plant so deal with it as soon as it appears.
Vine weevil The beetles attack the leaves of the plant, but the larvae in the soil cause the real damage. Water the soil with malathion regularly at fortnightly intervals.

PROPAGATION

Although painstaking in terms of the effort and time required, a successfully propagated cyclamen in the home is well worth the trouble.

Seed may be sown either in late summer to flower in the late autumn and Christmas period in the following year or at any time from late summer through until spring to flower up to approximately 15 months later. Sow the seed in shallow pans or trays, using a seed and cutting compost and lightly covering the seed. Germinate at a constant 65–68°F (18–20°C), keeping the seed in the dark.

Check regularly for germination, which may take up to several weeks and normally appears rather patchily. As soon as the seedlings are seen to develop place the pan or tray in a well-lit position and grow on until large enough to handle. Maintain a temperature of 55–60°F (13–15°C) with a free-moving supply of air. Prick out the individual seedlings when large enough into 3½–4¼in (9–11cm) pots of peat-based potting compost and continue to grow on at 55–60°F (13–15°C). Avoid draughts, but ensure a good exchange of air to prevent a stuffy dank atmosphere, which the cyclamen hates.

Cyperus

The cyperus is one of the few water plants that can be recommended for indoor culture as, with reasonable care, it will do well. The plants grow in clumps and have rather thin, pale green, grassy leaves that are not in themselves attractive, but the 3ft (1m) tall umbrella-like flower adds much to the general appearance. The simple way of producing new plants is to allow clumps to develop to a reasonable size, then to remove the plant from its pot and, with a large sharp knife, simply cut the clumps into sections. These can then be potted individually using a houseplant potting mixture.

VARIETIES

Umbrella plants can be quite difficult to obtain, but in the summer two varieties may be available in the shops.
C. diffusus This variety may reach a height of 3ft (1m). It is a striking plant with a wide spread of leaves.
C. alternifolius (*see below left*) This is a much smaller plant, usually growing to around 12–18in (30–46cm). It has narrow sparse leaves.
C.a. 'Albo Variegata' (*below*) This is a variegated attractive houseplant which has white-striped leaves.

Healthy plant Umbrella Plants grow wild all over the tropical and sub-tropical regions of the world. Their natural habitat is swamp-land and the shores of sluggish rivers and lakes. The two species most commonly found as houseplants in this country (*C. diffusus* and *C. alternifolius*) both originate in Madagascar. Water is therefore essential to their healthy growth, and if they are allowed to dry out, their foliage will very quickly turn a yellowish-brown. When looking for a healthy Umbrella Plant in a shop, choose one with fresh green lush-looking leaves. The necessity of keeping them moist makes Umbrella Plants ideal for the beginner, as they can never be overwatered! The other point to check when buying one of these plants is that the umbrella growths are free of signs of mealy bug and other pests.

PESTS AND DISEASES

As long as the Umbrella Plant is well watered, it should remain quite healthy.
Mealy bug To check for these, look into the green flowers at the top of the plant. They can be removed with an insecticide.
Green and **white fly** These may attack young leaves.

Diseased plants If the leaves turn brown at the edges and develop brown patches (*bottom*), the cause may be insufficient watering. It could also be that the plant needs more light, so it should be moved. Other danger signs are split leaves or holes in leaves (*below*). Check for pests if this occurs.

AVOIDING PROBLEMS

Light and position

The Umbrella Plant can be grown equally well in full, bright sunlight or slight shade. Highly adaptable, it will, with time, adapt itself to almost any location. If few stems are produced, however, the plant is getting too little light.

Temperature range

Cool   Intermediate   Warm

The Umbrella Plant will tolerate most temperatures between 50°-70°F (10°-21°C), provided there are no extreme fluctuations. In winter the temperature should not go below 50°F (10°C). *Cyperus papyrus* will need a minimum temperature of between 60°-65°F (15°-18°C).

Watering

Being aquatic, the Umbrella Plant must be grown in pots placed in a shallow pan of water. The water should be changed daily. During growth periods the plant will require more water than at times of rest. Do not totally immerse the pots which can cause the stems to rot.

Feeding

Because the plants sit in water, the best way to feed is with fertilizing tablets pushed well into the soil, Otherwise, a standard liquid fertilizer can be applied at monthly intervals during the active growth period.

Seasonal care

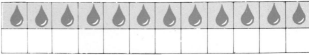

Winter   Spring   Summer   Autumn

Throughout the year, the Umbrella Plant needs a constant source of water to keep the roots saturated. If kept in dry, heated environments, the water level should be checked frequently. Feed at regular intervals except in winter. The plants can be propagated by division in spring. As the green plants die, cut them off at intervals throughout the year to allow for new growth.

Soil

The soil should have a high loam content to prevent it from disintegrating in the water. Pieces of charcoal can be added to the soil to keep it fresh and lessen unpleasant odours caused by souring compost. As they grow, the plants will require larger pots.

Dieffenbachia

Although these plants do produce insignificant spathe flowers, they are grown entirely as foliage plants – the vast quantities produced each year are a testimony to their popularity. Some of the more robust forms can grow to a height of about 6ft (2m) in only six years, but they are grown principally as compact plants that seldom get out of hand if confined to reasonably sized pots.

New plants can be raised from pieces of stem cut into sections and placed in a peat and sand mixture at a high temperature, or by removing the small plantlets that cluster around their parents, potting them individually in smaller pots.

Healthy plant *D. amoena* 'Tropic Snow' (**below**) is a variety of *D. amoena*. It is highly attractive, its dark green foliage being relieved by interesting white blotches. The detail (*right*) shows new growth after the plant has been cut back for propagation. Always wash your hands thoroughly after taking cuttings or removing old leaves. Dieffenbachia sap is poisonous.

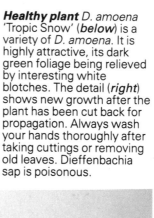

Two varieties *D. exotica* (**near right**) and *D. camilla* (**far right**) are two popular varieties. The former is extremely compact, with blotched green and white leaves. The latter is a more recent introduction. Its attraction is the creamy white centres of its leaves. Both plants need warmth and high humidity.

D. amoena This detail of the leaf of 'Tropic Snow' shows the sturdy, fleshy quality and the spread of pale markings from the centre.

D. exotica The blotchy leaf markings of this variety are less regular than those of 'Tropic Snow', although the colouring is similar.

D. camilla The creamy colour of the leaf, edged with green, is particularly striking, making *D. camilla* an unusual plant for display.

VARIETIES AND PURCHASING

These highly attractive houseplants can produce flowers, but these are of little interest. Their main appeal is their attractive shape and their striking foliage. This is usually green, but it is often intermixed with shades of white or yellow. When you buy these plants, remember that dieffenbachias love heat. They originally came from Brazil and were given their name by Dieffenbach, the gardener to the Hapsburg rulers of Austria, in 1830.

D. amoena A vigorous-growing plant, this is popular since it is relatively easy to care for.

D. camilla This plant is a fairly recent introduction, noted for its combination of pattern and colour.

D. exotica Striking blotched white and green foliage, with leaves spreading outwards and arching downwards make this an attractive plant.

D. bausei This has lance-shaped yellow-green leaves, up to 1ft (30cm) long, marked with white spots and dark green patches and margins.

D. bowmannii This dieffenbachia has oval leaves 2ft (60cm) long and 1½ft (45cm) wide on long stalks. The colouring is less striking than that of some varieties, being chiefly a mixture of pale and dark green.

D. imperialis This has leathery, oval leaves, splattered with yellow.

D. maculata Spotted Dumb Cane has many varieties, most with elegant pointed, lance-shaped leaves, coloured dark green with irregular off-white markings.

145

PROPAGATION

Stem Cutting

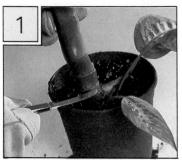

1

Cut stem carefully with sharp knife.

2

Ensure cut is made cleanly.

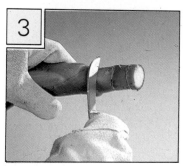

3

Cut stem into 3in (7.5cm) pieces.

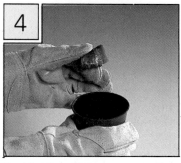

4

Dust lightly with hormone rooting powder.

5

Press gently onto compost surface.

6

Ensure stem is not buried and cover with plastic bag.

Tip Cutting

1

Remove 4–5in (10–12.5cm) tip cutting.

2

Dip in hormone rooting powder, insert in 3½–4¼in (9–11cm) pot and cover with clear plastic bag.

Although a number of plants are poisonous it is worth taking particular care when handling the dieffenbachia. Before starting to propagate the plant, try to wear gloves and avoid all contact with the sap due to its poisonous and violently irritating effect. Remember also to wash your hands and exposed skin, and to clean tools after the procedure.

For the best results propagate dieffenbachia from mid-spring to early summer.

Tip cuttings of 4–5in (10–12.5cm) should be cut with a sharp knife and prepared by removing any lower leaves that would be buried in the compost. The cutting should then be dipped into a hormone rooting powder and inserted in a 3½–4¼in (9–11cm) pot of a peat-based seed and cutting compost.

The cutting should be covered with a clear plastic bag and kept out of direct sunlight at a temperature of 72–75°F (22–24°C) until rooted. This can take up to two months. Remove the bag from time to time to trim off any decaying leaves to avoid the spread of a fungal rot.

Once rooted, remove the bag and commence feeding before potting on when large enough into a 5in (13cm) pot of a peat-based potting compost.

Large overgrown dieffenbachias with long bare stems may also offer propagation material in the form of the stem. This may be cut into sections measuring about 3in (7.5cm) which are gently pressed into the surface of a peat-based seed and cutting compost and cared for in a fashion similar to the tip cuttings technique. Stems will normally produce one plant, but if you are lucky and two are generated, take care to divide the stem carefully and pot up each plant separately.

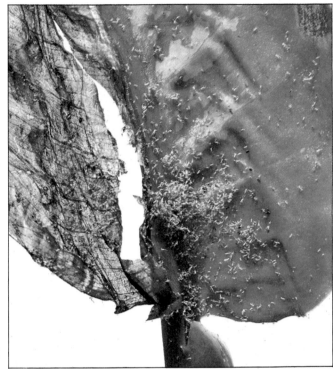

Leaves dying naturally It is common for the leaves of this plant to die back naturally (*above*). This happens first with the lower leaves. Plants should last at least three or four years with proper care.

Scorch This problem is caused by placing the plant either too near a radiator or too close to a sunny window (*below*). The best remedy is to move the plant to a more suitable location, although the damaged leaves will not recover.

Aphids This common houseplant pest will sometimes attack the dieffenbachia (*above*). It is best to treat aphids with a systemic insecticide in the form of either a spray or granules added to the soil.

Overwatering Brown patches on the edges of the leaves can indicate overwatering (*below*). Although this plant requires watering all the year round, water sparingly in winter.

Stem rot Plants kept in conditions that are too wet and cold may well develop rotting problems either on the stem (*above*) or foliage. Try not to overwater, and keep the plant in a temperature of at least 60°F (15°C).

Physical damage It is important to protect plants from damage by household pets (*below*). This leaf shows signs of scorch and of being eaten. There is no cure for such damage, but ensure that the plants cannot be attacked again.

AVOIDING PROBLEMS

Light and position

Place a dieffenbachia in a fairly light position, but shaded from direct sun. It should not be within range of heat from a radiator or cold draughts from a door or window. The colour of a variegated plant will suffer if it has poor light.

Temperature range

Cool   Intermediate   Warm

A dieffenbachia will live in a temperature of 60°F (15°C) but would probably prefer nearer 70°F (21°C). In higher temperatures it is important to keep up a good level of humidity. A cool, moist atmosphere can be tolerated for a short period, but may cause some falling of the leaves.

Watering

Moisture is required all year round, but the plant can be watered less in winter than in summer, when tepid water should be used. During spring and summer growth, watering should be generous and frequent.

Feeding

While the dieffenbachia is producing new leaf growth it should be fed with every watering, using weak, liquid fertilizer introduced through the soil. Feeding with every other watering is sufficient at other times.

Seasonal care

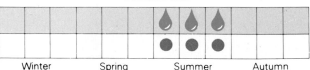

Winter   Spring   Summer   Autumn

Light and moisture all year round are vital to the health of this plant. A dark location or cold draughts will result in general decline, spindly growth and loss of leaves. In cold and wet conditions the leaves will brown at the edges. Propagation is most successful from stem cuttings, placed in peat and sand and kept moist and in a high temperature of 70°-75°F (21°-23°C). The plant requires the most attention, receiving plenty of food and water, during the summer months.

Soil

If the plant seems too large for its pot when purchased, it can be repotted immediately. Otherwise, wait until the plant is well established and repot in summer, using an open potting mixture containing loam and peat.

Dizygotheca

This genus comprises fragile-looking tropical plants that may reach 5–6ft (1.5–1.8m) in height, with a spread of 20in (51cm).

Dizygotheca elegantissima (also known as *Aralia elegantissima*) is a very slender plant. The leaves of older plants are almost black in colour, but when young they are coppery-red. Very slender and delicate, they have an almost fili-greed appearance. However, as the plant ages, the leaves gradually change colour and become much coarser. Older leaves radiate in palmate fashion with stiff petioles that are attached to a solid woody stem. Overall, the plant presents a fine canopy of greenery.

This is not the easiest of plants to manage, but when properly cared for, it can be one of the most attractive of all foliage plants. It is excellent in groupings.

To do well, *Dizygotheca elegantissma* needs light shade in temperatures of around 65°F (18°C). Be careful when watering that the soil does not remain soggy for long periods of time. Dizygothecas are slow growing and need to be potted on only once every two years. Use a soil-based potting mixture for this.

DIZYGOTHECA

Light and position

These plants like plenty of bright light, but they should not be exposed to strong sunlight.

Temperature range

Cool   Intermediate   Warm

The winter months can be critical, as the plants hate low temperatures. A minimum temperature of 65°F (18°C) should be the aim. Low and fluctuating temperatures can be damaging.

Watering

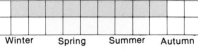

Water sparingly and carefully in winter. Allow the top of the mixture to dry out before watering again.

Feeding

Feed only in the spring and summer. Apply standard liquid fertilizer every two weeks during the growth period.

Seasonal care

Winter	Spring	Summer	Autumn

Frequent potting on is not necessary, as these plants are slow-growing. Spring is the best time to pot on, and because they grow upright, rather than branching out, several dizygothecas can be planted to good effect in one pot.

Soil

Use a rich, peaty mixture for potting on. Topdress about an inch of fresh mixture every spring.

Dizygothecas are delicate-looking foliage plants, with leaves divided into radiating leaflets. *D. elegantissima* (***top***) shows the characteristic very dark green colouring of a healthy plant. This species has deeply toothed margins to the leaflets, giving the leaves (***detail above***) an almost filigreed appearance. Plants are slow growing, and need careful management.

Dracaena

This is a diverse group of plants that look as though they should be growing on a tropical island. Many are stately plants that grow on slender stems, but there are also those with a more prostrate habit, such as *D. godseffiana*, and the more colourful ones such as *D. terminalis*. Almost all dracaenas are a little difficult to care for in rooms where the light and temperature are inadequate.

Propagation methods vary; some plants can be raised from stem cuttings and others from rooting fleshy roots that develop as the plants age. Both these methods need temperatures in the region of 70°F (21°C).

D. deremensis This variety may grow to 10ft (3m) but can be contained by pruning.
D. marginata 'Tricolor' (*below*) At the top of this plant's stout stem is a cluster of narrow green leaves, edged with red.
D. souvenir de Schriever (*below left*) This plant has bold green leaves which have a margin of yellow.
D. terminalis (*bottom left*) This attractive plant may reach a height of 30in (75cm). Young plants have green leaves but as they mature they turn a brilliant red.
D. godseffiana This has yellow mottled foliage on wiry stems and may, in ideal conditions, grow to 6ft (2m).

Healthy plant Healthy dracaenas are most attractive plants. When buying a dracaena, check that the leaves are not discoloured and that their tips have not gone brown. The topmost leaves should also be examined, as the white, powdery mealy bug could be present. Although many species do grow to a great height in their natural environment, they can be kept to a reasonable size and pleasing shape by judicious pruning. All varieties like light and will not achieve their best colour and contrast unless given the maximum amount of light possible. Homes that have central heating provide ideal

environments for these often exotic-looking plants. A group of dracaenas of different heights and colours, arranged artistically in a large window, can make a most attractive display.

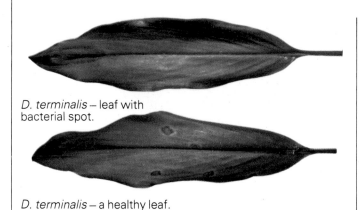

D. terminalis – leaf with bacterial spot.

D. terminalis – a healthy leaf.

D. marginata – a healthy leaf.

D. marginata – a scorch-damaged leaf.

D. 'Souvenir de Schrievar' – a rotting leaf.

PESTS AND DISEASES

Mealy bug Young bugs wrapped in a tell-tale substance like cotton wool are a sign that there are adult bugs in the foliage of the plant. They are normally found among the topmost leaves and can be eradicated by repeated use of malathion insecticide or by cleaning the bugs from the foliage with a sponge soaked in methylated spirits.
Root mealy bug If these are found in the roots, immerse the rootball in malathion.
Red spider mite This is quite common. The pest will be found on the underside of the leaf and brown patches may develop. Treat with insecticide.

Damaged leaves The effects of mealy bug can be seen in this *D. deremensis* leaf (*above left*). Dracaenas can be watered freely in summer. However, care must be taken not to overwater them and they should be kept rather dry in winter. The effects of overwatering can be seen in the picture of a *D. godseffiana* (*above*).

AVOIDING PROBLEMS

Light and position

All dracaenas need good light but care should be taken to avoid putting them in very bright sunlight as there is then a possibility of scorching. They should also be protected from cold draughts. Taller plants can be placed on the floor.

Temperature range

Cool   Intermediate   Warm

Dracaenas can survive quite low temperatures in the region of 50°F (10°C), although their leaves will droop in such conditions and eventually fall off. However, a couple of weeks in such temperatures will do no harm. The ideal temperature is somewhere between 60°-70°F (15°-21°C). They also need a humid atmosphere, so stand the plants on trays of damp pebbles or moss.

Watering

The plant needs plenty of water, especially during the growing period, throughout which the potting mixture should be kept very moist. Be careful, however, not to stand the pot in water, and in the winter months, keep the soil fairly dry.

Feeding

Fertilizer should be given to the plant during the growing period but it should not be fed during the winter. Either use a liquid fertilizer or place a slow-release pellet in the soil. Do not use a foliar feed as dracaenas do not do well if their leaves become wet.

Seasonal care

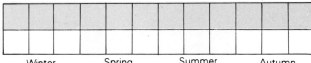

Winter   Spring   Summer   Autumn

During the summer months, when the plant is growing, water is the most important thing to remember. Making the roots excessively wet should be avoided, so allow the plant to dry out to some extent between each watering. Do not allow it to get bone dry in winter. Many of the taller growing plants will need cutting back, and this can be done at any time of the year. The cuttings can be used for propagating new plants.

Soil

Use loam-based potting mixture and pot on the plants during the summer months, ensuring that the new pots are not too large. It is a good idea with some plants to remove the top layer of old soil and replace it with fresh mixture. Pot on only when the plant is nearly pot-bound.

151

PROPAGATION

Stem Cutting

Cut stem with secateurs.

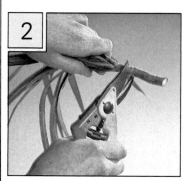

Cut stem into 2–3in (5–7.5cm) pieces.

Take care to keep stem right way up, dip into hormone rooting powder and insert in 3½in (9cm) pot. Cover with clear plastic bag.

Tip Cutting

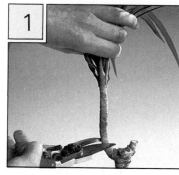

Remove 4–6in (10–15cm) tip cutting.

Dip into hormone rooting powder.

Insert in 3½in (9cm) pot, gently firm and cover with clear plastic bag.

Dracaena will grow to produce large, often multi-stemmed, plants that may need to be pruned to keep in check, an ideal time to consider propagation.

Dracaena may be propagated by tip or stem cuttings. Shoots produced from the base of the plant may also be used. Tip cuttings and shoots produced at the base of the plant should be removed with a sharp knife and trimmed to 4–6in (10–15cm).

Stem cuttings, consisting of the bare stem, should be cut with a pair of secateurs or pruning shears into 2–3in (5–7.5cm) pieces, taking care to ensure that each piece has a dormant shoot-bud. It is also important to ensure that the pieces of stem are kept the right way round; it can be very embarrassing to pot them upside down!

Dip each cutting into hormone rooting powder, stripping off any unwanted leaves and dibble each one into 3½in (9cm) pots of seed and cutting compost. Enclose the cuttings in a clear plastic bag at a temperature of 75°F (24°C) out of direct light. The compost should be kept barely moist.

After a period of up to two months rooting should have taken place. The bag should be removed as soon as the cuttings show signs of growth and start developing a reasonable root system.

The cuttings are then ready to be grown on and fed with a liquid fertilizer as required to help form a reasonable plant.

For the best results from propagating the plant it is worth avoiding the height of summer and to aim for propagating in mid- to late spring or late summer to early autumn.

Although quite different in form, dracaenas such as *D. sanderiana*, *D. fragrans* and *D. deremensis* may all be propagated similarly.

Episcia

Episcias are excellent flowering as well as foliage plants. Leaves are oval and hairy; flowers are brightly coloured and dainty. Episcias are commonly called Carpet Plants because of their creeping stolons.

Episcia cupreata is a striking plant that can be encouraged to trail as it ages. The leaves are all shades of silver and pale green, and the small flowers are an intense shade of red. The combination is very appealing when plants have developed into fairly large clumps – in hanging baskets, for example. This tender plant will not take kindly to lower temperatures, and needs a minimum temperature of 65°F (18°C).

Episcia dianthiflora is an easier plant to grow and should fall within the scope of almost all indoor-plant growers. Pale green leaves are formed in rosettes and are attached to rapidly growing pendulous branches that are much enhanced when gleaming white flowers appear from within the foliage. The plant is commonly named Snowflake Flower because of the tubular flowers that are prettily frayed around their margin. These are fine hanging plants that grow and propagate easily.

Episcias are grown both for their attractive trailing foliage and for their small, often brightly coloured flowers. *E. dianthiflora* (**right**) is the easiest species to manage, rewarding the grower with dainty white flowers with unusual frayed margins (**above**).

EPISCIA	
Light and position	**Feeding**
Bright light is desirable, with a few hours of direct sunlight a day. If humidity is high, reduce the amount of direct sunlight.	Apply liquid fertilizer at every watering. Do not give any feed in winter.
Temperature	**Seasonal care**
Cool Intermediate Warm These plants do best at temperatures between 60°F (16°C) and 85°F (29°C). They require high humidity and do very well in terrariums.	Winter Spring Summer Autumn Frequent potting on is not necessary — you need only repot when the roots appear to fill the pot.
Watering	**Soil**
Water as necessary throughout the growing period, but never stand the plant in water. In winter water sparingly.	Use a rich peaty mixture with some loam.

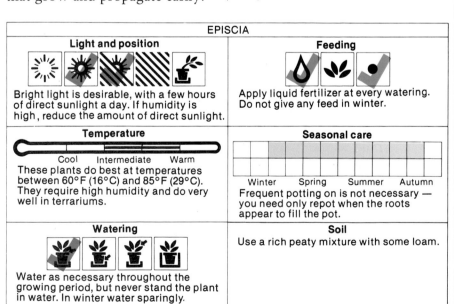

Euphorbia pulcherrima

In the past 25 years, Poinsettias have come from virtually nothing to being far and away the most popular Christmas-flowering plant. This is due to the development of greatly improved strains and growth-retarding chemicals which control the eventual height of plants.

There are varieties with pink, creamy white and bi-coloured bracts, but the important colour is the brilliant red of the Christmas Star. The plant's leaves are pale green and the flowers uninteresting, but the brilliantly coloured bracts are a magnificent attraction. The bracts are, in fact, coloured leaves that begin to develop in the topmost branches of the plant in autumn.

Cuttings about 4–6in (10–15cm) long are taken in mid-summer from top sections of the stem. These are rooted in moist peat and sand in humid conditions at a temperature of around 70°F (21°C).

Healthy plant A Poinsettia will always be striking because of its colour, and is usually displayed alone (*right*) to considerable effect. The coloured bracts that cluster round the plant's flowers (*above*) can grow up to 10in (25cm) long.

154

AVOIDING PROBLEMS

Light and position

The Poinsettia, like other flowering plants, especially winter varieties, must have plenty of light to maintain the colour of its bracts. It will not be harmed by weak, winter sunshine once established, but young plants should be protected from direct sun and cold draughts.

Temperature range

Cool   Intermediate   Warm

Keep the plant in intermediate temperatures. Room temperatures of 60°-70°F (15°-21°C) are fine. When the Poinsettia is not in colour it will survive in a cooler atmosphere, but should on no account be exposed to frost. The plant appreciates a moist atmosphere and may be adversely affected if there is a gas fire in the room.

Watering

Keep the compost moist and make sure it is not allowed to dry out while the plant is growing and in flower. The watering can be reduced once the plant has flowered, but return to the normal amount after pruning or repotting in midsummer. Water from the top of the pot.

Feeding

Add liquid feed to the water during the active period for the plant. When the Poinsettia begins to die down naturally, stop feeding it until signs of growth are resumed.

Seasonal care

Winter   Spring   Summer   Autumn

When the plant begins to die down after flowering, cut back the main stems to a length of about 4in (10cm). Store the plant in a warm, dry place and wait until new growth is apparent. This will take about six weeks, and as soon as the plant resumes activity, it can be watered and repotted. Be careful not to overwater a Poinsettia as this can cause root rot and leaf discoloration.

Soil

Use a loam-based potting mixture for repotting in late spring. Remove the old soil and replant in the same container. Water the plant after potting but keep it only just moist until new growth has fully taken hold.

Unhealthy leaves Botrytis (*above*) often attacks Poinsettias. It is a grey mould that causes nasty wet blotches on the foliage, attacking the lower leaves first. It is unwise to buy a Poinsettia that has very few lower leaves, as they may have been removed because the plant is already suffering from this mould. To cure, remove badly affected leaves and treat with fungicide. Leaves regularly suffer discoloration (*top*) and this may simply be age, or alternatively, root-rot. This develops if the soil is kept too wet, and air is unable to circulate round the roots of the plant. Eventually the leaves will drop off. There is no cure so excessive watering should be avoided.

PESTS AND DISEASES

White fly This is by far the most troublesome pest, and can easily be detected on the undersides of the leaves. It is notorious for increasing rapidly, and being fairly difficult to kill. There are numerous insecticides available – dichloran and malathion sprays are recommended – but they must be used intensively. Having killed off the parent flies, insecticide treatment must be repeated at four-day intervals to dispose of any larvae. A Poinsettia must be checked regularly for white fly throughout its life.

Botrytis This can occur (*see illustration above*) causing the plant to give off dust when it is moved or shaken. Household chemical sprays will cause spotting of a much smaller type than botrytis patches.

Root rot Another regular cause of discoloration in Poinsettias (*see illustration above*), this causes a dramatic fading in the colour of leaves.

155

Fatsia and × Fatshedera

The fatsia and the fatshedera are very closely related in as much as the fatsia is one of the parents of the fatshedera – the hedera obviously being the other. Both are hardy out of doors, and reasonably trouble-free plants in the home. While the fatsia has large, shallowly indented, fingered leaves, the fatshedera has similarly shaped leaves that are very much smaller. Both are green, but there are also variegated forms of each. The fatsia produces a compact bush while the fatshedera is much more upright, and will generally branch out if the growing tips are removed.

The best method of propagating the fatsia is by means of seed. To grow new fatshederas, tip or stem cuttings should be taken during spring and summer.

VARIETIES AND PURCHASING

These are both robust plants which are quite easy to grow. Check the leaves when buying the plant and choose one with glossy, bright green foliage. An overall browning of the plant may indicate the presence of red spider mites, so avoid a plant which does not look in the peak of condition.
Fatsia japonica This is often to be found under its other name of *Aralia sieboldii*. There is also a variegated form which is very decorative, but this is more difficult to manage and is seldom seen on sale.
× **Fatshedera lizei** This fresh green plant has upright growth and is an ideal climbing plant, for instance, on an open staircase where the temperature may be too low for other plants.

Healthy plant The spreading leaves of *Fatsia japonica* (**right**), form an attractive, almost tropical display. The mature plant may reach a height of 4ft (1.3m) but remains rounded and bushy, unlike the fatshedera, which grows vertically. However, both plants are susceptible to aphids, which especially enjoy the young shoots (**below**) in the top growth of the plants. Mealy bugs and red spider mites may also attack both these plants.

AVOIDING PROBLEMS

Light and position

These plants are quite tolerant of bad conditions, but prefer good light, so long as it is not harsh sunlight. A room which is bright but not sunny, or an airy hallway, is ideal, but keep plants away from draughts coming through doors or windows.

Temperature range

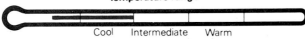

Cool   Intermediate   Warm

A temperature of below 60°F (15°C) is required but the plants are quite hardy and anywhere in the range 45°-60°F (7°-15°C) is suitable. Keep them well away from radiators, which exude dry heat which the plants cannot enjoy. The lower temperatures in the preferred range are adequate in winter.

Watering

Water the plants regularly but do not let them stand in water. They will require less moisture in winter, especially if the temperature is low. Be quite generous with the watering, but allow the soil to dry out slightly before repeating.

Feeding

Established plants will require frequent feeding. Add liquid feed to the water at regular intervals. As is usually the case, the plants may be fed less as watering is reduced, in this case during the inactive winter period.

Seasonal care

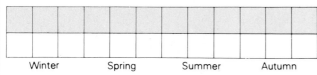

Winter   Spring   Summer   Autumn

Both plants will enjoy being placed out-of-doors in summer, if they are placed in a sheltered position, though not in full sun, and if their need for food and water is not neglected. Spray the leaves regularly when the plants are indoors. Cut back the stems if the plant becomes too leggy or the leaves have suffered from dry heat. The plants may be propagated from stem tip cuttings potted in the spring.

Soil

Plants in small pots will need potting on soon after they are bought. Once the plant has reached a pot of 5-7in (12.5-17cm) it can stay there quite happily for two or three years. Use loam-based mixture at all stages as peat is too thin.

PROPAGATION

Remove 3–4in (7.5–10cm) tip cutting.

Dip in hormone rooting powder and insert in 3½in (9cm) pot.

Place clear plastic bag over cane supports.

Secure bag with elastic band.

While × *Fatshedera lizei* may be rooted in a seed and cutting compost and potted on as required, it may be worth considering direct sticking to save time and hasten establishment and development.

From mid-spring to early summer take 3–4in (7.5–10cm) tip cuttings, as the plant starts to develop new growth, using a sharp knife or pair of scissors.

After having removed any surplus lower leaves, dip the cutting into hormone rooting powder and insert one per pot in a 3½in (9cm) pot. Alternatively put three per pot in a 4¼–5in (11–13cm) pot filled with a peat-based potting compost.

Cover the cutting with a clear plastic bag and to reduce water loss keep it in moderate light at a temperature of around 65–68°F (18–20°C).

Rooting should take place within a few weeks, provided the compost is not kept too moist; otherwise the cutting will rot off. After rooting, remove the plastic bag and grow the plant on, taking care to allow the compost almost to dry out in between waterings as this will help to stimulate the development of the root system.

PESTS AND DISEASES

Red spider mite Both plants are vulnerable to this pest, fatsia more than fatshedera. Browning of the leaves and hardening of soft new growth is the sign of spider mites. Thorough and repeated spraying with malathion is vital.

Aphids These greenfly are found on the younger leaves (*see illustration left below*) and are easy to see. Treat the plant by spraying with diazinon.

Mealy bug It is not difficult to detect this pest. At an early stage, wipe off the white bugs with cotton wool soaked in malathion.

Botrytis If the conditions in which the plant grows are cold, dank and shaded, it may develop mould. Remove badly affected leaves and spray the plant with dichloran.

Leaf problems Plants which are taken out of doors in summer are especially prone to damage from slugs and caterpillars which eat the leaves. Slug damage is more serious than the less voracious attentions of the caterpillar (*above*). These creatures can find their way into the house even if the plant has not been outside. Cut away badly eaten leaves and remove all slugs from the plant.

Ferns

Fine-foliage ferns

The finer-foliaged ferns must rank among the oldest of houseplants, and they are as popular today as they were in the other heyday of indoor plants, the Victorian age, when they were well adapted to the relatively dark rooms of most homes. There are some varieties with silvery variegation to their foliage, but the vast majority are grown and enjoyed for their cool, soft greenery.

Coarse-foliage ferns

It is probably more correct to say that these have large, rather than coarse, fronds as the Bird's Nest Fern, *Asplenium nidus-avis*, has just about the smoothest and the most exquisite leaves of any green-foliage plant. The Stagshorn Fern, *Platycerium alcicorne*, is coarser in appearance, on account of the waxy coating that completely covers the antler-shaped fronds. The asplenium has pale green fronds that in very mature specimen plants can be 3ft (1m) long arranged in the shape of a shuttlecock, and these can be a most impressive sight. As the name suggests, the Stagshorn Fern has decorative leaves that have a definite antler appearance to them. The fern also has anchor leaves, which attach it to trees and other forms of aerial support, where the plant makes its natural home.

Healthy plants The Bird's Nest Fern, *Asplenium nidus-avis* (**above**), is one of the most popular varieties, its distinctive leaf pattern giving rise to its common name. Its fronds, which are undivided and glossy, spread themselves upwards to form a bowl shape, similar to that of a bird's nest. The fronds themselves are delicate during the first few weeks of growth and thus, since they can be easily damaged, should not be dusted. Mature fronds, however, benefit from an occasional dusting.

AVOIDING PROBLEMS

Light and position

Most ferns prefer a fairly shady location, and will deteriorate quickly if exposed to strong sunlight. They do not care for sudden changes in conditions, abhor draughts and even those which like warm temperatures should not be placed near heating appliances.

Temperature range

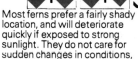

Cool   Intermediate   Warm

There are a great number of different ferns and as a group they cover quite a wide range of preferred temperatures. In general, fine foliage ferns such as the nephrolepis and pteris need intermediate conditions of 55°-65°F (13°-18°C). The ferns with coarser foliage, such as the platyceriums, require more warmth, in a range of 60°-70°F (15°-21°C). Some ferns are quite hardy but are happiest in a humid atmosphere.

Watering

Ferns enjoy moisture on the foliage and can be sprayed quite generously. Watering should be frequent to help maintain humidity, but the plant container should not be allowed to become waterlogged. Avoid overwatering especially in lower temperatures.

Feeding

Feed the plants with weak liquid fertilizer at every watering while they are active and producing new foliage. Little or no food is needed in the winter.

Seasonal care

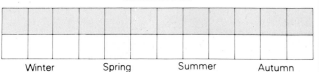

Winter   Spring   Summer   Autumn

The plants must be kept moist throughout the year and may prefer to be given rainwater. Although you must guard against overwatering, it is also important to take care that the roots are not allowed to dry out. Thorough cleaning in the centre of each plant during the autumn will reduce problems with rotting leaves which clog the plant and make it unsightly.

Soil

An open, peaty mixture is essential to the well-being of all types of ferns. The containers must be well-drained and a plant which is newly potted should be wetted mainly on the leaves and the soil kept only just moist.

VARIETIES AND PURCHASING

Though flowerless, ferns are extremely popular houseplants. The family consists of many different varieties with common characteristics. Their method of reproduction is unusual; unlike most other plants, they reproduce by means of spores, rather than flowers or seeds. Ferns can be bought in many sizes, but, whatever their size, they will grow at a prodigious pace, given suitable conditions. Small plants, therefore, can be just as good a buy as large ones. Check any plant carefully before you buy it. The leaves should be fresh and green. Any plant with dry and shrivelled foliage should be passed over, although browning of leaf ends is only a sign that the plant was allowed to become too dry at some time and is not, in itself, a reason not to buy it. Watch out for signs of scale insects and mealy bugs, the chief pests. Their presence is normally easily detectable if you examine the leaves. Any asplenium should be checked for blemishes along the margins of its leaves, as these are very susceptible to damage. The anchor fronds of a platycerium should be green, fresh and not dried out; the latter is a sign of neglect. All ferns prefer shaded locations and quickly deteriorate if exposed to strong sunlight. Avoid draughts and do not position them near heating appliances. Grouping plants together is a good idea; they will invariably grow and look better.

Blechnum Many different varieties of fern are included in this genus, ranging from small creepers through to upright plants with small trunks. The most popular is *B.gibbum*, an attractive plant with a tidy rosette of fronds crowning its trunk. Other popular versions are *B.brasiliense*, whose pinnae are copper coloured when young, turning green as the plant ages, and *B.occidentale*.

Pellaea rotundifolia The Button Fern is one of the two species of pellaea grown as houseplants. The other is *P.viridis* or Green Cliffbrake. The former's fronds arch downwards, carrying pairs of button-like pinnae. *P.viridis* has a bushy look.

Cyrtomium falcatum The Holly Fern is extremely decorative and long-lasting.

Phyllitis Only one species, the Hart's Tongue Fern, is commonly grown as a houseplant.

Polypodium The fronds of *P.aureum* rise from a long rhizome part-embedded in the potting mixture.

Davallia Two popular varieties are *D. canariensis* and *D.fejeensis*. The rhizomes are furry and will spread over the pot so that it is hidden.

Platycerium alcicorne The easiest of this family to grow indoors, it needs to be acclimatized gradually. It does best growing on bark or in a basket.

Pteris Three species do well as houseplants – *P.cretica*, *P.ensiformis* and *P.tremula*.

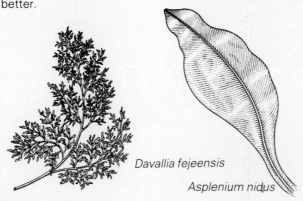

Davallia fejeensis

Asplenium nidus

Davallia

Phyllitis

Pellaea

Polypodium

Types of fern The possibilities of the fern family are almost endless. Many varieties are available in addition to the ones illustrated here; the commonest include the adiantum, asplenium, blechnum, cyrtomium, davallia, nephrolepis, pellaea, phyllitis, platycerium, polypodium, polystichum and pteris ferns. Because they invariably grow in places sheltered from direct sunlight in the wild, they thrive in places in the home where other houseplants are prone to languish. They like normal room temperatures, though high humidity is essential, as a surprising amount of water can be lost through the fronds of a fern in room conditions.

Cyrtomium

Blechnum

Platycerium

Three favourite ferns
Another popular version is *N. cordofilia*, the Erect Swordfern. *Adiantum capillus-veneris* (**centre**), the Venus Hair, is one of the best known of all the pot ferns. The triangular green fronds are comprised of fan-shapcd, fragile pinnae. Though the Venus Hair likes a humid atmosphere, take care not to overwater it; it should be kept only slightly moist at the rootball. Other varieties of maidenhair ferns include *A. hispidulum, A. raddianum* and *A. tenerum. Microlepia speluncia* (**bottom**) is a new coarse fern raised in Holland. It should be treated in the same way as the nephrolepis ferns. They grow well in normal room temperatures, though the roots must never be allowed to become dry; the potting mixture should be kept moist. In common with nephrolepis ferns, cut out any unusual rogue fronds if they appear. This is a sign that the variety is reverting to the base species.
Pteris (*top*) has many species all with intricate lacy fronds. Shown here is *P. cretica albolineata*, with attractive, variegated fronds.

PESTS AND DISEASES

Coarse-foliage ferns are relatively easy to care for, being less temperamental than some houseplants. Remember that an open, peaty potting mixture is essential and that pots and containers must be well drained. Some varieties, notably the platycerium, like to be rooted in bark. Do this by wrapping the roots in sphagnum moss soaked with liquid fertilizer. The roots can be attached easily to the bark and, eventually, will cling naturally by their anchor fronds. Such plants make very fine specimens indeed. They are watered by plunging the plant and anchorage into a bucket to soak them thoroughly. With all coarse-foliage varieties use rainwater for preference, plus a weak liquid feed. When the plant is well soaked, allow it to dry out a little before repeating the process. At no time should the roots be allowed to become excessively dry. All fine-foliage ferns prefer shaded locations and quickly deteriorate if exposed to strong sunlight. Keep the plants moist at all times; in dry conditions, it is a help if plant pots can be plunged up to their rims in moist peat. It is important to maintain humidity in the surrounding atmosphere, though the potting medium should never be allowed to become sodden for a long period. Feed weak liquid fertilizer at every watering while the plants are producing new foliage. A peaty, open mixture should be used at every stage of potting, following which, the soil and the foliage of plants should be well watered with a fine rose. Guard against too wet winter conditions when temperatures are low. A thorough cleaning out of the centres of plants each autumn will reduce the risk of leaves rotting and falling off.

Scale insect These present by far the most serious problem, as far as pests are concerned, since they can soon infest plants if left unchecked. To start with, they mostly trouble the reverse sides of the leaves. These should therefore be examined carefully as a matter of routine, so that remedial action can be taken at the earliest possible stage. Chemical treatment is best, but check carefully first to make sure the necessary insecticide, diazinon or malathion for example, will not damage the plant itself, as many of the ferns are sensitive to chemicals. Treat a specimen section of the plant to see if there is any reaction. The fronds of the asplenium can be wiped gently with a damp cloth to remove scales; this, however, is not recommended for the wax-covered fronds of the platycerium. When treating fine-foliage ferns, wipe the insects carefully off the infected plant; brown scales may be scraped with a thumbnail. Again, check the insecticide is suitable before using it on the whole plant. Test a leaf, waiting about 10 days to see the result.

Mealy bug This is a less serious problem. The bugs can be eradicated by soaking a cotton wool bud in methylated spirits and dabbing directly onto the powdery white adult bugs. Take care also to treat the young bugs in their waxy white protective coverings. Mealy bugs are difficult to locate in older fine-foliage ferns. Part the foliage for close inspection and, if bugs are present, remove them as for the coarse ferns.

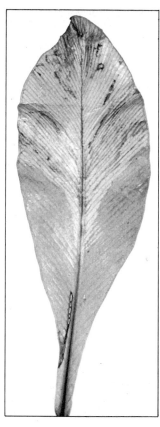

Unhealthy and healthy ferns The asplenium (*left*) has been affected dramatically by a sudden change in its environment. Careful observance of a few simple rules will ensure your plants remain healthy. Keep the room temperature constant, avoiding extremes of either hot or cold. If the temperature rises above 70°F (21°C), remember to increase the humidity. A simple way to achieve this is to spray the plants with water. If the temperature falls below about 60°F (15°C), reduce watering accordingly. With an asplenium, remember it is important to water plentifully during active growth, but that afterwards less is required. The fronds of a nephrolepis fern (*below*) illustrate a common cause of confusion. The top illustration shows scale, which should be treated with an insecticide; the bottom one shows brown areas, which are often thought to be scale insects, but, in fact, are spores.

Three common problems
The adiantum (*far left*) is underwatered, while the plant (*left*) is overwatered. The trick with these ferns is to keep them only slightly moist at their roots; if the rootball is allowed to dry out and the plant is then overwatered to compensate for this, the results can be disastrous. When watering, try to control it, so that the plant is given sufficient water to moisten the potting mixture throughout its depth, but ensure that the top layer of the mixture dries out before watering is repeated. The asplenium (*right*) is suffering from slug damage. This is a common problem but is minor compared to the two other pests that can attack ferns — mealy bugs and scale insects. The marks are not only damaging, but also unsightly. Usually, the smooth pale green shuttlecock leaves of the *Asplenium nidus avis* place it among the cream of potted plants.

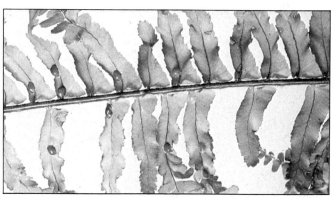

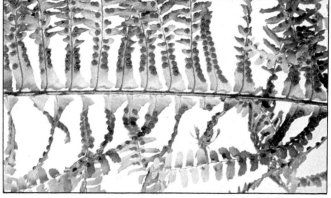

PROPAGATION

The **nephrolepis** may be propagated by two techniques, the first being probably much more practical and effective than the latter.

As the plant produces runners complete with little plants that form at the end when the runner touches compost, this technique may be utilized to propagate new plants.

Active runners may be laid onto compost and young plants should form as the runner begins to

root. When this occurs the runner may then be cut off and the young plant grown on.

This technique may be carried out whenever the plant is in active growth and particularly during the spring and summer. 3½in (9cm) pots filled with seed and cutting compost or potting compost are acceptable, taking care to ensure that the compost is kept reasonably moist.

Try to maintain a reasonable level of humidity and a temperature of around 65–68°F (18–20°C).

Alternatively, and more complicatedly, nephrolepis may also be propagated from spores produced on the undersides of the fronds. Collect the spores as they mature and are released on a white sheet of paper. Sow them very thinly onto the surface of seed and cutting compost lightly filled and even in a seed tray or half-pot or pan.

Cover with a sheet of clear plastic, glass or polythene and keep at 70°F (21°C) until germinated, which tends to be relatively poor, slow and patchy. When the young ferns are large enough to handle at ½–1in (1–2.5cm) prick them out and pot them up singly in 2½in (6cm) pots of potting compost and thereafter, when more developed, into 3½–4¼in (9–11cm) pots. Always keep out of direct light, and water from below by gentle and partial immersion.

The **asplenium,** like most ferns, can be difficult to propagate, but the keen enthusiast will find it well worth attempting.

Spores are produced from gill-like protrusions on the underside of mature fronds. These may be collected by lightly tapping the fronds over a sheet of white paper. The brown spores may be seen as a fine dust-like powder on the paper.

Prior to sowing the spores, fill a seed tray, pan or half-pot with a peat-based seed and cutting compost and lightly moisten.

Sow the spores very thinly on the surface of the compost and cover, with a piece of newspaper over the top to keep out excessive light.

Aim to maintain a temperature of around 70°F (21°C) until the spores germinate. If they germinate too thickly, prick them out to give them more space, treating them in much the same way as germinating the spores of *Platycerium bifurcatum*. However, this problem is unlikely to occur as germination is usually slow.

When the young plants are large enough to handle, approximately ½–1in (1–2.5cm), pot them up singly in a 2½in (6cm) pot using a peat-based compost, and then later into a 3½–4¼in (9–11cm) pot.

Tap spores onto a sheet of paper.

Sprinkle spores thinly onto the surface of the moistened compost.

The *Adiantum capillus-veneris*, or Venus Hair, is a beautiful, but delicate, plant, which must be looked after carefully, as it dislikes excessive heat, direct sunlight and a very dry atmosphere. It rarely grows higher than 12in (30cm).

Ficus

Many houseplants are drawn from this diverse family of plants whether they are large, small or creeping. Most have green foliage, although there are some variegated forms, which have a limited degree of popularity. All are propagated by means of cuttings of one kind or another, and need temperatures of around 70°F (21°C) to get them under way.

The leaves of the *F. benjamina* have a weeping habit and can be most attractive in many settings – especially placed over water by an indoor pool. The plant's small, oval-shaped, glossy green leaves are produced in abundance, and lost in abundance as well if the light levels are inadequate.

New plants are made by removing tip cuttings that are reasonably firm and about 4in (10cm) in length. In moist peat and a temperature of 70°F (21°C) rooting is not too difficult.

The well-known ubiquitous Rubber Plant is one of the most popular houseplants. *F. robusta* is the name of the modern version of an earlier plant, *F. elastica*, which has long been discontinued. The Rubber Plant today is a much tougher individual than its predecessor and is more able to withstand the vicissitudes of life in the home.

VARIETIES AND PURCHASING

Because there are so many varieties of ficus, there is sure to be one to fit each personal requirement. When purchasing, look for clean, blemish-free leaves. The plants should have a little sparkle to them too. Those with dull and dowdy foliage will have less chance of surviving when introduced to the conditions of the average living room. Look also for missing leaves, which is a sign of old age and poor culture. Besides *F. benjamina* and *F. robusta*, the most popular varieties, there are other members of the ficus family that make excellent houseplants.
F. 'Europa' This cream and green variegated form is one of the most attractive.
F. pumila This is also called the Creeping or Climbing Fig. It has little in common with the other plants being a small, creeping variety with thin, heart-shaped leaves. *F. pumila* is generally used as a trailing plant, and it grows very well in moist, shady locations.

F. lyrata The Fiddle Leaf Fig has violin-shaped leaves attached to woody stems. The plant can reach tree proportions and will require regular pruning. It grows quickly and tends to stay on a single stem. In poor conditions, rapid shedding of the leaves will occur.
F. benghalensis The Banyan Tree is valued for its branching habit and dark, oval leaves, which can grow to 1ft (30cm) in length.
F. retusa This ficus, the Indian Laurel, may occasionally bear small inedible fruit. The plant has dark green, elliptical leaves, which grow to about 3in (8cm) on stems that branch profusely.
F. rubiginosa This plant is the Rusty Fig, a small tree with leathery, oval leaves rust coloured underneath. *F.r.* 'Variegata' has leaves that are marbled with yellow markings.
F. sagittata This is a good trailing plant with leaves 2–3in (6–8cm) long.

AVOIDING PROBLEMS *(GENERAL)*

Light and position

There are many ficus varieties, each requiring slightly different lighting and positioning. All, with the exception of *F. pumila,* require good light and shade from direct sun. Healthy specimens will grow quite large and thus need ample space and positioning.

Temperature range

Cool   Intermediate   Warm

All except *F. diversifolia* require a minimum temperature of 60°-70°F (15°-21°C). *F. diversifolia* can withstand temperatures down to 45°F (7°C), provided watering is infrequent. The maximum temperature for all these plants is 75°F (23°C).

Watering

None of these plants like to be overwatered. A symptom of overwatering is yellowing and falling leaves. Water twice a week in summer and once a week in winter. Never let a plant stand in a dish of water.

Feeding

Liquid fertilizer can be added to the water every few days during the active growth period. Generally, ficus plants should be given larger and stronger doses than those recommended by the manufacturer or retailer.

Seasonal care

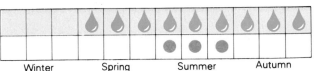

Winter   Spring   Summer   Autumn

All varieties need to be kept moist throughout the year, although less water is needed in winter than at other times. Water thoroughly and allow the soil to dry out before repeating. Repotting can be done annually in spring. Mature plants which do not need repotting can have the topsoil replenished. Prune the plant in spring and remember to dust the cuts with charcoal to prevent bleeding. As they age, some of these plants will develop aerial roots which should never be cut. Instead tie them back.

Soil

All large specimens need loam-based mixtures. The plants should be repotted when they have a solid rootball. Larger plants tend to push their roots through the pot bottom. Draw these back by carefully removing the rootball, pulling the roots with it.

AVOIDING PROBLEMS (F. BENJAMINA)

Light and position

F. benjamina is one species of the this family which requires plenty of light, but not direct

sunlight. If adequate light is not provided, the leaves will turn yellow and drop off.

Temperature range

Cool   Intermediate   Warm

The Weeping Fig is happiest in temperatures between 65°-70°F (18°-21°C). The maximum temperature it will tolerate is 75°F

(23°C). This plant does not like draughts, so if near a window, make sure there are no cold breezes coming through.

Watering

As with all the ficus varieties, *F. benjamina* should not be overwatered or the leaves will inevitably go yellow and drop off.

Water no more than twice a week in summer and every 7 - 10 days in winter.

Feeding

Established plants will need copious feeding in whatever form you choose. Less feeding is required in winter, but plants that

continue to produce new growth will need a small amount even at this time.

Seasonal care

Winter   Spring   Summer   Autumn

Liquid fertilizer should be added to the water during the active growth period. A daily spraying of water will benefit this plant throughout the year. Repot once a year at most in the spring. Mature

plants need not be repotted but can have the topsoil replenished. Prune in spring but do not remove any aerial shoots. The plant can be propagated from stem cuttings taken in the spring.

Soil

Like many of the strong ficus plants, this will soon push its roots through the bottom of the pot. Withdraw the plant from its pot and carefully tease back the

roots through the drainage holes. When the rootball is a mass of roots, repot in a loam-based mixture.

AVOIDING PROBLEMS (F. ROBUSTA)

Light and position

Although the Rubber Plant will tolerate fairly shady conditions, it grows more quickly in good light. It will also benefit from direct sunlight for a few hours a day.

F. robusta prefers cool environments to dry and hot, otherwise it is a very adaptable plant.

Temperature range

Cool   Intermediate   Warm

Temperatures between 50°-60°F (10°-15°C) are best, but the Rubber Plant will tolerate a minimum of 40°F (4.5°C) in winter.

In very hot rooms, above 85°F (29°C), the leaves tend to lose their turgid appearance.

Watering

With most houseplants, the temptation is to overwater. This is one plant that should never be overwatered. In

winter the soil should be just moist, and in summer water twice a week at most.

Feeding

When plants are first purchased and brought indoors they should be fed immediately. Feeding should continue thereafter using a weak fertilizer with each

watering. Less is needed in winter. Plants which have just been repotted need no food for at least three months.

Seasonal care

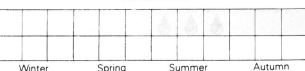

Winter   Spring   Summer   Autumn

Overgrown, larger plants can be pruned in autumn by cutting through the stem just above the leaf. Check the resultant flow of sap by covering the wound with moist peat. Clean the leaves

periodically with leaf cleaner, but avoid frequent use of chemicals; wiping with a damp sponge is usually sufficient. Less watering is required in winter when the plant is inactive.

Soil

A loam-based houseplant mixture is essential. Once in pots 7in (17cm) in diameter, sustain with regular feedings. The plant should be well rooted before repotting.

Water after potting and keep on the dry side for one month afterwards to allow the plant to root in the new soil.

Healthy plant Along with the ubiquitous Spider Plant, *F. robusta*, the Rubber Plant (*left*), is the most popular houseplant today. The central stem usually grows straight, but branching can be induced by cutting off new growth. When purchasing, the leaves should be free from blemishes, dark green, shiny, and leathery in texture.

F. 'Europa' (*above*) has cream and green variegated leaves. The leaves of *F. robusta* (*below*) are thick and leathery with prominent midribs.

F. benjamina, the Weeping Fig (**below**), grows into a large, graceful tree. As it grows, its 'weeping' appearance becomes more pronounced. The plant does not have a definite rest period, but its leaves often turn yellow and drop off in winter. The leaves of *F. benjamina* (**left**) are 3–4in (6–10cm) long. They are light green when young, and they darken with age.

The common name of *F. lyrata*, the Fiddle Leaf Fig (**above**), is well expressed by its violin-shaped leaves (**left**). *F. pumila* (**below**) is a compact plant with branching leaves that tend to creep. It is also attractive if trained onto a pole.

PESTS AND DISEASES

All these plants can contract pests and diseases, but which type will depend on the individual plant.

Scale insect These can become a major problem if left unchecked to go about their destructive business. Black, crusty, adult scale insects, or softer, flesh-coloured, young insects attach themselves to leaves, branches, and almost every other part of the plant. *F. benjamina* is especially prone to these pests, so check the undersides of leaves frequently. For minor attacks, wipe the pests forcibly with malathion. More stubborn adults may need the encouragement of a thumb-nail to dislodge them. Control bad attacks with thorough and repeated saturation with malathion.

Mealy bug These usually appear on older plants and can be removed by spraying or wiping with malathion.

Root-rot This is aggravated when roots are deprived of oxygen, which in turn is caused by soil that is too wet and does not allow air to penetrate it. Because the plant is deprived of moisture and nutrition, the roots will turn brown and lifeless and the plant will shed its foliage. Let the soil dry out thoroughly so the plant may produce new roots. The obvious precaution is never to overwater the plant nor let the plant stay wet for long periods of time.

Mealy bug When found on an *F. lyrata* leaf (*above*) mealy bugs will lodge in the veins of the leaf. Saturate the leaf with a sponge soaked in malathion or methylated spirits.

Sooty mould Dark mould on an *F. benjamina* leaf (*left*) grows on the excreta of scale insects into which fungus mould then settles. To cure, wipe the leaves clean with soapy water. Scale insects (*above*) are either black and crusty as adults, or flesh-coloured when young. They will attach themselves anywhere on the plant. Sponge away with an insecticide. Root-rot (*right*) tends to make the leaves yellow and eventually fall. Let the plant dry out thoroughly and do not overwater it in future.

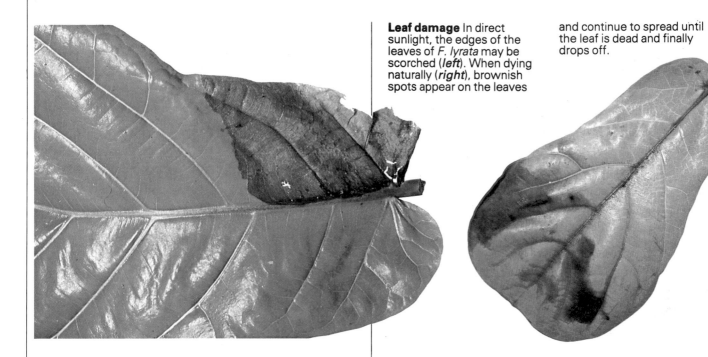

Leaf damage In direct sunlight, the edges of the leaves of *F. lyrata* may be scorched (*left*). When dying naturally (*right*), brownish spots appear on the leaves and continue to spread until the leaf is dead and finally drops off.

Underwatering To maintain healthy, lush growth, *F. pumila* (*above*) needs careful watering. Never allow the plant to become too dry or the paper-thin leaves will shrivel. Allow only the top ½in (12.5mm) of soil to become dry between waterings.

Overwatering This is a common mistake with *F. robusta* (*right*). A symptom of overwatering is drooping, lifeless leaves, which will soon turn yellow and drop off. These plants need only moderate watering, even in active growth.

PROPAGATION

Ficus benjamina may be propagated from mid-spring to early summer.

Tip cuttings measuring 3–4in (7.5–10cm) should be removed with a pair of secateurs or pruning shears and dipped into hormone rooting powder. As they are slow to root and easily put off, they should be inserted one per pot in a 2½in (6cm) pot of seed and cutting compost with a lower nutrient status than a standard potting compost, which could inhibit rooting.

Covering the cuttings with a clear plastic bag may be useful, but is not essential provided the atmosphere is not too dry. The cuttings should be kept at a minimum of 70°F (21°C) and up to 75°F (24°C) for rooting to take place. This may take several weeks. Sudden leaf drop is a sign that the propagation is failing.

However, if successful, the cutting should then be allowed to grow on and develop a healthy root system before being potted up into a 4¼–5in (11–13cm) pot of peat-based potting compost.

Ficus pumila (opposite) is easier to propagate, starting from mid-spring to early autumn, although cuttings taken earlier may propagate more readily.

Use scissors, not a knife, to cut off tip or stem cuttings measuring about 4–5in (10–12.5cm).

Strip off sufficient lower leaves to allow 1–1½in (2.5–4cm) of stem to be inserted in the compost. Dip the lower stem into hormone rooting powder and insert five to seven cuttings in a 3½in (9cm) pot of peat-based seed and cutting compost, ensuring that the compost is reasonably moist. Cover the cuttings with a clear plastic bag and keep them at 65–68°F (18–20°C) in moderate light. Rooting will occur within a few weeks, with the appearance of new growth and even aerial roots signifying the event.

Remove the plastic bag and feed with liquid fertilizer until a well-formed plant is produced, after which it may be potted on into a 4¼in (11cm) pot or 5½in (14cm) half-pot filled with peat-based compost.

Remove 3–4in (7.5–10cm) tip cutting.

Dip in hormone rooting powder and insert in 2½in (6cm) pot of seed and cutting compost.

Remove 4–5in (10–12.5cm) tip or stem cutting.

Gently remove lower leaves from bottom 1–1½in (2.5–4cm) of stem.

Dip in hormone rooting powder.

Insert five to seven cuttings per 3½in (9cm) pot.

PROPAGATION

The popular and easy-to-grow houseplant **Ficus robusta** requires a high rooting temperature to propagate successfully.

From mid-spring to mid-summer, cuttings consisting of a leaf and a piece of the main stem may be taken. This obviously means that the parent plant has to be pruned somewhat, a point worth considering before embarking upon the process.

Using a pair of secateurs or pruning shears, cut the stem into several pieces each with a leaf, leaving the stem approximately up to ½in (1cm) above the leaf and up to 2in (5cm) below it.

Wherever cut surfaces ooze the milky white latex, sprinkle powdered charcoal to help the sap congeal and wipe off any drops with a damp cloth before it becomes sticky and difficult to remove.

Taking each leaf and piece of stem, dip the stem into hormone rooting powder and insert it in a 2½in (6cm) pot of seed and cutting compost. Curl the leaf around a stick inserted vertically in the pot and secure it with a rubber band to support the cutting.

Maintain a temperature of up to 80°F (27°C) in moderate light, using a clear plastic bag to cover the cutting as necessary to improve its humidity. After about two months a new shoot will appear in the leaf axil. Pot the cutting in a 5in (13cm) pot of potting compost.

Alternatively, *Ficus robusta* may be air layered by selecting a length of shoot, ideally 6–10in (15–25cm), and cutting into the middle and then upwards for 2–3in (5–7.5cm).

The wound should then be eased open with moist sphagnum moss, which should be inserted between the cut faces and packed around the cut area. Then wrap the shoot carefully and tightly, with clear plastic tied above and below the wound. After this the wrapped area should then be closely covered with kitchen foil to keep out the light.

After a period of about two months, the area should contain roots, provided that the moss has been kept moist. The shoot may then be cut off below the initial wound before being potted up in a 5in (13cm) pot of potting compost.

Stem cutting

Tip Cutting

1. Cut leaf with stem to allow about ½in (1cm) above leaf and 2in (5cm) below leaf.

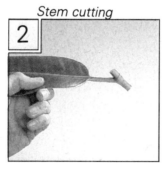

2. Dip base of stem in hormone rooting powder.

3. Insert stem in 2½in (6cm) pot of seed and cutting compost.

1. Remove 4–6in (10–15cm) tip cutting with at least three mature leaves. Dip into hormone rooting powder, having congealed oozing sap with powdered charcoal.

4. Gently firm cutting, taking care not to bury leaf axil.

5. Insert cane to provide support for leaf.

6. Place elastic band over slightly curled leaf to secure and cover with clear plastic bag.

2. Insert tip cutting in 3½in (9cm) pot and cover with clear plastic bag.

PROPAGATION

Air Layering

Select length of shoot 6–10in (15–25cm).

Carefully cut diagonally into stem.

Cut upwards in centre of stem for 2–3in (5–7.5cm).

Insert match-stick at top of wound to hold open.

Remove match-stick and allow stem to flex back onto sphagnum moss.

Dust wounded area with hormone rooting powder.

Gently place moist sphagnum moss between cut surfaces.

Gently lever open wound, taking care not to snap shoot off.

Pack moist sphagnum moss around stem.

Gently compress sphagnum moss and wrap with clear plastic film.

Holding stem enclose sphagnum moss to form a 'ball' around stem.

Secure plastic film with plastic-covered tie at top and bottom.

Having applied ties to top and bottom, check to ensure ties are secure but not too tight.

Wrap aluminium foil around air-layered area.

Form foil around area, gently crimping to secure as necessary.

Periodically check moss for dryness, moistening as necessary by adding water through loosened top tie.

Fittonia

Fittonias are creeping plants indigenous to tropical rain forests. Leaves are small, oval, with fine coloured veins. Plants produce small yellow flowers but seldom bloom indoors.

There are perhaps three species one can find in a good plant shop, and all of them are compact and low growing. All of them can be a problem indoors if the temperature is inadequate; 65°F (18°C) and above is essential. Roots should be kept moist but not wet.

The paper-thin leaves of *F. verschaffeltii* have a base colour of olive-green, but what makes the plant so attractive is the multitude of red veins, which makes the leaves seem entirely red in colour. Shaded, moist conditions are required, and weak feed only. When potting on, use peaty soil and shallow pots, not pots of full depth.

Very similar in habit and requirements to *F. verschaffeltii* is *F. v.* 'Argyroneura', which has attractive veined leaves in silver. More

popular on account of its neat habit and slightly easier culture is *F. v.* 'Argyroneura Nana', a lovely plant for bottle gardens and conned moist areas. It is troublesome in winter if temperatures fall too low, but it is very easy to propagate and pests are not a problem.

Fittonias are small-leaved foliage plants. The thin green leaves of *F. verschaffeltii* (**top**) appear to have a net of red drawn over them, as the leaf veins are coloured red. The leaves of *F. v.* 'Argyroneura' (**right**) are veined in silver, but apart from this, the two species are very similar in their appearance and requirements.

PROPAGATION

The diminutive mini fittonia or miniature snakeskin plant (**F. verchaffeltii argyroneura 'Nana'**) is much easier to propagate than the more brightly hued *Fittonia verschaffeltii*.

The low-growing trailing plant may be propagated from mid-spring to early autumn by carefully pinching or cutting off tip cuttings measuring about 3in (7.5cm). Each cutting should consist of at least three pairs of leaves to take successfully.

Remove the lower pair of leaves and dip the base of the stem in hormone rooting powder before inserting five cuttings in a 3½in (9cm) pot of peat-based potting compost.

Cuttings may actually be rooted without having to be covered with a clear plastic bag, although this may help where problems of dehydration are encountered. Take care to ensure that the compost is not allowed to dry out, otherwise the cuttings will rapidly wither. Conversely, avoid over-watering, otherwise they are likely to succumb to rotting.

By maintaining them in a temperature of 65–68°F (18–20°C) in good light, but out of direct sunlight, rooting will take four to six weeks. After this the new plant may well be ready to take more tip cuttings from.

Fittonia verschaffeltii or the Snakeskin Plant is a plant that is reasonably easy to propagate, but more difficult to cultivate than the smaller-leaved variety.

Cuttings may be propagated from mid-spring to early summer, removing cuttings measuring about 3–3½in (7.5–9cm) and consisting of at least two pairs of leaves.

Dip the base of the stem of the cutting into hormone rooting powder and insert three cuttings in a 4¼–5½in (11–14cm) pot of peat-based potting compost.

Cover the cuttings with a clear plastic bag, allowing plenty of air space around the leaves to avoid them coming into contact with moisture on the plastic; otherwise, rotting will quickly occur.

Maintain a temperature of 68–70°F (20–21°C) in moderate light, keeping the compost just moist. Rooting should take place within a month or less, after which the plastic cover may be removed. Under better conditions of humidity it may be possible to root the cuttings without the need of a plastic cover, although unlike the mini snakeskin plant the larger leaves of this variety are more prone to dehydration.

AVOIDING PROBLEMS

Light and position

This plant is that unusual specimen which actually enjoys a shady position. Although it will grow in reasonable light, it cannot abide direct sun or even too much indirect light. However, it is also damaged by exposure to draughts.

Temperature range

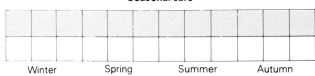

Cool　　Intermediate　　Warm

The fittonia must have warm temperatures, a minimum of 65°F (18°C) and preferably surroundings of 70°F (21°C). It will also tolerate higher summer temperatures, but it is then vital to keep up a high level of humidity. The plant appreciates an overhead spray with tepid water in any season.

Watering

The soil must be kept moist at all times, although the fittonia will require less water during the winter when it is inactive. To keep up humidity, stand the pot on a tray of damp pebbles, but make sure the base is not actually sitting in water.

Feeding

Feeding is not essential in this case, but a weak liquid feed with every watering will keep the plant in good condition. Stop feeding it altogether when it is dormant in winter.

Seasonal care

Winter　　Spring　　Summer　　Autumn

If the conditions in which the plant is kept are naturally dry, especially in the summer, create humidity by placing the pot on a tray of damp pebbles and moisten the fittonia with an overhead spray. Otherwise it will simply wilt, but if it does so, it should revive without further harm when watered. Stem tip cuttings can be taken in spring and must be raised in a temperature of 75°F (23°C).

Soil

This plant prefers a small, shallow pot and potting on is seldom required more often than every other year. Use a potting mixture with a good proportion of peat and repot during the summer months.

Grevillea robusta

With the cost of larger plants ever on the increase, it is surprising that this plant is not much more popular than it is. Easily raised from seed it will develop into a plant of considerable height in only a few years, reaching tree proportions in eight to 10 years. By removing the top section of the plant, it can be reduced in height at almost any time. A further advantage is that it not only tolerates cooler conditions, but actually prefers them to warmer temperatures. The leaves are fern-like and have a silky sheen to them, hence the common name. *G. robusta* is indigenous to Australia and although there are other varieties, this one is the best and the most easily obtained.

Healthy plant *G. robusta*, the Silk Oak, is a fast-growing, evergreen plant. The foliage, which is dark green, tinged with brown when the leaves are young, has a downy upper surface, silky to the touch. These plants go well in a mixed pot with other plants when young while they still resemble ferns. In a few years, however, they can reach 6ft (2m) and will need a sturdy pot of their own. Plants grown indoors will not produce flowers but will provide a pleasant feature for any cool room.

PESTS AND DISEASES

Red spider mite These can best be avoided by inspecting the undersides of the leaves at regular intervals with a magnifying glass. If the plant is affected, spray with insecticide or, if necessary, cut away the damaged leaves.
Sciarid fly This is a kind of fungus gnat which nests in the potting mixture and is not particularly harmful. The flies are black and can be cleared by watering the soil with malathion.

AVOIDING PROBLEMS

Light and position

Good light is essential to the grevillea, but it should be shielded from direct sun if in a window. It grows to quite a height and can be placed anywhere in a light, airy room, but in poor light it will shed some of the lower leaves.

Temperature range

Cool   Intermediate   Warm

Cool, but not draughty, conditions are required and extremes of temperature can kill the plant. Somewhere in the range 45°-55°F (7°-13°C) is suitable. At the other extreme, hot sun can scorch the leaves of the plant, leaving unpleasant brown marks, and in high summer the temperature in a sunny window may be far too high.

Watering

The grevillea dislikes extremes of any kind and it should be thoroughly but not excessively watered and allowed to dry out slightly before watering is repeated. However, at no time should the soil be allowed to dry out completely.

Feeding

Once established, the grevillea is a vigorous plant which requires regular feeding. The amount of fertilizer recommended by the manufacturer can be increased or administered more frequently, as the plant will respond well to a strong feed.

Seasonal care

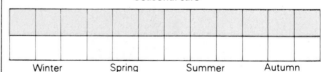

Winter   Spring   Summer   Autumn

The plant does not need any particular seasonal attention, but in common with many others, it is less active in winter and feeding can be decreased or stopped for a while until growth is stimulated once again. Overgrown plants can be trimmed back at any time, but should not be cut right down.

Soil

The soil should be a loam-based mixture with plenty of body to sustain the plant over a long period. Increase the pot sizes progressively and crock the bottom of a large container. The plant may remain in one pot for three years

Hedera

These are among the most popular of plants sold for indoor decoration, although they are not particularly suited to rooms that are heated. Perhaps one of their most appealing qualities is that once they appear to have failed indoors, they can be planted out in the garden, where they are likely to flourish.

There are many different varieties and almost all of them are propagated from easily rooted cuttings taken during the spring and summer months. Firm pieces of stem with two sound leaves attached are put into small pots filled with peaty compost and placed in a close atmosphere at a temperature in the region of 65°–70°F (18°–21°C). Several cuttings should be inserted in each pot to ensure that the eventual plant looks quite bushy.

VARIETIES AND PURCHASING

Never buy an Ivy with long lengths of leafless stem at the top of each stalk, as this indicates the plant has already been attacked by pests. What is more, all the other plants in the shop are likely to be infested as well. There are only a few hedera species, but there are many varieties, which have a wide range of leaves (*see illustration below*)

H. canariensis This is one of the tallest plants. It has large leaves 5in (12.5cm) long and 6in (15cm) wide which are the shape of a rounded triangle. The leaves are dark green with pale green veins. There is also a variegated form called 'Gloire de Marengo', which has leaves bordered in cream and blotched with grey-green.

H. helix This is the English Ivy of which there are many varieties. Its familiarly shaped leaves have three or five lobes.

H.h. 'Chicago' This has medium-sized green leaves. There is a variegated form *H.h.* 'Chicago Variegata' which has creamy bordered leaves. It is more difficult to manage but worth growing as it is a very colourful plant.

H.h. 'Glacier' This is perhaps the hardiest of all the variegated Ivies. It has light and dark grey colouring.

H.h. 'Little Diamond' This also has grey-coloured variegated foliage. Its leaves are a particularly pleasing diamond shape. The stems have a twisting appearance.

H.h. 'Sagittaefolia' As its name, derived from the Latin for 'arrow', suggests, the dark green leaves of this Ivy are arrow shaped. There is also a variegated form, *H.h.* 'Sagittaefolia Variegata' which has green and pale yellow leaves. This makes an excellent trailing plant.

H. ivalace This hedera has glistening green leaves and reddish-brown stems. It is excellent for both indoor and outdoor use. It is seen to its best effect when grown as a hanging plant in the window of a cool room or out of doors on a sheltered patio where there are no cold winds.

Healthy plant When choosing hederas, avoid those that look dehydrated and have a number of dead leaves gathered at the base of the plant.
H. canariensis (**above**) is a tall species that can be grown quite easily. If you want the plant to become more bushy, pinch out the growing tips as they develop.

PESTS AND DISEASES

Black spot Ivies are particularly susceptible to this. It will appear on plants that have been kept crowded together or in very damp conditions. It is a damaging fungus which should be treated immediately with a reliable fungicide.

Thrips These insects, which are also called thunderflies, are sometimes present in Ivies. They can be detected by grey streaking on the softer leaves. Remove any very badly damaged leaves and spray thoroughly with an insecticide such as pyrethrum.

Scale insect These will lodge on the stem of the plant, or under its leaves. They should be wiped off with a wad of cotton wool soaked in methylated spirits after which the whole plant should be treated with pesticide.

Aphids One of the most common houseplant pests, aphids may be detected on the leaves. Treat with a systemic insecticide. Aphids may also spread virus.

Unhealthy plant
If an Ivy is allowed to get too dry, it will become withered and unattractive (*left*). To cure this, mist the plant daily with water and move it to a cooler position. Light brown discoloration of the foliage and a dry appearance (*below*) suggests that red spider mites are present. The grey furry blotching (*below*) is caused by botrytis, which should be treated with a fungicide.

AVOIDING PROBLEMS

Light and position

Ivies require light, cool environments. If poorly lit, variegated types will lose their colouring and should thus have 2-3 hours of sunlight each day. Keep other types out of direct sunlight and away from dry heat which can encourage red spider mites.

Temperature range

Cool · Intermediate · Warm

Ivies are generally sturdy enough to withstand a broad range of temperatures but they do not like wide fluctuations. Most respond well to temperatures between 50°-60°F (10°-15°C).

In temperatures higher than 65°F (18°C), provide a moist environment. In winter, let the plants rest in a cool temperature of 50°F (10°C).

Watering

Keep the compost moist in summer with regular waterings. In winter, water sparingly but do not let the compost dry out. Ivies like humidity, especially if the atmosphere is dry, as in summer. Mist frequently at these times, and also in winter if the room is dry and warm.

Feeding

Ivies are not fussy about feeding, and any fertilizer recommended by the manufacturer may be used. Feed actively growing plants with a standard liquid fertilizer every two weeks. Most Ivies grow prodigiously without assistance, so feeding may not be necessary.

Seasonal care

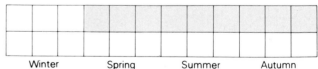

Winter   Spring   Summer   Autumn

In their growth period, Ivies can create dense foliage which should be cleaned out in autumn and spring by removing all dead or dying undergrowth. Water frequently in all seasons except winter when the soil should be kept fairly dry. Repot Ivies every two years in the spring in pots no larger than 5-6in (10-15cm) in diameter. Plants which are not repotted should have the top layer of compost replenished annually.

Soil

Peaty compost mixtures tend to produce soft growth, so use a mixture which contains enough loam to sustain the plant over a long period. This will also eliminate the need for frequent repotting. Tip cuttings should be potted in a mixture of moistened peat moss and coarse sand.

Heptapleurum

This little-known plant came on the houseplant scene not much more than a decade ago and has made a considerable impression, as it is elegant, free growing and reasonably easy to care for. There is a variegated form and also varieties with smaller leaves, but they all grow in a similar way. Naturally glossy green leaves, elliptic in shape, are arranged like fingers on slender stalks attached to a stout central stem. By removing the growing tip at an early age, plants may be encouraged to branch quite freely and take on a very bushy form. Alternatively, they can be left to grow on, in which case they simply extend to about 8–10ft (3m) as slender specimens.

Stem cuttings can be rooted in a temperature of around 70°F (21°C) if the conditions are close and moist. At potting time, three plants put into a 5in (12.5cm) pot will provide plants of considerable beauty as they mature.

VARIETIES AND PURCHASING

Inspect young leaves for aphids and avoid plants with yellowing foliage or any other leaf discoloration. Parasol Plants that have been very wet and cold will wilt, and should also be avoided.

H. arboricola The original variety, this is the most elegant plant and is probably the best type to choose.

H.a. 'Geisha Girl' With more rounded individual leaves, this is less free growing, although it is similar to the original *H. arboricola* in other respects.

H.a. 'Hong Kong' This has green foliage too, but is much smaller and more compact than the other varieties. It is also slightly harder to care for than other Parasol Plants.

H.a. 'Variegata' This has yellow and green variegated leaves that make it more colourful than the other varieties. It is fairly difficult to propagate, and requires a brighter location indoors than the other Parasol Plants if it is to retain its colouring. The contrasting leaves of the *H. arboricola*, *H.a.* 'Geisha Girl' and *H.a.* Variegata are pictured below.

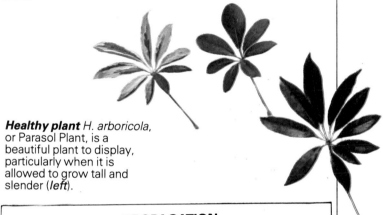

Healthy plant *H. arboricola*, or Parasol Plant, is a beautiful plant to display, particularly when it is allowed to grow tall and slender (*left*).

PROPAGATION

The **heptapleurum** usually becomes rather lank and straggly in the home, an ideal time to consider propagation.

In mid- to late spring, prune back the plant as required with a pair of secateurs or pruning shears and cut into 7.5–10cm tip and stem cuttings.

Remove any surplus leaf and stalk that would otherwise be below soil level, then dip the base of the cutting into hormone rooting powder and insert it in a 3½in (9cm) pot of seed and cutting compost. Cover with a clear plastic bag and keep out of direct light at a temperature around 70°F (21°C) until new growth is evident, either at the top of the tip cutting or in the leaf axils of a stem cutting. The plastic bag may be removed and the new plant grown on a little more, applying liquid fertilizer to help the plant's development.

Once it is well formed, the plant may be gently removed from its pot and potted up in a 5in (13cm) pot of potting compost.

The *H.a.* 'Variegata' (**below**).

HEPTAPLEURUM

AVOIDING PROBLEMS

Light and position

All heptapleurums require good light. At least two to three hours a day are needed, but avoid direct sunlight. If lighting is poor, the leaves will grow abnormally long. Position the plant well away from radiators, draughts, and cold windows and doorways.

Temperature range

Cool Intermediate Warm

H. arboricola requires a minimum temperature of 60°F (15°C) all year long, and a maximum temperature of 70°F (21°C). In winter, keep the plant warm at not less than 60°F (15°C).

Heptapleurums also enjoy a moist, humid environment which can be created by standing the plants on trays of pebbles covered with water.

Watering

H. arboricola needs moderate watering. Allow the top inch (2.5cm) of soil to dry out between waterings. The soil should not dry out more than this, nor should it be watered so that it is thoroughly wetted. The plants also enjoy frequent misting.

Feeding

Do not overfeed. Feed only when the plants are well rooted in their pots. This can be determined by turning the plant out of its pot to check the amount of root growth. A standard fertilizer may be used every two weeks from spring until late autumn.

Seasonal care

Winter Spring Summer Autumn

Heptapleurums should never be overwatered, but they should be watered more frequently during the active growth period between spring and summer. In spring the plants should be moved to pots 2in (5cm) larger. Continue to repot during the growth period as required. The plants can be propagated in spring from tip or stem cuttings.

Soil

Peat mixtures with a small amount of loam are best. Press the mixture down firmly in the pot, but not too tightly. Before repotting, make sure the plants have enough root growth to justify the move. When propagating, plant cuttings in a mixture of moistened peat moss and coarse sand.

Stem rot This can affect Parasol Plants, causing them to become slimy, black and rotten near the base (*above*). The leaves will start to drop off as the condition becomes worse. Stem rot is usually brought on by overwatering, and there is no easy cure. If the rotten section is fairly high up the stem, however, the top half of the plant can be cut off in the hope that the remaining healthy stem will sprout again. Heptapleurums will become droopy and discoloured if they are overwatered (*left*).

PESTS AND DISEASES

Aphids These occasionally attack young leaves and cause spotting. They can be controlled by using one of the many effective insecticides.
Mealy bug This is normally only found on larger plants with a tangled mass of growth in which it can go undetected. Spray thoroughly with insecticide or wipe bugs off the plant with a sponge that has been soaked in methylated spirits. Large yellow blotches often appear on the topmost leaves of heptapleurums. There is no simple explanation or cure, but fortunately most plants seem to grow out of this condition.
Red spider mite These may attack heptapleurums, particularly if the surroundings are unusually hot or dry. They are very small, and hard to detect with the naked eye as a result. Light brown leaf discoloration is a sign of their presence, which can be confirmed by thorough scrutiny of the undersides of the leaves with a magnifying glass. Treat with insecticide.

183

Hibiscus rosa-sinensis

This is another much improved potted plant for indoor decoration, owing much of its undoubted success in recent years to the scientist rather than the grower of the plants. The discovery of growth-retarding chemicals has made it possible to grow these plants so that they can be in full flower when they are little more than 15in (38cm) high. This makes them ideal for the average room, ideal for handling and packing, and ideal in that they require less heated space on the benches in the greenhouse than many other houseplants. *H. rosa-sinensis* is woody, has glossy green leaves, and produces quite superb flowers in both single and double forms.

VARIETIES AND PURCHASING

H. rosa-sinensis (*see illustration below*) This is the original Rose of China from which many hybrids have been produced. The flowers may be crimson, pink, yellow or white, and have long golden stamens.
H.r-s 'Cooperi' This is a variety of the Rose of China. Its leaves have olive-green, pink and white markings and its flowers are red.
H. schizopetalus This is the Japanese hibiscus. Its delicate stems support orange-red flowers.
'Hawaiian hybrids' This group of hibiscus all have very large flowers. They include 'Surfrider', 'Elegance' and 'Firefly'.

Healthy leaves Despite the differences in shape, these four leaves all came from the same plant.

PROPAGATION

The **hibiscus** or Rose of China may be propagated from mid-spring to late summer, as soon as the plant starts to produce new season's growth.

Try to select tip cuttings without signs of flowers and remove any with a sharp knife, or pair of secateurs or pruning shears. Alternatively, gently remove the cutting by pulling off a side-shoot complete with a heel, taking care not to tear off too much of the mother plant's bark.

Cuttings should measure about 3–4in (7.5–10cm) and should be dipped into hormone rooting powder before being inserted in a 2½–3in (6–7.5cm) pot filled with seed and cutting compost. They may then either be regularly misted or covered with a clear plastic bag and kept at around 70°F (21°C) in reasonable light out of direct sunlight.

As soon as the cuttings start to produce fresh growth, stop misting or remove the plastic bag and wean the plant, taking care to keep the compost just moist. Feed the plant with liquid fertilizer until it starts to form a good framework and then pot up in a 4¼–5in (11–13cm) pot containing a peat-based potting compost.

Healthy plant A hibiscus (*below*) has glossy leaves and brilliant flowers. The leaves should grow right down to the top of the pot. When choosing one, check the buds and undersides of the leaves for aphids.

Dehydrated plant This hibiscus has not been given enough water with the result that the leaves are wilting.

Aphids These insects will attack both the buds and the open flowers, as well as the upper leaves. Remove aphids by running a finger and thumb along the plant, but if the attack is severe, immerse the plant in insecticide.

AVOIDING PROBLEMS

Light and position

In common with all flowering pot plants, the hibiscus needs very good light to retain its buds and go on to produce a satisfactory flowering. Keep the plant away from draughts and any place in the home which is likely to have sudden changes of temperature.

Temperature range

Cool   Intermediate   Warm

The plant prefers an even, moderate temperature of around 60°F (15°C) although the range in which it can exist without problems is 55°-65°F (13°-18°C).

Any radical change in the temperature to either end of the scale may damage the plant and cause the buds to drop.

Watering

Water the plant well during dry weather and evenly all year round, allowing the top of the compost to dry before watering again. Do not make the plant waterlogged or the roots will rot. When the plant is in bud, it benefits from a daily overhead spray.

Feeding

Feed the hibiscus with weak liquid fertilizer, given at each watering, while the plant is in active growth. This can be discontinued in winter while the plant is resting.

Seasonal care

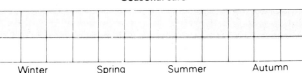

Winter   Spring   Summer   Autumn

When the plant is being well watered in the summer months, it is important that it should drain quickly through the soil when applied at the surface. In winter, even though the compost is kept at the right moisture content, some leaves will fall from the plant, but the new growth in spring refurbishes it. Pruning is only needed if growth is really out of hand and is best done when the plant has just finished flowering.

Soil

The hibiscus does not do well in peaty compost, but will enjoy a loam-based potting mixture. Pot the plant into a slightly larger pot each spring. It is not good practice to transfer a small, new plant into a large pot and wait for it to fill it.

Hoya

Hoyas are naturally climbing plants that twist and twine around everything in sight. Their common name is Wax Flowers because of the waxy star-shaped flowers that bloom in clusters.

Hoyas are very easy plants to manage. They need good light and careful watering, especially in winter when growth is less active. Possibly the greatest difficulty is keeping the twisting branches under control.

The two species grown indoors are *Hoya bella* and *Hoya carnosa*. *Hoya bella* has pale to dark green leaves that are attached to wiry stems that fan out almost horizontally from the container in which it is growing. The branches do not hang pendulously as one would expect from a hanging plant, because the flower clusters form on the under-side of the branches. With the branches fanning out as they do, the exquisite waxy flower clusters are seen to perfection.

H. carnosa has dark green leaves and white to pale pink flowers that bloom in clusters of 10 to 30. There are two variegated-leaved cultivars: *H. c.* 'Exotica' and *H. c.* 'Variegata'.

HOYA	
Light and position  Three to four hours of sunlight a day is desirable for healthy growth, but shade the plant from the hot midday sun.	**Feeding** During active growth, feed with a liquid fertilizer once every two weeks.
Temperature range Cool — Intermediate — Warm Keep these plants at room temperature. The temperature should not drop below 55°F (13°C) at any time. In spring and summer maintain a humid atmosphere.	**Seasonal care** Winter Spring Summer Autumn Hoyas in pots can be potted on each spring, as necessary. Trailing hoyas need only be moved once very two years.
Watering Water moderately during the growth period. Use a spray-mist regularly, except when the plant is in bloom.	**Soil** Use a peaty mixture with some loam added.

Hoyas are pretty climbing plants with sweet-smelling, star-shaped waxy flowers. They are vigorous growers and even the dwarf species *H. bella* (**top**) needs care to keep its fanning branches under control. The flower clusters of *H. bella* (**above left**) hang from the underside of branches, making this a plant to suspend at head level so that its beauty and fragrance can be fully appreciated. *H. carnosa variegata* (**above**) is a variety with pink-edged leaves.

Hydrangea macrophylla

Hydrangeas are available in the spring in white, pink and blue, the latter in fact being pink plants artificially treated with alum to persuade them to change colour. Blues will often vary, sometimes being nothing more than washed-out pink. This happens when the colouring chemical is used incorrectly. These plants will be out of doors most of the year, coming inside in the middle of winter to be forced into flower. If they are to do well for years after they have been bought, hydrangeas should be out of doors all summer, coming into a cool place in the autumn, then to a warmer place in mid-winter to encourage flowering in the spring.

VARIETIES AND PURCHASING

Plants are available from early until late spring. Look for fresh green colouring and sturdy leaves. Avoid plants that are thin and weak with discoloured foliage. Multi-headed plants are usually the better buy. Try to obtain plants with both flowers and buds.

Hydrangeas are not usually offered by name but by colour and general appearance.
H. macrophylla One of the best varieties for growing indoors, this has much larger flowers than other types. The flowers are either pink, red, blue or deep blue.

Healthy plant Hydrangeas are attractive flowering plants but they need careful attention. The many different colours of the flowers are produced by the acidity of the soil in which they are grown. By changing the acid content, the owner can alter the colour of the flowers to blue (**see illustration above**), purple, pink, red or deep blue. A group of hydrangeas in individual pots of differing soil can be placed in a large tub to produce a delightful rainbow of colours.

PESTS AND DISEASES

Aphids These are found on softer leaves and should be treated with an insecticide.
Red spider mite These appear on the underside of leaves. In time, the mites produce tiny webs. Remove the worst leaves and treat with pest control.
Mildew This is seen as a white, powdery deposit on the top of leaves. Remove the worst leaves and treat with a fungicide.
Botrytis This fungus develops in large, wet patches on the leaves. Remove affected leaves and spray with a solution of dichloran.

Underwatering This is easily detected in the hydrangea because its leaves are normally thick and healthy. The first signs of underwatering will appear on the edges of leaves, which will turn brown and curl under (*below*). In extreme cases, (*bottom*), the whole plant will wilt dramatically. To revive, immerse the pot in water and continue watering at regular intervals.

AVOIDING PROBLEMS

Light and position

Hydrangeas prefer to be positioned in a light, cool place. Leaf scorch may result if the plant is placed too close to a window, but this is usually minimal. If put out-of-doors, keep in light shade.

Temperature range

Cool   Intermediate   Warm

Keep in fairly cool conditions of 50°-60°F (10°-15°C). This will ensure that the plant will go on flowering much longer than if placed in a hot, dry location. Avoid direct sunlight and heat. When properly situated, hydrangeas will produce abundant, lush growth.

Watering

During active growth, the plants will need frequent watering. Allow the topsoil to dry out before watering, but avoid letting the plants wilt. Pots should have large drainage holes and a healthy layer of crocks and rotted leaves to help retain moisture.

Feeding

Hydrangeas usually have an abundance of strong foliage and will need weekly feeding to keep them strong and healthy. The acid in some soil can cause the flowers to go blue; adding alum will ensure that the flowers remain blue and do not revert to pink.

Seasonal care

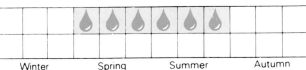

Winter   Spring   Summer   Autumn

Copious watering is required when the plants are in active growth, but none while the plants are in their dormant phase towards the end of the year. After flowering, shoots should be cut back to about half their length. Top sections of shoots that have not flowered can be treated in a heated propagator. The cuttings should have two leaves attached. Prune in early spring, removing any dead material, as well as dead flower heads.

Soil

Hydrangeas prefer heavier soil and a loam-based mixture is best. Pot in the spring when flowering is over. An all-purpose potting soil can be used. Make sure enough room is left at the top for heavy watering. The pots should also have good drainage.

Impatiens

This is another common plant that has undergone many changes in recent years. The plants today are generally more robust in habit, the flowers are more colourful and attractive, and the variegated foliage of many of the varieties is as colourful as the flowers. Cuttings about 4in (10cm) long, with the flowers removed, will root very readily either in water or in a peaty potting mixture. The cuttings should be provided with moist conditions, shade from the sun and a temperature in the region of 65°F (18°C). When the cuttings have rooted and started to grow, the tips should be removed to encourage branching.

Healthy plant Busy Lizzies are too often straggly, leggy plants with yellowing foliage and few flowers. A healthy plant (*below*) should be of compact shape, with glossy leaves and a profusion of bright flowers. When choosing one, make sure the leaves are clean and fresh, the flowers open, and lots of buds are visible. A well cared for Busy Lizzie will hardly ever stop flowering. Old plants tend to lose their beauty, so keep the stock fairly young, and be ruthless about pruning. The pathetic, straggling, limp Busy Lizzie is not a pleasant sight, but when in the peak of condition they are among the most attractive and cheering of houseplants.

VARIETIES AND PURCHASING

The Busy Lizzie is one of the most popular houseplants. Today there are many hybrids, which are compact plants with many flowers.
I. petersiana This one has burgundy-coloured foliage and rich red flowers. It grows to a height of 2–3ft (70cm–1m) and can attain a very attractive shape. It is rather prone to red spider mite and so the undersides of the leaves should be inspected carefully when buying.
I. wallerana It is from this species that many hybrids have been produced. It tends to grow too tall and droopy, unlike its descendants. The flowers of the hybrids can be all shades – white, pink, orange, or a combination of any two. Most of them do not have names but a few have been specially bred.
I. 'Red Magic' This is similar in appearance to *I. petersiana*. However, it is not as vulnerable to red spider. It usually grows to a height of 2ft (7cm) and has scarlet flowers. It is a hybrid of *I. wallerana*.
I. 'Arabesque' This is another hybrid of *I. wallerana*. Its leaves are veined with red and have yellow centres.
I. 'New Guinea' hybrids These are the latest version of the Busy Lizzie. With their large flowers and vigorous growth they are possibly the best buy, although they are slightly more expensive than the other varieties.

AVOIDING PROBLEMS

Light and position

If the Busy Lizzie is to produce a lot of flowers, it must have the lightest possible position although it is wise to protect it from very strong sunlight. It does not like draughts and will not do well in a shady position.

Temperature range

Cool   Intermediate   Warm

The Busy Lizzie will not flourish in temperatures below 55°F (13°C). Normal room temperatures are ideal. It may be possible to put the plant outside in summer, provided it is in a warm and sheltered spot. At very high temperatures over 75°F (23°C) the plant needs a humid atmosphere, so stand it on a tray of damp pebbles or moss.

Watering

The Busy Lizzie should be given moderate amounts of water at rest times, and plentiful supplies while it is growing. Never let the potting mixture dry out, and never let the plant stand in water for too long.

Feeding

This vigorous plant responds well to liberal feeding. During the spring and summer, which are periods of fast growth, it can be fed once a week with a standard fertilizer. Extend the interval to three weeks during the rest of the year.

Seasonal care

Winter   Spring   Summer   Autumn

Because the Busy Lizzie is so susceptible to pests it is important to keep a regular look-out for pests. Never neglect its water or feed if the plant is to remain at its best. In winter it should be kept a little warmer. In autumn, trim large plants back hard as otherwise they will be difficult to care for. Cuttings should be taken and rooted, to replace older plants when they are past their best.

Soil

For the vigorous growth of this plant, a peaty, loam-based mixture should be used. Young plants can be put into 5in (12.5cm) pots on purchase. In the first year, plants can be potted on twice.

PESTS AND DISEASES

Aphids Like all sucking insects, aphids love Busy Lizzies. They are usually found on the new growth and they should be treated with one of the many pesticides available.

Red spider mite Treat with insecticide, paying particular attention to the undersides of leaves. Smaller plants can be immersed in a bucket full of the insecticide.

White fly These are easy to spot as they fly away from the plant when it is moved. Treat with doses of insecticide.

Stem rot Wet and cold conditions may cause this – parts of the stem will be black. Remove the affected parts and treat with fungicide.

Sooty mould This is a fungus that develops on the honeydew of the aphids. Remove with a damp sponge.

Unhealthy plants White fly (*above top*) are a big problem with Busy Lizzies. They are difficult to eradicate – the insecticide should be used four times at four-day intervals. Red spiders (*above*) have a very detrimental effect on plants and Busy Lizzies are particularly vulnerable to them. Signs of their presence are poor growth and discoloured foliage. Wear rubber gloves if immersing plant in insecticide. The effects of dehydration and starvation are shown on this Busy Lizzie (*above centre*). Moderate feeding and watering are essential to these vigorous plants.

Jacobinia

This genus includes about 300 species, but only two are commonly grown indoors. Stems and branches are soft and woody; leaves are somewhat coarse in their appearance. Jacobinias' chief attraction is the appealing tubular flowers they produce.

Jacobinia carnea, a species which also masquerades under the splendid name of *Justicia magnifica,* is a shrubby, upright plant with soft grey-green leaves that are red on their undersides. Mature plants will produce a wealth of rose-coloured bracts at the top of the several stems that develop as the plant ages.

Jacobinia pauciflora grows to approximately 18in (45cm) in height and bears scarlet flowers with yellow tips. This plant can be placed out of doors during the summer, but should be moved inside when weather starts to deteriorate.

Jacobinias need moist, humid, warm conditions. The temperature should be a minimum 65°F (18°C), and plants should be placed in light shade. Water and feed freely in summer, and pot on into loam-based houseplant soil.

Plants need plenty of room in which to grow and will generally do best when growing in pots about 8in (20cm) in diameter. Jacobinias become very straggly looking unless properly pruned, and are usually discarded after one or two years. The top sections of stronger stems may be used for propagating new plants in spring. Removing the growing tops will also encourage plants to bush out and become more compact.

Jacobinias are shrubby plants with attractive tubular flowers. *J. carnea* (*right*) is one of two species commonly grown as houseplants. Like *J. pauciflora,* it is usually discarded when it becomes straggly.

JACOBINIA	
Light and position  This plant needs bright light, but should be protected from direct sunlight in summer.	**Feeding** Feed should be given while the plant is in bloom, but do not feed during the winter months.
Temperature range 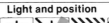 Cool Intermediate Warm Average warmth is sufficient for these plants, but the temperature should not drop below 55°F (13°C) in winter.	**Seasonal care** 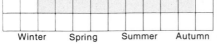 Winter Spring Summer Autumn Pot on in spring, or when roots appear through the drainage holes of the pot. Pinch out tips of young plants to encourage a more compact habit. After flowering, plants should be cut back almost to soil level.
Watering Water mature plants well in summer; keep them on the dry side in winter.	**Soil** Use a loam-based mixture that is free to drain.

Kalanchoe beharensis

This is one of the most majestic of the many fine kalanchoes available, but it is also one of the most difficult to obtain as it is more of a botanical specimen than a commercial houseplant. The plant has triangular-shaped leaves, which are attached on their undersides to stout greyish green petioles, and these in turn are borne on stout stems that become very woody with age. Young leaves are also greyish green, maturing in time to an unusual dark brown colouring. The strong upright main stem will reach a height of around 10ft (3m) when roots are confined to pots 10in (25cm) in diameter, and it will not normally need to be staked.

The plant's leaves stand stiffly away from the central stem, and they have a natural tendency to die at a lower level as the plant increases in height. Many of the kalanchoes can be propagated from pieces of leaf and stem extremely easily, some of them not requiring any form of soil to encourage rooting. *K. beharensis* has the fascinating ability to develop perfectly shaped young plants along the fractures of broken sections of mature leaves. A leaf should be bent over until it fractures, with the broken piece left hanging, and new plants will then form along the fracture. When large enough to handle, these can be potted in sandy potting mixture.

AVOIDING PROBLEMS

Light and position

Good light is essential to the Felt Plant and it will even tolerate quite bright sun without coming to undue harm. Sunlight tends to enhance the appearance of the leaves. It cannot thrive in poor light or in a draughty position.

Temperature range

Cool   Intermediate   Warm

The kalanchoe survives happily in a broad temperature range, as high as 75°F (23°C) or down to 55°F (13°C). In fact, it can exist in even cooler conditions, but this is inadvisable, and the temperature should never be lower than 50°F (10°C), especially in a damp atmosphere.

Watering

Water the plant sparingly, but enough to keep the soil moist throughout the year, which means that it will requre little watering in winter. Overwatering is particularly damaging in cooler temperatures and when growth is less active.

Feeding

If the potting mixture is sufficiently nutritional, little feeding is needed and it is certainly not essential. A little feeding in spring and summer when the plant is developing new growth is beneficial.

Seasonal care

Winter   Spring   Summer   Autumn

The kalanchoe does not need special care, but it is not entirely easy to grow and the watering and conditions of light and temperature which it requires should be strictly adhered to. Although the fleshy leaves can survive temporary neglect, remember to check the soil carefully and moisten it whenever necessary.

Soil

Use a loam-based potting mixture and repot the plant in spring if this is necessary. Propagate from stem tip cuttings, which should root easily, or pot out baby plants which will form along a fractured leaf.

PESTS AND DISEASES

Botrytis This is mould on the leaves and stem (*see illustration*) caused by overwatering.
Red spider mite If the plant should be found to be inhabited by this pest, immediate action is vital. Spray the leaves with diazinon and repeat the treatment at intervals of a few days.

Damaged leaves Since the leaves stand out from the plant they are liable to damage from rough handling (*above left*). Botrytis (*above right*) occurs in damp conditions. Remove badly affected leaves and spray the plant with dichloran.

PROPAGATION

The popular flowering succulent **Kalanchoe blossfeldiana** is a relatively easy plant to propagate.

In mid- to late spring remove 3in (7.5cm) tip cuttings with a sharp knife. Then prepare them for propagation by leaving them for two or three days to start to form a callus, taking care to store them out of direct sunlight at normal room temperature of 65–68°F (18–20°C).

The cuttings may then be gently inserted into 3½in (9cm) pots of cacti and succulent compost in reasonable light, but out of direct sunlight, at a temperature of 70–71°F (20–21°C). Take care not to allow the compost to become too wet, but keep it barely moist. As rooting occurs and the plant begins to grow, more water may be supplied, but still take care not to overdo it.

Take care, also, to ensure that any damaged or rotting tissue is removed as soon as possible before any disease spreads and affects other cuttings: something which can happen very quickly.

Remember towards the autumn that the plant must be exposed to short days and long nights; the short number of hours of daylight and long hours of darkness will encourage it to flower for the Christmas period.

Maranta

Marantas are low-growing plants with the common name of Prayer Plant, because as daylight fades, leaves close together like hands in prayer. *M. leuconeura* is the only species grown indoors, but there are several varieties of it.

M. leuconeura 'Erythroneura' has a flat habit of growth, but can be encouraged to produce longer and more erect stems if the plant is provided with a supporting cane to which developing branches can be tied. Leaf colouring is a velvety olive-green with red veins; the underside is dull red. Flowers are small, insignificant and die off almost as soon as they appear, so their removal will tend to improve the appearance of the plant. Despite the exotic colouring of the foliage, this is one of the easier plants to care for, needing little more than average conditions and care.

M. leuconeura 'Kerchioviana' has pale green leaves well endowed

with central spots, giving the plant the common name of Rabbit's Tracks. This is another easy plant to raise if protected from bright light.

Marantas are foliage plants with leaves beautifully marked with distinctive patterns and colours. *M. leuconeura* 'Erythrophylla' (**above left**) has red-veined dark green leaves with lighter patches. The leaves of all varieties are rolled up when young.

Healthy plant Calatheas and stromanthes also belong to the Marantaceae, but they are rather more delicate and subtly coloured than the marantas. *Calathea makoyana* (**above**), commonly called the Peacock Plant, has thin, almost transparent leaves (**below**), predominantly green on the top with light markings and a rich reddish brown on the undersides.

VARIETIES AND PURCHASING

Exercise careful choice when buying plants of the Marantaceae family, especially with the delicate calatheas. If the retailer has allowed the plants to be exposed to cold temperatures for any length of time, the plant will be damaged and may soon die. Avoid plants with brown leaf tips, or leaves that have any sign of ill health. These are not plants that will recover happily once given the correct care.
Maranta leuconeura 'Kerchoviana' has green colouring with dark blotches on the leaves. It is a plant of compact habit, seldom growing very high at all.
M. leuconeura 'Erythrophylla' This may alternatively be labelled *M. leuconeura* 'Tricolor', a name suggested by the bright markings and rich red vein pattern on the dark green leaves. It is one of the easier plants to care for in this species.

Calathea makoyana The paper-thin leaves of this plant, commonly called the Peacock Plant, are carried on slender petioles and are reddish brown on the undersides. The veins of the leaves form a delicate pattern and the plant itself is extremely sensitive and cannot be revived after a period of neglect or ill treatment.
C. zebrina This is sometimes known as the Zebra Plant, although this common name is more generally used for another houseplant. *C. zebrina* has stripey leaves of dark and light green, slightly velvety in texture and the undersides are a rich reddish purple.
Stromanthe amabilis Another typical member of the Marantaceae, and not the most difficult to care for, the stromanthe has a fresh, open arrangement of leaves.

The leaves of a maranta will curl and wither if the plant becomes too dry and cold. Raise the temperature and humidity gradually.

This leaf shows the drastic effects to a plant that is cold and overwatered. The limp leaf is brown and patchy, curling at the edges.

PESTS AND DISEASES

Most of these plants will be marked because of rough handling or bad culture. They may also develop spotting if exposed to household aerosols such as spray polish or air freshener. Marantaceae are as vulnerable to even momentary carelessness as they are to pests.
Red spider mite Marantas may be slightly more liable to this pest than calatheas. It is extremely difficult to detect but hardening of leaves and a general lack of vigour in the plant may be signs of infestation. Inspect the undersides of leaves with a magnifying glass as soon as you suspect spider mites, because once they have taken hold they are difficult, if not impossible, to eradicate. If the trouble is still at an early stage, spray the plant with malathion, with particular attention to the undersides of leaves. Alternatively, insert a

systemic insecticide such as disulfoton in the soil. Test the solution on a single leaf of a plant and allow a day or two for it to take effect before spraying the whole plant. Repeated treatments will be necessary, but may be to no avail if the mites have really taken hold.
Symphalids These small white insects which dance in the soil may affect a calathea. They are quite harmless but unsightly. If you wish to get rid of them, water the soil with malathion.
Sciarid fly Plants that stand in the same pot over a long period may be visited by these small black fungus gnats. Again, they live in the soil and are not especially harmful. Overwatering, causing dank conditions around the plant and in the pot, encourages both sciarid flies and symphalids. Watering with malathion removes both pests.

Dehydration This is extremely damaging to Marantaceae, as shown by this *Maranta leuconeura* 'Erythrophylla' (***below***), which has been neglected to a catastrophic degree. Whole leaves are limp and discoloured and the stems are spindly and weak. If the plant can be retrieved, be careful not to shock it further by swamping it with food and water. Gradually moisten it with tepid water and keep it warm.

A plant which suddenly acquires torn and ragged edges may be suffering from the unwanted attention of a curious cat or dog.

AVOIDING PROBLEMS

Light and position

These plants must have a shady position as sunlight will damage the foliage. The colouring is actually improved by poor light.

As they require warmth, a location in a window or near a door is unsuitable, being too cold and draughty.

Temperature range

Cool   Intermediate   Warm

The temperature must be no lower than 65°F (18°C) and preferably higher. A stable temperature of 70°F (21°C) is ideal for all types and the calathea can be warmer still, at 75°F (23°C).

Moisture in the atmosphere is essential and to encourage this, a group of small plants can be placed together in a shallow container filled with moist peat.

Watering

Regular watering is necessary but wait until the soil feels fairly dry as overwatering is as bad for the plant as lack of moisture. Put in

the water at the top of the pot and let it drain through the soil, but do not leave the plant standing in the excess.

Feeding

Occasional doses of a heavy feed will not be beneficial. Give the plants weak liquid fertilizer when they are watered, except during

the winter, when they will require feed once a month at most, and then only if they are active.

Seasonal care

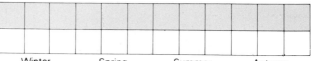

Winter   Spring   Summer   Autumn

In common with the majority of plants, marantaceae need more attention in the summer and during the growing period than in the winter. Plants can be cleaned and freshened occasionally by

sponging the leaves gently. Never use plant cleaning chemicals and take care not to damage the leaves which are quite tender and vulnerable. Tepid water is better appreciated than cold.

Soil

A peat-based mixture is the best choice, but it should contain some loam to provide nourishment to the plants.

Frequent potting is not necessary and a plant should never be put in a pot that is too large. A 7in (17cm) pot should be the maximum size.

Monstera deliciosa

Blessed with numerous common names, the monstera has immense appeal. Indigenous to Mexico, it now grows naturally in most tropical regions, and in almost every collection of tropical and indoor plants. Easily raised from seed, the monstera is therefore an ideal plant for the commercial grower, who can produce uniform quality plants with little difficulty, so long as the reasonably undemanding cultural requirements are provided. Indoors, the naturally glossy green leaves, interesting habit of growth and ease of culture ensure that the monstera will always be among the top 10 foliage houseplants.

Endless questions are asked about this attractive plant, chief among them being what should be done about the natural aerial roots that protrude from the main stem of the plant. Where there is an excessive amount of these roots, it will do no harm to remove some of them, but it is really much better to tie the roots neatly to the main stem of the plant so that they may grow naturally into the soil in the pot when they are long enough. The important thing to remember is that these roots will draw up food and moisture to nourish the plant, so any drastic removal of the roots would weaken it.

PROPAGATION

The trouble with the **monstera,** commonly known as the Swiss Cheese Plant or Mexican Breadfruit Plant, is that in time it really can become a monster, and attempts to restrain it may finally result in the need to start off a new plant and discard the old.

Sever the growing point with two to three adult leaves, using a sharp knife, and pot it in a 5in (13cm) pot of seed and cutting compost. Use a cane and appropriate twist-tie or string to support the cutting, otherwise it will fall over. Pot just below the surface, ensuring that the growing point is fully exposed.

Maintain a temperature of 70°F (21°C) in moderate light, taking care to improve the humidity level by covering the plant with a clear plastic bag.

Mid-spring to early summer is probably the best time to carry out this process, enabling the cutting to establish during the late summer months. The plastic bag may be removed as soon as the plant starts to grow, at which time liquid feeding should be regularly carried out. Another method of propagation is layering, encouraging the plant to root its aerial roots into a new pot of compost and then severing the new part of the plant from the old.

The seed may also be propagated at 70–75°F (21–24°C), sown in a seed tray or pan filled with seed and cutting compost. Prick out the seedlings initially into 3½in (9cm) pots of potting compost and then grow on before potting up.

Remove a growing point with at least two to three adult leaves.

Dip base of stem into hormone rooting powder.

Place in 5in (13cm) pot and fill with peat-based seed and cutting compost, taking care not to bury leaf axil.

Use cane to support, securing loosely with wire twist tie, and cover with clear plastic bag.

Healthy plant The *Monstera deliciosa* (***right***) is a hardy plant with tough, glossy leaves. Mature plants can reach a height of 20ft (6m) and look attractive displayed on their own. The leaves are neat and rounded, deeply serrated and perforated in older plants. The leaves benefit from occasional cleaning with a damp cloth, but do not attempt to clean new, soft leaves, as these are easily damaged.

PURCHASING

Select a firm, compact plant, with glossy, green, unblemished leaves. Check that the soft, new leaves at the top of the plant are undamaged. Other common names for the monstera include Splitleaf Plant and Window Plant.

199

Damaged leaf A dark brown colour around the outside of a leaf (*below*) is a sign that the soil is much too wet and that the temperature is also too low. Increasing the temperature and reducing the watering is the cure, but steps may also have to be taken to dry out the soil. Leaves damaged in this way will not recover and should be removed.

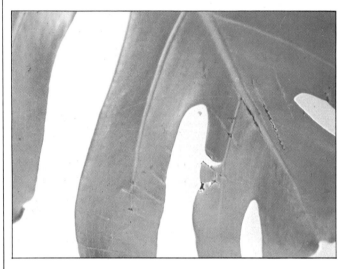

Underwatered plant This plant (*above*) is suffering from underwatering, causing the leaves to wilt and eventually die. Signs of underwatering will only show if the soil is extremely dry and the atmosphere is dry as well. The remedy is to water the plant regularly and provide a moister atmosphere. Monsteras should be watered and sprayed liberally in the spring and summer; in the winter it is sufficient just to keep the soil moist.

AVOIDING PROBLEMS

Light and position

Ideal conditions will produce a large, healthy plant. Avoid strong sunlight and dark corners. Sun will scorch the leaves, while poor light will restrict growth and result in smaller, less serrated leaves. Monsteras are happiest in locations with ample space.

Temperature range

Cool   Intermediate   Warm

A temperature range of 60°-70°F (15°-21°C) is ideal. Excessive heat should be avoided or the lush leaves will begin to curl and droop. Avoid wet conditions around the roots if lower temperatures are likely to prevail which may cause the roots to rot.

Watering

Monsteras should be kept moist, especially if in dry surroundings. The roots which grow from the main stem can be put into containers of water, reducing the plant's need for frequent watering. Sponge the leaves with water to keep them clean.

Feeding

This plant produces masses of roots in its active period, so it must be given regular feeding at this time. During less active periods, feed only if new leaves are being produced. Large plants which have been in their pots a long time need frequent feeding.

Seasonal care

Winter   Spring   Summer   Autumn

When in the active growth period, feed and water monsteras generously. Give less of both at other times. Clean the leaves occasionally, but never wipe soft new leaves at the top of the stem because these are easily damaged. If the plant is healthy, potting can be done at any time of year but should be avoided during the colder months.

Soil

The potting mixture for monsteras should be primarily composed of peat, sand, and an appropriate fertilizer. Older plants will benefit from a mixture containing a good amount of sterilized loam.

200

Musa

In the genus *Musa* are 35 species of evergreen perennials, including several exotic banana plants. Of these, *Musa cavendishii* is the most suitable for indoor culture, being smaller and less vigorous. Plants are upright and attain a height of 5ft (1.5m) in time, developing stout trunks of a brownish-yellow colour. Leaves are bright green, produced three and four at a time. Plants will naturally shed lower leaves as new top leaves are produced.

Musa cavendishii needs sufficient space for spreading leaves to develop and a light but not sunny position. The temperature should be a minimum of 60°F (16°C), and the soil should be kept moist at all times. While in active growth, plants will need regular feeding. Mist the leaves daily to produce adequate humidity.

Although it is optimistic to expect *Musa cavendishii* to produce fruit indoors, plants will occasionally do so in a heated greenhouse when high humidity can be maintained. The main stem will die down, but plants will almost invariably produce new shoots at the base. These will go on to form new plants.

It is possible to successfully germinate seed from *Musa cavendishii* and other banana plants, but bear in mind that these are large plants; keep only one seedling if several should germinate. Red spider mites sometimes trouble these plants.

Musa Cavendishii (*above right*) has only recently been grown as a houseplant. Yellowing leaves (*above*) at the base of the plant need not cause concern, as these older leaves are shed naturally.

MUSA		
Light and position  Give plants maximum light. Protect plants from fierce sun during the summer.		**Feeding** This is a large, fairly quick-growing plant and it needs plenty of nourishment. Feed it every time it is watered, except in winter.

Temperature range

Cool — Intermediate — Warm

A minimum temperature of 60°F (15°C) is vital to the Banana Plant and it will do better in a range of 65°-70°F (18°-21°C). Keep the atmosphere quite humid.

Seasonal care

Winter — Spring — Summer — Autumn

Keep the plant clean and remove the lower leaves when they yellow and begin to die. This happens quite naturally and is not a sign of ill-health. The plant is propagated in spring by splitting off new suckers and potting them on separately.

Watering

The Banana Plant needs plenty of water, but should not be left to stand in a full saucer.

Soil

Pot on a plant in loam-based mixture at any time during spring or summer if it seems necessary.

Orchids

Magnificent, mysterious, fascinating, beautiful: Many superlatives have been rightly used to describe the greatest family of flowering plants – the Orchidaceae. Yet, along with the mystique of orchids go the myths and fallacies that surround them – that they are expensive, that they are parasites, that they need expensive osmunda fibre imported from Japan, that they all require high temperatures.

The truth is that today's modern hybrids are available at reasonable prices and are not too difficult to cultivate. Orchids thrive in a wide range of conditions, and, by the way, no orchid is parasitic!

Though unknown in Europe until the mid-seventeenth century, orchids have a long history. Certainly the ancient Greeks were aware of them. The Greek philosopher Theophrastus (372–287 B.C.) referred to a group of plants called 'orchis' in his manuscript 'An Enquiry into Plants', and the name orchid derives from the Greek word 'orchis', which means 'testicle' – a term that describes the roots of orchids, testiculate tubers occurring in pairs. This part of the plant was considered of great medicinal value for many centuries. Scientists now believe that orchids originated as early as 120–100 million years ago, probably in Malaysia.

Orchids grow in one of two ways, either in a monopodial growth pattern or a sympodial growth pattern. Most orchids are sympodial, including the cymbidiums, paphiopedilums and odontoglossums. These orchids produce a succession of growths connected by a short rhizome. They often produce a pseudo-bulb as well. This is not a true bulb, but a swelling at the base of growth. It enables the plant to store water and nutrients used in adverse conditions.

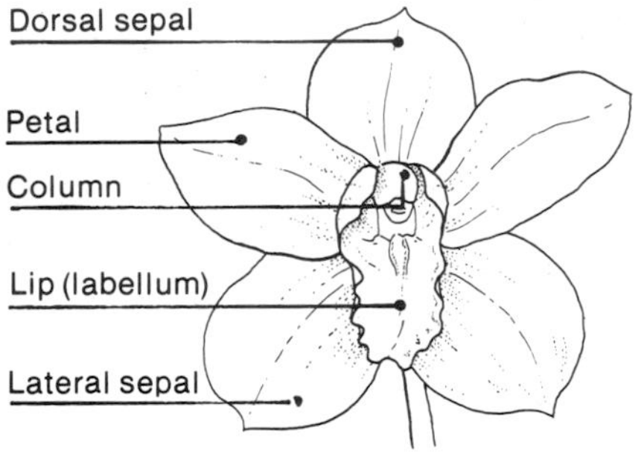

Flower structure (Cymbidium)

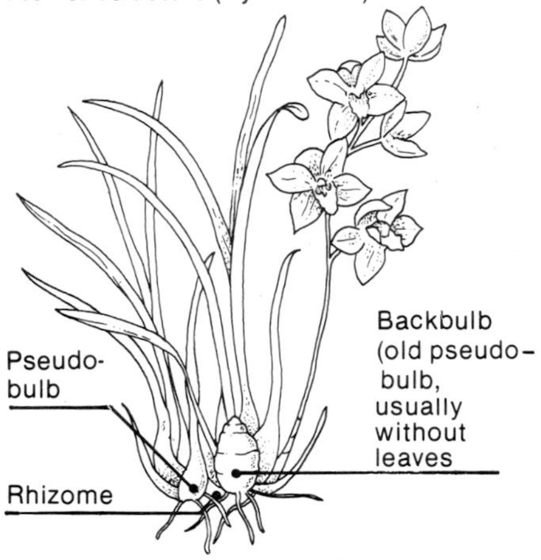

Dorsal sepal
Petal
Column
Lip (labellum)
Lateral sepal

Sympodial growth (Cymbidium)

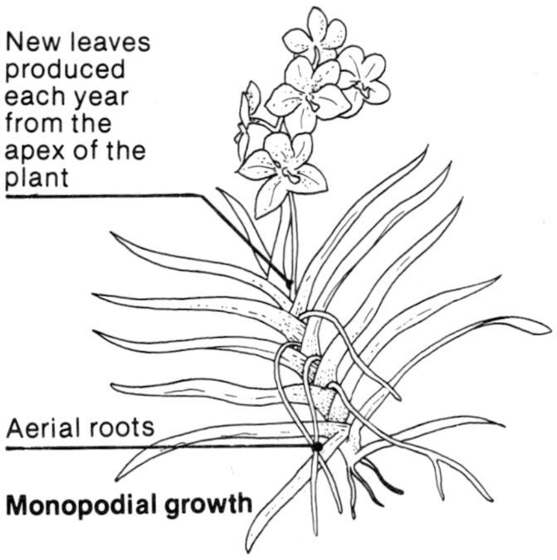

Pseudo-bulb
Backbulb (old pseudo-bulb, usually without leaves
Rhizome

Monopodial growth

New leaves produced each year from the apex of the plant
Aerial roots

All orchids have the same flower structure (*top*). Shown here are two examples of growth patterns – sympodial (*centre*) and monopodial (*bottom*).

Phalaenopsis and vandas are examples of monopodial orchids. They have a single stem that each year produces new leaves from the apex of the plant, and they often have aerial roots. Most of the monopodial orchids are epiphytic, originate from the tropics and do not produce pseudo-bulbs.

All orchids are alike insofar as they have three outer floral segments (the sepals), and three inner segments (the petals), one of which is modified into a lip or labellum. The stamens and the stigma – the sexual parts of the plant – form what is known as the column. This structure is common to all orchids, but the great variety in orchids is probably more striking than their similarity. Approximately 100,000 orchid species and hybrids exist today. Flowers range from massive blooms to those that almost require a magnifying glass to be seen. Some orchids are flamboyant and colourful; others are dull and insignificant. Some have delightful perfumes, other give off noxious odours. Flower structure also varies.

Much of this variety is due to the work of modern hybridizers. In nature, only a very small percentage of seeds ever develop into plants. New scientific advances, however, have enabled hybridists to grow larger populations of seedlings. The production of plants by tissue culture, a technology developed in the 1960s, was an immense breakthrough for orchid breeders, making it possible to propagate, or 'clone', several thousand plants from a single piece of orchid tissue.

Partly because of their increased availability, partly because orchids are such good value for money – many orchids will last up to three months in flower and, provided instructions are followed, will flower the next year – orchids are now increasingly common as houseplants. Some of these magnificent flowering plants, classified according to genus, are described in the section that follows. Though there are many genera of orchids, the four represented here encompass those orchids most suitable for indoor cultivation.

Hybrid varieties of orchids like these (*above*) have been produced in large quantities by the tissue-culture method developed in the 1960s. The materials used in this method are shown below.

Dissecting microscope, used during the removal of tiny slivers of tissue from the shoot tip of the plant.

Flasks containing nutrient jelly. Sterilized, they are planted with divided tissue from the test tubes.

Sterile petri dishes containing orchid tissue ready for sectioning.

Instruments and materials within a sterile work cabinet.

Test tubes containing nutrients, sugar and glucose, vitamins and growth hormones in liquid form. Slivers of tissue are grown in this solution to many times their original size.

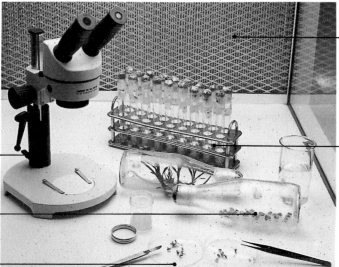

Flasks containing growing orchid tissue (*left*). The flask in the foreground shows tissue ready for removal and further sectioning. The flask behind contains tissue which has been allowed to go on to produce roots and shoots. The cloned plants — thousands from a pinhead-sized piece of tissue — are grown on in special trays (*right*).

Temperature

Orchids are grown in three temperature ranges. The cool-house varieties need a minimum winter night temperature of 50°F (10°C). In summer, night temperature should not rise above 65°F (18°C). Intermediate varieties need a minimum temperature of 55°F (13°C) and summer night temperature is best at 60°F (16°C). Warm-house varieties should be raised in a night temperature not less than 60°F (16°C) in winter. In summer, night temperature should be a minimum of 65°F (18°C).

In all cases, daytime temperature should be at least 9°F (5°C) higher than night temperature. Most orchids do poorly if daytime temperature rises above 90°F (32°C), although they can tolerate higher temperature levels for a short time if humidity is also high.

Watering

With today's peat-and-perlite mixes, it is best to wait several days after the surface of the plant becomes dry before watering. When you do water, give a thorough soaking from the top, using a watering can. Rainwater is preferable to tap water.

Feeding

The orchid growers of the past thought that giving orchids fertilizers was the road to certain disaster. Now, however, orchid growers realize that the orchid plant, like other members of the plant kingdom, needs some form of nourishment. The main nutrients required by most plants are nitrogen, phosphate and potassium – a threesome often referred to as n.p.k. During the spring and early summer months a fertilizer containing n.p.k. in the ratio of 20:10:10 is most suitable. During the late summer, early autumn and winter months, a fertilizer containing equal concentrations of nitrogen, phosphate and potassium (20:20:20) is ideal; during the early autumn period a high-potash fertilizer is beneficial. Most fertilizers should be used at half the prescribed strength and given at regular intervals. It is of great importance to flush out the compost with pure water periodically; the best practice, therefore, is to feed your plant with each watering (giving water with the levels of fertilizer indicated), changing to pure water every fourth time. Make sure that you give the compost a really thorough soaking, so that any build-up of salts will be flushed away.

Light

Orchids need good light, but also some protection from direct sunlight. Therefore, place plants in an east- or west-facing window in spring, summer and autumn, moving plants to a south-facing window during winter. Protect plants in the greenhouse from sun with either lath blinds or a greenhouse shading material.

Humidity and ventilation

Orchids need a humid atmosphere in order to thrive. Plants grown indoors should be placed on a tray of gravel that is kept moist at all times. Growing several plants together is also a good practice, for plants will then create their own micro-climate.

Orchids also need ventilation. The normal opening and closing of windows that goes on during the course of the day should provide indoor plants with adequate refreshment of air. However, if orchids are grown in greenhouses, ventilators are required.

Compost

In different parts of the world, orchids are grown on various types of compost, including bark, rice husks, peach stones, peat, perlite, pumice, charcoal, sand and gravel. The most popular compost in the U.K. is one based on sphagnum moss, peat and perlite, used at a ratio of 2 parts peat to 1 part perlite.

TIPS ON ORCHID CARE

Observing the following points will keep your orchids in top condition.

1. Select plants that have properly trained flower spikes to show the flower to best advantage.

2. Plants in flower will bloom for a longer period if the temperature is slightly lower than optimum.

3. Never stand a plant on or close to radiators.

4. If possible, grow plants together in groups.

5. Try to provide plants with some sort of gravel tray or bowl and keep the base material on the tray or bowl moist. This will help create humidity around the plant.

6. Plants will lose the odd leaf now and again. Do not worry. This is quite normal.

7. When the plant finishes flowering, cut the stem within 1in (3 cm) of the base.

8. Do not water until the compost has become partially dry. Then give a thorough soaking.

9. Give the plant fertilizers as recommended. Do not increase the concentrations; plants cannot utilize the nutrients, and excessive fertilization can cause other problems.

10. When repotting, choose a pot that provides enough space for one year's growth (the plant may look crowded in the pot) rather than overpot.

11. After repotting, soak the compost three times. The compost should then dry out – this may take as long as two to three weeks – before it is watered again.

1 Propagating an orchid. This plant is ready for division. First, remove dead bracts. Each new division should have two bulbs with leaves and, if possible, new growth.

2 Use a sterile knife to sever the short rhizome that connects the bulbs, but ease the bulbs apart before severing the rhizome.

3 The plant can now be removed from its pot and the divisions pulled apart. If necessary, cut the roots in order to ease the divisions apart.

4 At this stage, trim back any decayed or broken roots to healthy tissue or unbroken roots. Broken roots are likely to decay and poison the new compost.

5 Remove the leafless bulbs (called back bulbs) from the main divisions. Sever the short rhizome that connects them and trim the roots right back.

6 Here two divisions have been made and three back bulbs obtained. The roots of the divisions have been trimmed and the back bulbs cleaned up.

7 For the division select a pot that allows for one year's growth and place a good layer of drainage material at the base.

8 For each back bulb, which will probably be without roots, select a pot just large enough to accommodate it with plenty of drainage at the base.

9 Place the back bulb in the centre of the pot. Repotted divisions and back bulbs should be given a thorough soaking, allowing the compost to dry before the next watering. Seal the back bulbs in a plastic bag and hang in a warm position until they begin to shoot.

Repotting an orchid The first step is to clean up the base of the plant by removing dead bracts and weeds. Remove plant from pot.

Select a pot that allows for one year's growth. Place a layer of drainage material – polystyrene or perlag will do – at the bottom of the pot.

Place plant on top of the drainage material and start filling in round the root ball with compost. Continue to pour compost around the root, tapping the pot a few times on the bench to ensure good packing. Apply firm finger pressure down the sides and top up with compost to within 1in (2.5cm) of the top.

The pH of the mix should be adjusted to pH 6.0 by the addition of limestone and Dolomite of lime; a fertilizer that contains an even balance of nutrients and trace elements should also be added. Some growers find perlite mixes difficult, especially with regard to watering, and they often add bark to open up the compost.

Propagation

Propagate sympodial orchids during the early spring or directly after the plant has finished flowering. Clean and trim the plant before dividing it. Do not make divisions of less than two or more than three bulbs. Sever the short rhizome that connects the bulbs, using a sterilized knife. Once all the cuts have been made, knock the plant from its pot, pull the plant apart and sort out your new divisions.

It is also possible to increase your stock of sympodial orchids by removing leafless back bulbs and potting into small pots. The bulbs should be placed in warm shaded positions, or, alternatively, enclosed in a polythene bag and hung up. After a few weeks, most will have made a new growth, and can be removed from the bag and grown normally.

Monopodial orchids propagate with difficulty. However, 'keiki' (small plantlets produced as offsets) sometimes sprout from the base of the plant or the node of the flower stem. Once these keiki have produced roots, sever plantlets and pot in the normal way.

Pests and diseases

Orchids are not particularly susceptible to pests. Slugs and snails may attack young plants, flower spikes and flower buds, but a pellet of metaldehyde and bran, placed between spike and bulb before the buds emerge, should prevent damage. (If growing small plants, it is good practice to scatter pellets among the plants to prevent slug damage.) Red spider mite, aphids and scale insects sometimes appear but can usually be controlled with insecticides.

Prevent disease by purchasing good, clean stock. Should a plant show signs of virus, destroy it immediately. If it remains in your collection, it will endanger your other plants.

Repotting

Orchids should be repotted at different intervals depending on the particular species or hybrid. When repotting, always be sure to trim and tidy the plant first. (In the case of sympodial orchids, remove the dead leaf bracts around the pseudo-bulbs.) Then, knock the plant out of its pot and check the compost to see if it is still in good condition. At the same time, look at the root system for evidence of decay.

If roots and compost are in excellent condition, select a pot that will allow for one year's growth. At the base of the pot, place chunks of polystyrene or coarse perlag to give free drainage. Place the plant in position, pouring the new compost around the root ball. Tap the pot a few times to ensure that the compost is evenly packed around the root ball. Then apply firm finger pressure down the sides of the pot, filling it to within ¾in (2cm) of the top.

If the roots and compost are decayed, remove all the compost and trim the roots so that only healthy ones remain. If orchids are sympodial, remove any leafless pseudo-bulbs by cutting with a sterilized knife the short rhizome that connects the bulbs. Plants with decayed roots should be divided into pieces that contain two pseudo-bulbs and a new growth. Repot as above.

Cymbidiums

Cymbidiums are by far the most popular orchid the world over. The reason for their popularity is obvious to anyone who has seen a well-grown and flowered collection of them. These sympodial plants have very graceful foliage. They produce flowers in a wide range of colours and have lip markings that may contrast or harmonize with the rest of the flower. The word cymbidium derives from the Greek 'kymbe', meaning 'boat', and refers, in fact, to the boat-like appearance of the lip. Cymbidiums are the easiest of all orchids to cultivate. In nature, they grow in a variety of climates, from tropical rain forest to desert.

Two types of cymbidium are available. Growers refer to them

Miniature Cymbidiums
Flowering time – late autumn.

Miniature cymbidiums have the species *Cymbidium pumilum* in their background. This fine selection (**above**) shows the range of colours available during the pre-Christmas period.

Cymbidium Strathbraan
(*C*. Putana x *C*. New Dimension)
Flowering time – late autumn.

This outstanding new hybrid (**left**) flowers very early in the season. It is extremely free-growing and easy-flowering. Clones range in colour from very fine white to ice green to blush pink. Lips are beautifully marked, often heavily splashed with deep crimson.

as 'standard' (large-flowered) or 'miniature' cymbidiums. The latter are more suitable for houseplants, as the large-flowered types tend to be too big for most modern rooms. If you do have the space, however, then nothing is so spectacular as a well-grown standard cymbidium in full flower.

Most miniature cymbidiums today have been bred from the Japanese species *Cymbidium pumilum*. This species figures two generations back in the pedigree of most cymbidiums available today, which are thus termed the second-generation types. These miniature cymbidium hybrids are compact in stature and grow and flower easily. They have attractive blooms in a wide range of colours and last up to 12 weeks in flower.

Hybrids of the miniature species *Cymbidium devonianum* have arching and sometimes pendulous spikes of flowers. These can be green, yellow, bronze, or shades in between, and most flowers have well-marked lips.

Hybrids of *Cymbidium ensifolium* have attractive flowers and a lovely fragrance. However, flowers often last only a few days,

Cymbidium Mary Pinchess 'Del Rey'
(*C. pumilum* x *C.* Pajaro)
Flowering time — mid-winter.

Although the variety illustrated (*above*) was produced many years ago in the United States, it still remains one of the finest early-flowering yellows. While it is not as easy to grow as *C.* Strathbraan, it does flower easily when mature.

CYMBIDIUM	
Light and position	**Feeding**

Cymbidiums need good light conditions throughout the year. Do not place plants in flower in strong sunlight.	Use a high-nitrogen fertilizer during spring and summer, and a high-potash fertilizer during the autumn.
Temperature range	**Seasonal care**
Cool Intermediate Warm	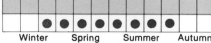 Winter Spring Summer Autumn
A temperature between 50°-65°F (10°-18°C) is ideal. If plants are developing flower spikes, then the night temperature must not be above 58°F (14°C).	In autumn, when the flower spikes are developing, stake and support them, placing a slug pellet between bulb and spike to ensure that the buds will not be damaged. Repot plants in spring; do not over-pot.
Watering	**Soil**
	A mixture of 2 parts sphagnum moss peat to 1 part perlite with the pH adjusted to 6.00 is ideal for this orchid.
Do not overwater, but give a thorough watering from the top when the compost has dried out.	

Cymbidium Annan 'Cooksbridge'
(*C*. Camelot x *C*. Berwick)
Flowering time – late winter.

This plant (*right*) is by far the finest clone in its colour range, with one of the most spectacular lips in the whole of the *Cymbidium* genus. The plant grows and flowers very easily; blooms are carried on fine upright spikes. The first flowering on a young plant will often be during December and January, but in subsequent years the plant will bloom during April and May.

Cymbidium Western Highlands 'Cooksbridge Ice Green'
(*C*. Western Rose x *C*. Miretta)
Flowering time – early spring.

The crossing of the fine green breeding plant *C*. Miretta with the white-flowered *C*. Western Rose has produced many outstanding varieties. The illustrated clone (*above*) is by far the most impressive in the ice-green coloration, having up to 18 large flowers carried on long semi-arching spikes.

Cymbidium Sutherland
(*C*. Vieux Rose x *C*. Miretta)
Flowering time – spring.

The pink coloration is unusual for this hybrid (*right*), which can bear as many as 16 blooms.

Cymbidium Bullbarrow 'Our Midge'
(*C*. Western Rose x *C*. devonianum)
Flowering time – spring.

The hybrid *C*. Bullbarrow (*right*) is the most exciting yet produced from the species *C*. devonianum and the hybrid *C*. Western Rose and has been highly awarded both in England and overseas. It produces plants with medium-sized spikes. The flowers are nicely shaped and come in green, bronze and pink shades. Most have beautifully marked crimson lips.

Cymbidium Highland Wood 'Cooksbridge Poly'
(*C*. Wood Nymph x *C*. Western Rose)
Flowering time – late winter.

Late-flowering miniature cymbidiums have proved very difficult to produce. The miniature species *Cymbidium tigrinum* has been used to attain this objective. In the case of *C*. Highland Wood (*left*), the species features two generations back in the pedigree.

Cymbidium Castle of Mey
(*C*. Putana x *C*. Western Rose)
Flowering time – late winter.

The large-flowered *C*. Western Rose has been an outstanding parent and in combination with the miniature *C*. Putana has produced the superb *C*. Castle of Mey. This hybrid (*above*) produces upright spikes with flowers mostly in white and pastel pink with attractive crimson-marked lips.

209

Cymbidium Strathmore
(*C*. Nip x *C*. Rincon)
Flowering time – late autumn.

The large-flowered *Cymbidium* Rincon is the parent of many fine early-flowering cymbidiums. The hybrid has been combined with the exceptional miniature *Cymbidium* Nip to produce delightful plants with attractive pink flowers (*left*).

Cymbidium Angelicas Loch
(*C*. Angelica x *C*. Loch Lomond)
Flowering time – early winter.

Cymbidium Angelica has proved to be an exceptional parent for early-flowering hybrids. The combination of it and the beautiful, green *C*. Loch Lomond produces a range of varieties in the yellow and green shades, most having quite outstanding crimson-banded lips. The illustrated clone (*below*) has fine large flowers carried on upright flower spikes.

Cymbidium Strathdon 'Cooksbridge Noel'
(*C*. Nip x *C*. Kurun)
Flowering time – late autumn.

The hybrid *C*. Strathdon (*bottom*) produces pink-coloured blooms. The variety 'Cooksbridge Noel' is one of the finest yet produced.

Cymbidium Christmas Song 'Cooksbridge Flamboyance'
(*C*. Kurense x *C*: Rincon)
Flowering time – early winter.

Bright, attractive, bicoloured cymbidiums are a rarity, and this fine early-flowering clone (*above*) is one of the most exceptional in its class. It produces up to 15 flowers and is easy-growing and free-flowering.

Cymbidium Sylvia Miller
(*C*. Mary Pinchess x *C*. Sussex)
Flowering time – winter.

This hybrid (*left*) produces flowers in shades of yellow, orange and green. Most plants have strong, upright flower spikes and tend to be large. Hybridists are working to improve the plant growth habit. One or two clones are late-flowering.

and the foliage may develop unsightly black marks. Breeders are working to correct these problems.

The third most important miniature species is *Cymbidium tigrinum*, used chiefly as a stud plant because of its late-flowering habit and the fact that it produces dwarf plants that are compact, with short, broad leaves on small pseudo-bulbs. Until recently the colour range of hybrids derived from the species has been limited to yellow, green and bronze, but there are now hybrids available in some very attractive pastel shades as well.

Most of the large-flowered cymbidiums have been bred from Burmese, Thai, Vietnamese and north-eastern Indian species – *C. eburneum, C. grandiflorum, C. insigne, C. iansonii, C. lowianum* and *C. parishii*. The early-flowering types have the genes of *C. traceyanum* and *C. erythrostylum*. Due to the hybridists' work, it is now possible to obtain larger-flowered cymbidiums in almost every colour except blue. These plants flower from autumn until late spring.

The cymbidiums are cool-growing orchids. They can tolerate night temperatures near to freezing and day temperatures up to 110°F (43°C), though these extremes are not desirable. The best daytime temperature for mature plants is 55–75°F (13–24°C). Temperature in spring, summer and autumn will vary, but try to keep the daytime temperature below 85°F (29°C) and the night temperature about 60°F (16°C). In winter, the night temperature should be 50°F (10°C). Daytime temperature should be 10°F (6°C) higher.

Repot cymbidiums in spring, and place them out of doors in a sheltered position during the summer months.

Collection of miniature cymbidiums
Flowering time – mid-winter
 The fine miniature breeding plant *C.* Nip has produced many high-quality hybrids in the pink, red and orange shades. The plants illustrated (*left*) are typical. During early winter they produce flower spikes easily.

Cymbidium Aviemore 'December Pinkie'
(*C.* Putana x *C.* Kurun)
Flowering time – early winter.
 The crossing of *C.* Putana and *C.* Kurun produces superb-quality flowers in pastel shades through to deep pink and orange. The variety illustrated (*below*) is free-growing and easy-flowering.

Cymbidium Highland Surprise 'Cooksbridge Alba'
(*C.* Loch Lomond x *C.* Sussex Dawn)
Flowering time – late winter.
 The cymbidium hybridist has been hard at work in recent years, attempting to produce high-quality albino orchids. The variety illustrated (*above*) is free-flowering, with upright spikes of up to 10 flowers.

Cymbidium Caithness Ice
(*C.* Caithness x *C.* Miretta)
Flowering time – late winter.
 This fine hybrid is the product of two illustrious parents, *C.* Caithness and *C.* York Meredith. The progeny of this union have green flowers with attractive round, red-marked lips. The illustrated clone (*above*) is an easily grown, free-flowering plant.

211

Odontoglossums

The genus *Odontoglossum* was founded by W.H. Alexander von Humboldt in 1815 and includes approximately 300 species. Its name combines two words from the Greek – 'odous' meaning 'tooth' and 'glossa' meaning 'tongue' – and refers to the tooth-like projections on the lip of plants in this genus. The odontoglossum is sometimes called the 'Princess of the high Andes'; most species come from Central and South America and grow at high altitudes. In the last part of the nineteenth century and early part of the twentieth, when boat-loads of odontoglossum were brought to England, fine varieties of *Odontoglossum crispum* sold for as much as £1,000. In today's terms, this would represent between £80,000 and £100,000 for just one plant. These varieties were much sought after and were extensively used by the pioneers of orchid hybridization.

What orchid growers refer to as the 'odontoglossum alliance' encompasses odontoglossums and several other related genera, including *Brassia, Cochlioda, Oncidium* and *Miltonia*. From this group come some of the most beautiful flowers in the world and some of the best modern hybrids. Flowers have a 3in (8cm) to 4in (10cm) spread, and are carried on spikes of up to 30 blooms. Flowers are found in every colour imaginable; all sorts of patterned and spotted types are also obtainable. Many of the finest intergeneric hybrids have been bred from species of different genera in this alliance.

One of the most important species has been *Odontoglossum crispum,* which will be found in the background of numerous hybrids. Most crispums you see today are white, sometimes with purple or red spots.

Odontoglossum luteopurpureum, O. harryanum, and *O. triumphans* have bred the yellow odontoglossum hybrids, while the fine red odontioda hybrids seen today

The Odontoglossum Alliance
Flowering time – various.
Orchids in the odontoglossum alliance (**right**) possess a wide range of colours. These are very small first-flowering seedlings. Stronger plants would produce up to 15 flowers on arching sprays.

ODONTOGLOSSUM	
Light and position Odontoglossums need a light position, but the direct rays of the sun should not fall on its leaves.	**Feeding** Use a high-nitrogen fertilizer during spring and summer, and a high-potash fertilizer during early autumn.
Temperature range Cool Intermediate Warm The night temperature range should be 50°-58°F (10°-14°C) and the day temperature 60°-70°C (16°-21°C).	**Seasonal care** Winter Spring Summer Autumn Remove any decayed leaves and make sure the flower spikes are staked and properly supported.
Watering Do not overwater, but give a thorough watering from the top when the compost has dried out.	**Soil** The best mix for this orchid would be 2 parts bark, 2 parts sphagnum moss peat and 1 part perlite with a pH of 6.0. Potting should take place when the new growth is about 1½ in (4cm) high. Plants benefit from annual repotting; do not overpot.

have been bred from the small-flowered, brilliant red species called *Cochlioda noezliana*.

Two other intergeneric hybrids, odontoncidium (odontogloassum x oncidium) and wilsónara (odontoglossum x cochlioda x oncidium), are largely the result of the following species in the *Oncidium* genus: *O. tigrinum, O. wentworthianum, O. leucochilum* or *O. incurvum*. These species are native to Mexico and Guetamala.

Another intergeneric hybrid, vuylslekeara, has been bred from species of odontoglossum, cochlioda and miltonia. It particularly shows the influence of the latter, the 'Pansy Orchid', very clearly. The *Miltonia* genus is characterized by large flat flowers, and passes this on to its progeny. The most famous orchid in the world, certainly the one most propagated, is × *Vuylstekeara* Cambria var. 'Plush'. The quality of the flower, its ease of growth and its ability to thrive under varying conditions account for its popularity.

Plants within the odontoglossum alliance have a wide range of temperature requirements. Consequently, the 'ideal' temperature varies accordingly. Most, however, are happy at a night temperature of around 50–55°F (10–13°C). The day temperature should be controlled so that it does not rise above 80°F (27°C) if this is at all possible. Provided the plant is in good condition and well rooted, it will tolerate temperatures as low as 40°F (4°C) and as high as 90°F (32°C). These levels of cold and heat will, however, place a certain amount of stress on the plants, so limit their exposure to such extremes as much as possible.

Watering is critical for this group of orchids. It is most important not to overwater; in fact it would be better to slightly underwater. Use rainwater if possible.

Aphids sometimes trouble plants within the odontoglossum alliance, and in recent years there have been several instances of plants being attacked by false spider mites, which in some plants can be mistaken for virus disease. This pest can be eliminated by using an appropriate insecticide.

When potting these orchids, use a mix of 2 parts sphagnum moss peat, 2 parts Sequoia bark, 1 part perlite, with the pH adjusted to 6.0 and a base fertilizer added to the peat. Repot annually, when new growth is about 1½in (4cm) long. Ideally, odontoglossums should be in a greenhouse when not in flower. If this is not possible, place plants in a light location indoors but not in direct sun.

Vuylstekeara Edna x Odontioda Mardley Flowering time - various.
    This fine hybrid (top) has small to medium-sized flowers carried on a semi-arching spike. The broad flat lip is the characteristic that has been inherited from the miltonia orchid in its background.
Odontioda Le Nez Point
(*O.* Trixon x *O.* Fremar)
Flowering time - various.
    This beautifully shaped odontioda is made even more attractive by the lighter-coloured margins of its sepals and petals (above).

Odontoglossum and allied genera
Flowering time – various.

This display of orchids and ferns in a greenhouse (*left*) is just one example of the many ways orchids can be used in combination with other plants to create interesting flower arrangements. The orchids shown here can flower at almost any time of the year, although there are two main peak flowering periods. These occur in autumn and the late spring.

Odontoglossum Crutordo x Odontioda Elpheon
Flowering time – various.

This unnamed hybrid (*below left*), which is referred to by its crossing, is an excellent example of a heavily patterned odontioda. This first-flowering seedling bears large, well-shaped flowers. Mature plants may have a spike of up to 20 flowers.

Odontoglossum Royal Wedding 'Cooksbridge'
(*O*. Pancho x *O*. Ardentissimum)
Flowering time – various.

The superb hybrid (*above*) is bred from a line of superior odontoglossums, all of which have the albino characteristic. Flowers from this hybrid were included in the wedding bouquet of HRH The Princess of Wales. This plant is vigorous and free-flowering.

Paphiopedilum

Before they were re-classified, paphiopedilums used to be known as cypripediums, and many orchid-growers still use the latter name. The popular name for this orchid is Lady's Slipper because, instead of forming a lip as in most orchids, the modified third petal forms a pouch that looks somewhat similar to a lady's slipper. Species of this genus are found in the Far East, and in Southeast Asia. They encompass an immense range of sizes, shapes and colours.

Because it was valued as a cut flower, *P. insigne* was at one time the most common of all paphiopedilums. It is prominent in the background of many of today's spotted and yellow hybrids. *P. delenatii,* a delightful pink species, has produced a line of attractive pink-flowered hybrids, while *P. niveum* has produced some superb white-flowered hybrids.

Another important species used in the breeding of this genus is *P. bellatulum.* This plant is native to Burma and Thailand, and is responsible for the shape and broad petals of many of today's best paphiopedilum hybrids.

In recent years, there has been increasing interest in what is termed 'primary hybrids'. These grow and bloom easily, and are produced very quickly from seed.

Plants in this genus should have a night temperature of 58°F (14°C) and a day temperature between 65°F (18°C) and 75°F (24°C), although some growers keep their plants at lower temperatures. Try not to let temperatures rise above 85°F (29°C) for prolonged periods of time.

Pathiopedilums are low-light orchids and should not be subjected to the direct rays of the sun. Give them good light, but do not place them near the window. Repot plants directly after flowering, preferably before the end of spring. When watering, be careful that

Paphiopedilum Hybrids

Flowering time – winter.

This fine group of paphiopedilums (*above left*) shows some of the different colours and shapes of plants in this genus. While most flower in winter, some varieties do flower at different times of the year.

Paphiopedilum Brownstone

(*P. Hazella* x *P. Beedon*)

Flowering time – winter.

This high-quality paphiopedilum hybrid (*above right*) produces some exceptional striped flowers. It is a compact plant that grows and flowers very easily, usually in December-February.

water does not lie in the centre of growth. This will damage buds and flowers. Provide regular feeding during the summer.

PAPHIOPEDILUM	
Light and position Paphiopedilums are low-light orchids and must not be subjected to the direct rays of the sun. Give them indirect light	**Feeding** Use a high-nitrogen fertilizer during spring and summer, and a high-potash fertilizer during early autumn.
Temperature range Cool Intermediate Warm The best temperature range is 58°F (14°C) at night and 65°-75°F (17°-24°C) by day. Note that orchids with mottled leaves generally require warmer conditions.	**Seasonal care** Winter Spring Summer Autumn Gradually adjust the watering according to the season; the compost will require more frequent watering during the spring and summer period. When watering, make sure that water does not lodge in the centre of the growth. Repot in the spring; do not over-pot.
Watering  Allow the compost to partially dry out before giving plants a thorough watering.	**Soil** A mixture of 2 parts sphagnum moss peat to 1 part perlite with the pH adjusted to 6.00 is ideal for this orchid.

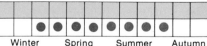

Phalaenopsis

The Dutch Botanist Karel Lodewijk Blume established this genus in 1852 when he discovered *Phalaenopsis amabilis* and thought the flowers looked like tropical moths. The generic name is Greek, 'phalaina' meaning 'moth', 'opsis' meaning 'appearance'.

These exotic, tropical orchids from the Far East are still popularly referred to as the Moth Orchid. They are monopodial in growth and have a single stem that continues to grow upwards, producing new leaves at regular intervals. These plants are mostly epiphytic. They grow on trees and frequently produce numerous aerial roots.

Hybridists have produced plants that are striped and spotted and come in a range of colours. The flowers can be 1in (3cm) to 5in (13cm) wide, and are often borne on long arching sprays.

Many species have gone into the breeding of these hybrids. *P. lueddemanniana* produces flowers that open successively on the spike so that a plant may be in flower for several months of the year. Hybrids are attractively barred or spotted in colour.

P. stuartiana has flowers that are white with a brownish-purple lip,

and the lower sepals are similarly marked. These characteristics are passed on to its progeny.

P. schilleriana is a magnificent species with beautiful foliage and attractive pink flowers, and it is in the background of today's fine pink phalaenopsis.

Native to the Philippines, *P. amabilis* is responsible for the large, white phalaenopsis orchid seen today, and figures in the pedigree of some other phalaenopsis as well.

Other species that today's modern hybrids have been bred from include *P. fasciata*, *P. fuscata*, *P. mariea*, *P. amboinensis* (mostly used to produce fine yellow types) and *P. equestris*. This is probably the commonest and has been used to breed the candy-striped and red-lipped types.

Phalaenopsis orchids need high humidity and high temperature. The ideal night temperature is around 65°F (18°C); the best day temperature is 70-75°F (21-24°C). Some orchid growers use a compost mix of 2 parts bark, 2 parts sphagnum moss peat, 1 part perlite with a pH of 6.0 for phalaenopsis. Excellent results can also be obtained with a bark compost – the size of the bark should be approximately ½in (1cm). When watering this orchid, try to keep the centre of the plant dry, as water here can cause rotting. If by chance you do fill the centre of the growth with water, make sure that this is emptied out before nightfall. Place plants in a light location.

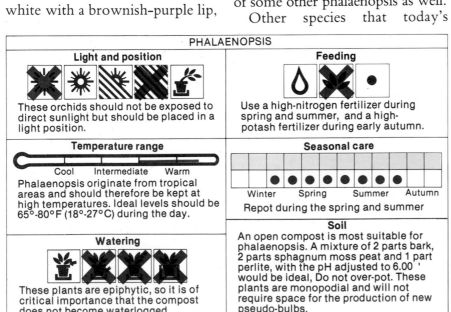

PHALAENOPSIS

Light and position

These orchids should not be exposed to direct sunlight but should be placed in a light position.

Temperature range

Cool — Intermediate — Warm

Phalaenopsis originate from tropical areas and should therefore be kept at high temperatures. Ideal levels should be 65°-80°F (18°-27°C) during the day.

Watering

These plants are epiphytic, so it is of critical importance that the compost does not become waterlogged.

Feeding

Use a high-nitrogen fertilizer during spring and summer, and a high-potash fertilizer during early autumn.

Seasonal care

Winter — Spring — Summer — Autumn

Repot during the spring and summer

Soil

An open compost is most suitable for phalaenopsis. A mixture of 2 parts bark, 2 parts sphagnum moss peat and 1 part perlite, with the pH adjusted to 6.00 would be ideal, Do not over-pot. These plants are monopodial and will not require space for the production of new pseudo-bulbs.

Phalaenopsis Temple Cloud 'Mount Hood' (*P.* Opaline x *P.* Keith Shaffer) Flowering time – various.

This fine example (*other page*) of a modern white phalaenopsis has been line-bred from the species *P. amabilis*. This hybrid is capable of producing a spike of up to 18 large flowers on a graceful arching spray.

Phalaenopsis Space Queen 'White Gold' (*P.* Temple Cloud x *P.* Barbara Moler) Flowering time – various.

On strong plants, this hybrid (*above*) gives good-size flowers on branched spikes of up to 20 blooms.

Phalaenopsis Solvang 'Portland Star' (*P.* Lena Martel x *P.* Barbara Moler) Flowering time – various.

Phalaenopsis Barbara Moler has proven to be an exceptional parent for the production of spotted, candy-striped and yellow flowers as well as the type illustrated (*right*). This hybrid can produce up to 15 blooms.

Pachystachys lutea

Although it belongs to the same family as the aphelandra and has similar yellow bracts, the pachystachys has very inferior foliage. While the aphelandra has attractive silver and green bars of colour across each leaf, this plant is a very dull, pale green in comparison. One compensation is that there are many more bracts and, if anything, the pachystachys is a little bit easier to care for. One drawback with this plant is that it does not travel very well, so, unless handling has been especially careful, plants are often not in particularly good condition when they reach the retailer.

Healthy plant. A well-cared for plant that is pruned slighty in spring retains a neat, bushy shape, showing the bracts to advantage.

The healthy leaf (*top*) is rather dull green but looks fresh and clean. Tiny holes (*above*) may be due to pests or a visiting caterpillar.

PURCHASING

Select a plant with a fresh and open appearance to the foliage. Plants that have been tightly packed for long before going on sale look sad and cramped. The Lollipop Plant may be bought with lots of buds developing among the top leaves, but avoid one that already has a mass of white flowers, as this is a sign of ageing. The bracts are continually developing as old ones are removed. The lower leaves will sometimes drop, so choose a plant with leaves all down the stem.
P. lutea This is the only variety that is truly suitable for indoor culture and is therefore the only one usually found on sale.

PESTS AND DISEASES

Aphids Check young growth regularly for the presence of these small green pests. They weaken the plant and cause distortion of the foliage. Spray the foliage generously with malathion.
Mealy bug These powdery white bugs attack only older plants and will be found amongst the bracts. Remove old bracts and burn them. Spray the plant with diazinon. Repeat after seven days to ensure their young are eliminated.
Botrytis Plants that are too moist and cramped may develop brown patches on their lower leaves. Remove affected leaves and spray the plant with dichloran.

AVOIDING PROBLEMS

Light and position

The plant requires the lightest position possible without being in danger from direct, hot sun which scorches the leaves. Weak winter sunlight or morning and evening sun will not harm it. The Lollipop Plant is quite delicate and must not be in a draught.

Temperature range

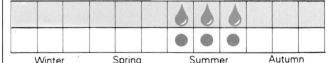

Cool   Intermediate   Warm

Warmth is an important requirement and the best temperatures are 65°-70°F (18°-21°C), although the plant is adequately warm at 60°F (15°C) or more, particularly in winter. In cooler conditions the leaves will drop. The plant will also appreciate a reasonable humidity, which can be achieved by standing the pot on wet pebbles, but the plant dislikes being sprayed when in flower.

Watering

Water from the top of the soil to keep it moist, but be sure the water drains through and do not leave the base of the pot standing in excess water. Make sure it is not waterlogged, but at the same time never let the compost dry out completely. Reduce watering in winter.

Feeding

Add liquid food to the water so the plant is well-nourished in the growing period. The food should be gradually reduced, along with the watering, when the plant rests in winter.

Seasonal care

Winter   Spring   Summer   Autumn

When the plant has flowered, the remaining yellow bracts should be removed. If they are left on the plant to rot it may develop botrytis. At the same time the stems can be cut back to half their size. The plant is kept to a neat shape if it is carefully pruned in the spring, and a leggy plant can be cut right down to about 2in (5cm) to start fresh growth. Keep soil moist at all times but water less in the winter.

Soil

Pot the Lollipop Plant in a loam-based mixture. A plant can be potted into a slightly larger container in the spring following the year when it is purchased, in time to encourage the new season's growth. Do not hurry it into a pot which is too big.

Palms

There are many types of palm, almost all of them fairly tough, but the majority are rather too vigorous for today's average living accommodation. The best known is the Parlour Palm, *Neanthe bella* (*Chamaedorea elegans*). This is a neat, slow-growing plant that many people have in their homes and which is very easily produced from seed by the commercial grower. Although there are many palm varieties most of them require similar treatment and temperatures, and they all attract the same sort of pests.

Two kentias are available – the Kentia Palm (*K. forsterana*), by far the most popular, and the Sentry Palm (*K. belmoreana*). The first has broader and fewer leaflets to each individual hand of leaves.

Kentias have been popular for indoor decoration since Victorian times and, in spite of the amount they cost, there seems to be little change in their popularity today.

Healthy plants *Neanthe bella* **(above)** does best in moist conditions. If the plant is allowed to become too dry, its leaf tips are liable to turn brown. Insufficient humidity may also lead to infestation by red spider mites. When mature it produces small yellow flowers, but its chief attraction is its mass of green leaves. *Kentia forsterana* **(left)** is easy to look after. Growth is very slow, so it is often best to grow several plants in a single pot. Kentias are often classified today as *Howea*.

AVOIDING PROBLEMS

Light and position

Most palms grow naturally in places where there is intense heat and sunlight. So, to encourage them to grow well indoors, place new plants where they will enjoy 2-3 hours of direct sun a day.

Temperature range

Cool   Intermediate   Warm

During the active growth period, a warm environment of 60°-70°F (15°-21°C) is best. During winter, hardier varieties, such as chamaerops, livistona and washingtonia, can tolerate temperatures down to 45°F (7°C). Other types should not be subjected to temperatures below 55°F (13°C).

Watering

The amount of water needed will depend on the individual palm. In general, water thoroughly during the active growth period. In winter, the cooler the room, the less water required. All palms like to be sprayed occasionally with tepid water.

Feeding

Smaller plants will do well with a weak feed every watering, but phoenix palms must have heavy feedings at weekly intervals during summer, and fortnightly in winter. For all palms, in winter use a weak feed or else stop feeding altogether.

Seasonal care

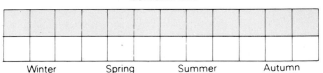

Winter   Spring   Summer   Autumn

All palms should be watered and fed thoroughly during the active period. Stop feeding and water only moderately during the rest period. Do not clean leaves with chemical mixtures; use a sponge and water instead. Most palms are very difficult to propagate and the seed can take up to two years to germinate. Palms are sensitive to changes in environment so if moving the plant out-of-doors in summer, acclimatize it gradually. Be sure to bring the plant back indoors before the temperature drops too low.

Soil

Smaller plants can be potted every two years using a loam-based mixture with leaf mould added. Good drainage is essential for all palms. Repot only when the roots have filled the pot and have begun to protrude through the drainage holes.

PROPAGATION

Propagation of the **howea**, or what used to be called the Kentia palm, can provide the home enthusiast with a challenge.

As with the chamaedorea, a relatively high temperature is required, up to 80°F (27°C). Seed should be sown in mid- to late spring in trays or 5½in (14cm) half-pots or pans filled with seed and cutting compost, the compost just covering the seed.

The temperature should be maintained for many weeks as germination is very patchy and may even take up to two to three months or more.

Keep the plant in light shade, with the compost just moist.

Germination is also poor and it is important to prick out seedlings as soon as they are large enough to handle.

Gently tease out the seedlings and pot up one seedling per 3½in (9cm) pot filled with a peat-based potting compost, growing on the new plant at a temperature of 68-70°F (20-21°C).

Grow the seedlings on in moderate shade. Keep the compost barely moist and take great care not to overwater.

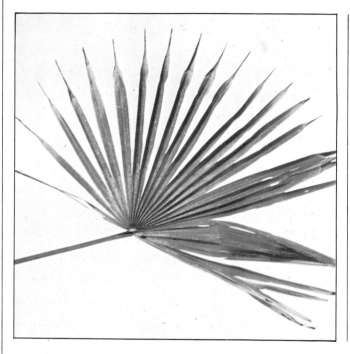

Dry conditions This leaf (*left*) is suffering from a lack of humidity, which has turned the tips of its fronds brown. To overcome this problem, stand the pot on a bed of peat moss, or a tray of moist pebbles. Mist-spray the plant regularly.

Two problems The *Neanthe bella* (*above*) has been underwatered. It also carries the symptoms of red spider mite — light brown patches on the edges and eventually over the whole of some leaves. Daily mist spraying acts as a preventative, since it keeps up the humidity.

Chemical danger All palms, like the *Kentia forsteriana* (*above*), are extremely sensitive to chemicals. Leaves should always be cleaned with a damp sponge, never a chemical cleaner. Similarly, always consult a retailer before using an insecticide.

Root growth The *Chamaerops humilis* (*left*) needs careful attention when grown indoors. They should be repotted every 2-3 years, the signal for this being the spread of brittle roots on the surface of the potting mixture. Repot the plant carefully, making sure the palm is planted firmly, but taking care not to damage its roots.

PESTS AND DISEASES

Red spider mite This is the chief enemy of all palms. As a preventative, keep the plant in fairly humid conditions and mist-spray regularly. If infestation is suspected, remove a sample and examine it under a magnifying glass as, in its initial stages, this tiny pest is easy to miss. Treat by thoroughly spraying the foliage with a recommended insecticide.
Scale insect These infest the stem and underside of the leaves. Like red spider mites, they are difficult to spot. Treat with insecticide.
Earthworms These can block drainage holes in the pot so that the soil becomes too wet, with the result that roots rot and die, shortly followed by the leaves.

VARIETIES AND PURCHASING

Palms fall into two main divisions – those with pinnate (feathery) fronds and those with palmate (fan-like) ones. Always choose plants that are free from blemishes and have a bright, fresh look to them. Check carefully for the presence of pests, such as the red spider mite and scale insect.
Caryota There are two common varieties, *C. mitis*, the Burmese Fishtail Palm, and *C. urens*, the Wine Palm. They like warmth, should be watered plentifully and fed once a month during the active growth period.
Kentia The slender build of *K. belmoreana* and *K. forsterana* belies their stamina. They are able to thrive even in difficult conditions, though they do not like temperatures below 55°F (13°C).
Phoenix *P. canariensis* is hardier than *P. dactylifera* or *P. roebelenii*. The last needs frequent repotting, as it grows quickly. Suckers can be used for propagation.
Chamaedorea As well as *C. elegans*, *C. erumpens* and *C.*

seifrizii are also popular. They all need plenty of water in the active growth period. In winter, however, water only just enough to moisten the potting mixture.
Microcoelum . *M. weddelianum* must not be potted in a pot that is too big for it and must be kept at a minimum temperature of 60°F (15°C).
Trachycarpus *T. fortunei*, the Windmill Palm, is a slender-stemmed plant, bearing attractive, fan-shaped leaves. These must be removed when age makes them unsightly.
Chrysalidocarpus *C. lutescens*, the Yellow Palm, produces clusters of reed-like stems. The small suckers that grow at its base can again be used for propagation.
Rhapis *R. excelsa*, the Little Lady Palm, and *R. humilis*, the Slender Lady Palm, are slow growing, producing fan-shaped dark green leaves. They will both do well in pots that seem a little small for them.

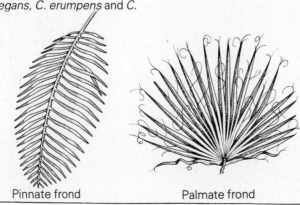

Pinnate frond

Palmate frond

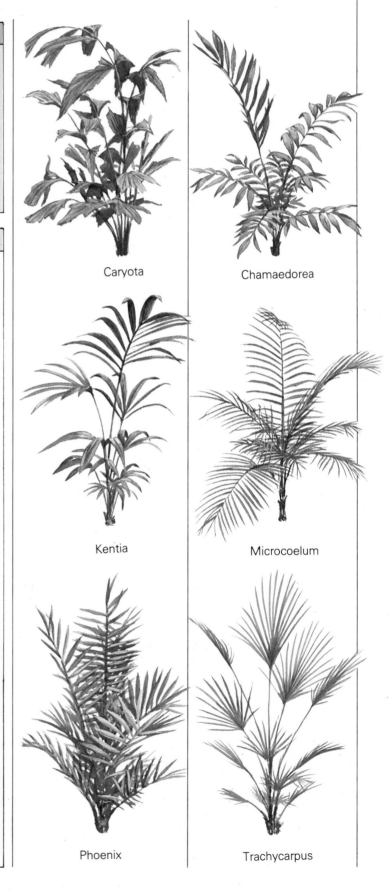

Caryota

Chamaedorea

Kentia

Microcoelum

Phoenix

Trachycarpus

Chrysalidocarpus

Rhapis

Propagation The *Neanthe bella,* which is also known as *Collinia elegans* and *Chamaedorea elegans* (**right**), is difficult but not impossible to propagate. Seeds can be gathered in the spring and placed in a heated propagator. A high temperature – at least 80°F (26°C) – is necessary, plus intense humidity. It is easier to propagate from the varieties that produce offsets. Allow these to develop leaves and roots, then cut them carefully from their parent. Plant them in moistened potting mixture, covering the pot with a plastic bag for a few weeks until they have taken root.

Pandanus

Pandanus leaves are clearly designed to protect the plant from interference. They are spined along their margins, viciously so on the leaves' undersides. Because of their spiteful nature, all plants in the *Pandanus* genus should be treated with respect and placed well out of reach. Leaves have no petiole and radiate in splendid fashion from a short central trunk. These are tough plants that will tolerate almost everything except wet, cold conditions.

Two species of pandanus are sold as houseplants. Both are grown purely for their foliage; there is no possibility of them flowering in room conditions.

Pandanus veitchii is the more compact species, with leaves that are white and green in colour. Plants grow 3-4ft (91cm-1.2m) tall with a similar spread when growing in 7in (18cm) and upwards pots.

Pandanus baptistii is a more magnificent plant. Foliage is bright golden-yellow in colour. The plant attains a height of 6ft (1.9m) with a similar spread. However, plants of such magnitude would be at least 10 years old and growing in ideal conditions.

Plants require the lightest possible location indoors, and it will help during the winter months if they can be placed under an artificial light during the evening. When potting, use a rich potting mixture and pot plants fairly firmly. Although plants must be kept on the moist side in spring and summer, it is important that they do not get too wet during the winter months.

Pandanus plants have long arching leaves with sharp spines. *P. baptistii (above)* is a large, spreading plant with golden-yellow leaves spiralling out from the central trunk. *P. veitchii (below)* is a smaller plant with striped leaves.

PANDANUS

Light and position

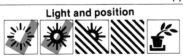

Good light is necessary for healthy growth, and these plants require at least three hours of sunlight a day.

Temperature range

| Cool | Intermediate | Warm |

Normal room temperature is suitable; the winter temperature should be in the region of 65°F (18°C). These plants need humidity — the leaves turn brown if the atmosphere is too dry.

Watering

Water plentifully during the active growth period. Plunge the plant in water during the summer and give less water in winter.

Feeding

Apply liquid feed once every two weeks, but avoid excessive feeding and do not feed in winter.

Seasonal care

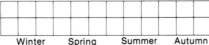

| Winter | Spring | Summer | Autumn |

New cuttings of these very tough plants can be made by pulling the offset away from the base of the parent plant and potting them on separately in pots filled with peaty potting mixture. Potting should be done as necessary, in the spring.

Soil

As plants get larger, it is advisable to use loam-based soil and clay pots for potting.

Passiflora

Indigenous to tropical South America, this plant grows at an extraordinary rate if the conditions are favourable. The intricately formed flower, which is predominantly blue, received its common name after Christian missionaries compared it to various elements of the Crucifixion. For example, they saw the crown of thorns in the purple rays of the corola. Whether or not it is a good houseplant is another matter, as there is not much to be admired in the foliage once the flowers have passed, and it is quite possible that after it has been bought the plant will not flower at all. In mild climates it will survive out of doors if it is given a sheltered position.

Healthy plant It is usual to buy the plant already trained around a hoop, which makes it look decorative. It is quite an easy plant to keep, although the attractive flowers (*above*) may take a long time to open fully.

VARIETIES

Plants may be bought at any time of year, but look their best in summer when the flowers are emerging. Look for a plant with fresh green leaves, as yellowing may be a sign that red spider mites are already in evidence. Check the buds on a plant carefully, and ensure that some of the flowers have already developed.
P. caerulea This is the best variety for indoor growing, and few others are likely to be seen for sale. The flowers are almost always a blue-purple colour but occasionally you may see pink or red. The plant has a natural climbing habit, having clasping tendrils that cling to anything within their range.

PESTS AND DISEASES

Aphids The young growing tips of the plant are vulnerable to this pest. Spray the plant with diazinon or malathion and repeat the treatment as necessary to clear them altogether.
Red spider mite These will be found on the undersides of leaves, which may look yellow and lacking in vigour. Thorough and repeated spraying with malathion is vital at the earliest possible stage.
White fly This is an infrequent visitor but may prove difficult to kill. Spray the plant with diazinon at four-day intervals and repeat the treatment at least four times to kill the flies and eradicate all their young.

AVOIDING PROBLEMS

Light and position

The best possible light is needed and the plant should be placed in a window, although it is necessary to watch for scorching in direct sun. The plant can be placed outdoors in summer, but be sure to remember it and attend to its needs.

Temperature range

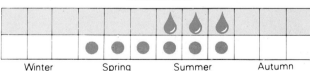

| Cool | Intermediate | Warm |

The passiflora likes a moderate temperature range, 55°-65°F (13°-18°C). It will not be harmed by warmer temperatures, but heat encourages red spider mite. In cooler conditions the plant maintains less active growth and will keep an attractive shape. In any temperature within the preferred range, keep the environment well ventilated.

Watering

Give the plant plenty of water, especially in summer when it may need watering three times a week. Reduce watering in winter, but do not let the soil dry out completely.

Feeding

The plant will flower more freely if the roots are confined, and if it is kept pot-bound regular feeding is essential. Give liquid feed with a high potash content, once a week in summer and about fortnightly in the autumn and cooler months.

Seasonal care

	Winter		Spring		Summer		Autumn	

Keep the soil moist at all times but be careful not to overwater in the winter. Growth can be extremely active so keep the plant in conditions which restrict it slightly and prune out unwanted stems in the autumn, after the plant has flowered. The passiflora is best grown on its own as it will tend to outgrow and swamp any companions.

Soil

Frequent potting on of this plant is not recommended, and when it is done, must be embarked upon carefully. Crock the bottom of the pot and use a loam-based mixture. Peaty soil will be of no use at all. Repot in early summer and press the soil well down around the roots.

Pelargonium

Most pelargoniums, which commonly tend to be called Geraniums, will do well indoors, but they must have the lightest possible position if their flowers are to open satisfactorily, and they are to continue to flower well. There are many types, but the Regal pelargonium is most associated with indoor culture. Cuttings can be taken at almost any time during the summer, but it is best to leave them until late summer so that young plants are over-wintered and ready for potting on and getting under way in the spring. Cuttings 3–4in (7.5–10cm) long root very easily and need no special treatment. Older plants that have flowered should be pruned back in the autumn and kept on the dry side until the following spring.

VARIETIES AND PURCHASING

There are so many varieties of pelargonium that it is impossible to give a full list. Flowers in colours ranging from white, through pink and red to deep plum are available, some as delicate sprays and others in rich, heavy flower heads. In addition, some varieties have leaf markings in dark red or cream. When selecting a plant, look for a full, bushy specimen and check the undersides of leaves to make sure there are no pests already at work. In all respects, pelargoniums are handsome, decorative plants that are quite easy to keep in the home.

P. × domesticum
Otherwise known as the Regal pelargonium, this is the most popular of domestic varieties and when well kept is a pleasing and impressive sight.

P. zonale This has red-brown markings on the leaves and bears it flower heads for several months.

Healthy plant Part of the great pleasure of these plants is the fresh and vigorous effect of the contrast between the clear, bright colours of the flowers and the rich green leaves, enhanced if several plants are kept together.

AVOIDING PROBLEMS

Light and position

Full light is essential for pelargoniums and they prefer an airy atmosphere, although they do not care for draughts. There are many varieties and they all enjoy sunshine, especially when flowering, but guard against scorched leaves in really hot weather.

Temperature range

Cool   Intermediate   Warm

Pelargoniums appreciate a cool or moderate range of temperature. They will exist happily in 50°F (10°C) but prefer a slightly higher temperature, nearer to 60°F (15°C). In summer they can tolerate rather warmer conditions for a while and a dry, rather than humid, atmosphere is best.

Watering

Introduce water at the top of the pot and let it sink down through the soil. After 15 minutes, empty the excess water from the saucer. The plants do not care for overhead spraying and this may start rotting in the leaves.

Feeding

Excessive feeding will encourage a leafy plant, but at the expense of the flowers. Give no more than an average amount of liquid feed in summer as the plants are watered. They will not require winter feeding.

Seasonal care

Winter   Spring   Summer   Autumn

Water the plants quite generously in summer, moistening the soil often, but keep them fairly dry during the winter and in the lower temperature of 50°F (10°C). The top growth of the plant can be severely cut back during the winter rest. This reduces the likelihood of disease in congested foliage and also allows for more attractive growth in spring. Cuttings taken in late summer provide plants for the following year.

Soil

Use a loam-based or peat-based compost. Repotting should not be done too frequently as the plant can benefit from being slightly pot-bound. Young cuttings should be potted on, but do not repot fully grown plants.

PESTS AND DISEASES

Aphids These little greenfly can be a nuisance on young plants. They suck the sap from soft growth and deposit sticky honeydew on the foliage (*see illustration right below*).

White fly This is a more prevalent problem and also more difficult to treat. The small white insects sit on the undersides of leaves (*see illustration below*) and dance about when the plant is disturbed. They may occur in great numbers and will spread quickly from one plant to another. Like the aphids, they weaken the plant by sucking the sap and again leave a sticky deposit. Spray the leaves with diazinon and repeat the treatment every four days until the plant is clean. Repeated spraying also kills the young flies that are hatching out.

Black leg This is a fungal disease that attacks the stems of pelargoniums. It occurs in conditions that are too wet and airless. There is no useful treatment and the plants must be destroyed, so make sure the same conditions will not prevail for plants that replace those affected.

Vine weevils Adult beetles can be damaging to the leaves, but it is the grubs, which live in the compost and attack the roots of the plant that are most dangerous. As soon as you notice this condition, soak the soil thoroughly with rotenone. Spraying the plant with this insecticide is a useful precaution which may prevent the outbreak.

Rust A disease that is not common in houseplants, this may appear on pelargoniums in dank, airless conditions. You will notice brown spores on the undersides of the leaves. Remove the diseased leaves and treat the plant with a suitable insecticide.

Virus There is no single, easily described symptom of virus infection. If certain areas of the plant are distorted or stunted, or the leaves develop pale green or yellow patches, it may have a virus. This may have been present when you bought the plant or insects may have carried in the infection. Either way, there is nothing to be done, so make sure there can be no other cause and then dispose of the plant.

Mealy bug These white bugs, the adults large and waxy and the young wrapped in cottony fluff, are easily seen on the plant (*see illustration right below*). A severe infestation is difficult to control and leads to the leaves of the plant yellowing and dropping. At this stage, spray the leaves generously with malathion, but if there are only a few pests, wipe them off carefully with cotton wool soaked in malathion.

White fly These can be clearly seen against the leaf colouring. They must be quickly treated before they do any more damage.

Pests White fly is a tricky pest to eradicate and causes great harm to the plant. The problem is compounded if the plant is at the same time suffering from botrytis (*left*). Any attempt to cure it would require a chemical assault, which would probably do more harm than good to a plant so weakened and it is doubtful that treatment could be effective. Remove and destroy a badly affected plant before the trouble spreads. A simultaneous infestation of mealy bug and white fly (*below left*) is not quite such a disaster, as spraying with malathion should kill both pests. Make sure the undersides of leaves are well soaked. Aphids alone (*below*) are destructive enough. Spray the plant as soon as you notice the problem and repeat as necessary.

Peperomia

These plants seldom reach a height of more than 10in (25cm). The Desert Privet has attractive cream and green variegation on rounded leaves that are attached to succulent stems. The Little Fantasy plant is very dark green with crinkled leaves that are small and rounded, sprouting not from stems but from soil level. This is a dwarf variety that rarely grows above 6in (15cm) in height.

Little Fantasy is propagated from individual leaves, while the Desert Privet is propagated from leaves with a piece of stem attached. They should be inserted in a peat and sand mixture in small pots and the temperature should be in the region of 70°F (21°C).

Healthy plant *Peperomia magnoliifolia,* the Desert Privet, is a small plant that generally grows to a height of 6in (15cm). It has attractive rounded leaves, which are variegated in cream and green. The leaves grow from thick, fleshy stems.

AVOIDING PROBLEMS

Light and position

Because of their neat size and shape, peperomias are essentially windowsill plants. The window should provide good light, but not direct midday sun.

These are excellent plants for mixing with other types. They are not, however, suitable for bottle-gardens.

Temperature range

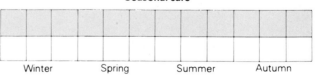

Cool   Intermediate   Warm

A modest temperature of 55°-65° F (13°-18°C) is best although this can drop to 50°F (10°C) in winter if

watering is also reduced. The maximum summer temperature should be 75°C (23°C).

Watering

Peperomias should be watered only sparingly, every 10 days in summer and every two weeks in winter. Use lime-free water. The

plants store water in their leaves, and if overwatered, these will quickly rot.

Feeding

Peperomias will usually be growing in a soil-less mixture which lacks essential nutrients, so feed with a weak fertilizer with each

watering. In summer, feed every two weeks using half the recommended dosage.

Seasonal care

Winter	Spring	Summer	Autumn

These can be difficult plants to keep growing from year to year, but it is well worth the effort. Peperomias should be watered very moderately throughout the year. Generally, these plants do

not develop extensive root systems and will not require repotting. If necessary, repot only in the spring. Propagate from cuttings.

Soil

These plants do much better in loam-based soil-less mixtures than in conventional soils. Repotting should be done every

second year at most. When repotting, use shallow containers rather than deep pots. Never repot in winter.

PROPAGATION

Select mature, but not old leaf and remove cleanly at base of leaf stem.

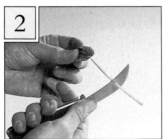

Trim leaf stem to about 1–1¼in (2.5–3cm).

Dip into hormone rooting powder and, gently holding by leaf, insert in 5½in (13cm) half-pot of seed and cutting compost.

Although the **Peperomia caperata** may be propagated from tip cuttings in a similar way to several varieties of peperomia it is not really the best technique to use, especially with small plants. A far better technique is that of simply removing leaves complete with the leaf stem from mid-spring to mid-summer. Select fully formed leaves, not old ones, and cut cleanly with a very sharp knife. Trim the leaf stem to about 1–1¼in (2.5–3cm), again using a very sharp knife and taking great care not to crush the leaf stalk

The leaf should then be dibbled into a seed and cutting compost in a tray or pan, using a small dibble or stick to allow its easy insertion into the compost. Do not compress the compost, but settle it with a light watering. The leaf should be just touching the compost and not buried.

Maintain a temperature of 68°F (20°C) in reasonable light, but not in direct sunlight, and take care to remove any leaves that start to rot before the infection spreads.

The cuttings will probably take up to two months to root. At the base of the leaf where it joins the leaf stalk, a new plant should form and when this is large enough to handle, at about 1¼–2in (3–5cm), it may be gently pricked out and potted up. Pot into a 3½in (9cm) pot using a peat-based potting compost, and grow on.

VARIETIES AND PURCHASING

When purchasing peperomias, select sturdy, compact plants with distinct markings. Look for damaged leaves and any discoloration. Carefully inspect the soil area for rot, which could quickly lead to irreversible problems. There are some 400 members of this family.

***P. magnoliifolia* 'Variegata'** This is also known as Desert Privet. It has green leaves with cream markings.
P. hederifolia has pale grey leaves that are indented.
***P. scandens* 'Variegata'** has small green and cream leaves.

Other varieties *P. lanceolata* (**above**) sends out shoots in an ivy-like fashion. The leaves of *P. lanceolata* (**below left**) have broad, pale green stripes with tiny veins. In good health. *P. obtusifolia* (**left**) has strong leathery leaves, which are a deep purplish green colour. The stems of the plant are purple. The leaves of *P. orba* 'Princess Astrid' (**below**) are round and fleshy with fine veins.

PESTS AND DISEASES

It is fairly easy to tell when something is wrong with most peperomias. If the leaves of the plant turn dull and pale, it is receiving too much sun. If the leaves begin to drop off, the plant could be sitting in a cold draught. Leaves that develop what look like blisters are suffering from overwatering. Besides regulating the water supply, check to make sure the plant is not standing in water and that proper drainage is provided. Let the plant dry out thoroughly and water only moderately thereafter. There are many pests and diseases common to these plants.
Red spider mite These can be an occasional problem. On variegated types, red spider can be difficult to see and a magnifying glass might be necessary to locate them. This should be carried out regularly anyway, even if their presence is not suspected, because once the pests appear, they usually maintain a firm foothold. In advanced stages, the plant will have a thick, dry appearance. Close inspection at this point will probably reveal fine webs on the undersides of leaves and the stems of the plant. If the plant has not been badly infected, an insecticide may clear up the problem. If the plant is overrun with the pests, it could prove pointless to attempt total recovery. Drastic as it might seem, the best action is to burn the plant to prevent the pests from spreading onto other plants that might be nearby.

Botrytis Due to incorrect watering, the disease starts at the rotting base of the plant. When the fungus begins to flourish, there is little hope. Treat with fungicide as soon as it is noticed, and cut out any rotting leaves, which may infect other parts of the plant.

Philodendron

Philodendrons are certainly some of the most important foliage houseplants. Although there are a few variegated forms, they are mostly green to reddish brown in colour. Some are majestic and upright, others are radiating and equally majestic, while others creep along the ground.

All philodendrons produce aerial roots of some kind from their stems, or trunks, which are used in their natural jungle habitat for entwining around tree trunks, so enabling them to climb into the upper air. Besides their climbing facility these roots can also spread out over the floor of the jungle and provide the parent with nourishment and moisture. Bearing this in mind, it is important not to remove too many of these roots from plants that are growing indoors. It is much better to tie them neatly to the main stem of the plant or its support and allow the tip of the root to enter the soil when it is long enough. With the low-growing, radiating types, any very long roots can be wound around the base of the plant on top of the soil, while smaller roots can be encouraged to enter the soil by making a hole with a pencil and carefully inserting the root into it.

New plants can be raised by a variety of methods. The most productive is from seed that is reasonably easy to germinate in a temperature of around 70°F (21°C). The seed should be sown in shallow boxes or pans filled with peat and sand that is not allowed to dry out. Most seed will be large enough to sow at approximately ½in (1.25cm) intervals before being covered with a very thin layer of the propagating mixture. Seedlings can be left in the propagating mixture until they have made several small leaves, when they can be transferred to small pots filled with a peaty potting mixture.

Except for stockier, radiating types, propagation can be from pieces of stem with one or two leaves attached. A peat and sand mixture can be used and a temperature of around 70°F (21°C) is necessary if the plants are to do well.

Healthy varieties P. 'Red Emerald' (*top*) is a hybrid, noted for its burgundy-red leaves. It is a slower climber than other philodendrons, but makes up for this by an increased spread.

P. hastatum (*above*) is distinguished by its broad, spear-shaped leaves (*left*). These are bright green in colour and attached to long stalks. They must be staked if the plant is to remain erect. It can reach a height of 20ft (6m) in optimum conditions. P. scandens (*right*) is known as the Sweetheart Plant on account of its distinctive heart-shaped leaves. These can be allowed to climb or trail, depending on requirements. The plant does particularly well in hanging baskets, where the trailing effect of its growth is most attractive.

PROPAGATION

Remove 3–4in (7.5–10cm) tip cuttings.

Dip base of stem into hormone rooting powder and insert three to five cuttings per 3½in (9cm) pot.

Insert two canes in pot for support.

Cover cuttings with clear plastic bag.

The popular climbing sweetheart plant **Philodendron scandens** is one of the easier philodendrons to propagate successfully.

Once rooted, however, it is not very tolerant of disturbance, and it is therefore better to strike the cuttings in the pot in which they are to grow on in. Although the concentration of nutrients is lower in a seed and cutting compost, it is a more suitable medium to strike the cuttings in. Nutrients can always be supplemented after rooting with a liquid fertilizer.

Tip cuttings measuring 3–4in (7.5–10cm) may be removed with a sharp knife and inserted three to five to a 3½in (9cm) pot filled with seed and cutting compost. The base of the cuttings should first have been dipped in hormone rooting powder.

Keeping the compost reasonably moist, but not over-wetted, maintain a temperature of around 68°F (20°C) in moderate light, covering the cuttings with a clear plastic bag to improve humidity and reduce transpiration.

Within a month or so rooting should have taken place, and the plastic bag removed. Feed regularly with a liquid fertilizer and grow on, providing support as required.

Cuttings may be taken at any time from mid-spring through until early autumn, although plants produced earlier in the season will probably form more compact and better-shaped specimens.

Pest infection Mealy bugs have infested the undersides of this philodendron's leaves (*above*) and its stem (*below*). To cure the plant, spray the infested area thoroughly with insecticide as necessary.

Sooty mould The black marks (*right*) are an indication of sooty mould. This grows on sticky honeydew deposited by aphids and other pests. To cure, wipe the leaves with a damp cloth.

Leaf damage Slugs have found the leaves of this *P. scandens* tender to eat (*above* and *left*). There is also leaf spot (*above*), which may be the result of either scorch or lack of water. If other similar marks are on the plant, the chances are that they are natural. Deal with the slugs by putting poison around the base of the plant.

Too dry The brown marks on the leaf (*right*) are natural, but the leaf is drooping because the plant is too dry. Soak the plant in a bucket of water and allow it to drain. Also check you are feeding it enough.

PESTS AND DISEASES

Once in their final pots, most philodendrons need little more than regular feeding and watering. The larger the plant, the more food it will require, though only moderate amounts of water are needed. All philodendrons should be protected from direct sunlight, while they are happiest at around 65°F (18°C).

Mealy bug These can be troublesome on some plants as they get older, but, fortunately, the open growth of most philodendrons makes it easy to deal with the pests. Spray insecticide heavily and directly onto them.

Black leg This attacks cuttings during the propagation stage in unhygienic conditions. There is no cure so the cuttings must be burned.

Root failure Due to wet and cold conditions, this can cause the plant's collapse. The same can happen in too dry conditions, but this can be avoided with care.

Slugs These can be troublesome on plants with soft, tender leaves. Use a recommended slug repellant around the base of the plant to eradicate them.

AVOIDING PROBLEMS

Light and position

All philodendrons must be given locations that will provide them with protection from direct sunlight and draughts. Choose a suitable position for each type.

Radiating plants will need ample space around them. Place climbing and trailing species where they have enough height to grow.

Temperature range

Cool   Intermediate   Warm

Philodendrons will thrive best in temperatures between 60°-70°F (15°-21°C) but above all should not suffer a drop in temperature below 55°F (13°C). The maximum

summer temperature at which they are comfortable is 75°F (21°C) and at all times they will appreciate occasional mist-spraying.

Watering

Water these plants in the growing period enough to moisten the potting mixture and then allow the top layer of the soil to dry out before watering again. In the

short mid-winter rest period give them just enough water to prevent the soil from drying out completely.

Feeding

The larger the plant and the longer it has been in the same pot, the stronger or more frequent feeds it will require. For smaller plants,

best results are obtained by including weak fertilizer in the water each time the soil is moistened.

Seasonal care

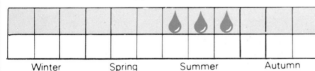

Winter   Spring   Summer   Autumn

These are plants for all seasons but they should be kept out of colder areas at all times. They have a short mid-winter rest period during which time they should have just enough water to

prevent the soil from drying out. Water in moderation for the rest of the year while the plants are in active growth and new shoots are being formed.

Soil

Use a peat-based mixture with some loam and pot on only when the roots completely fill the pot. Many of the larger plants (in pots over 10in (25cm) in diameter) are

best left where they are. Extremely large plants or those that will climb readily if tied to a stake should be started in tubs.

VARIETIES AND PURCHASING

Philodendrons are available throughout the year and are easy plants to handle and care for, as they do not require much in the way of special attention. One area in which they may need assistance is help in climbing. Here, wrapping a piece of dampened sphagnum moss around a stake so that the plant's aerial roots can cling to it is not only more attractive than training and tying, it is also better for the plant. Keep the moss moist and remember to apply enough to allow for the eventual growth of the plant. Your new plant should have no damaged or missing leaves. Remember, too, that the leaves of young plants can be entirely different in both size and shape when they reach maturity, so it is well worth a little research before you buy.

P. bipennifolium Commonly known as the Panda Plant, this is one of the many varieties whose leaves change as the plant becomes older. At first, they are heart shaped; as the plant matures, they shape themselves like a violin. The plant can grow to a height of 6ft (2m) and needs to be supported securely.

P. bipinnatifidum This is a radiating type, with fingered green leaves spreading from a central trunk. It can reach a

height of 10ft (3m), but this is seldom attained indoors. Its aerial roots are very strong. These should be directed into the soil when they are long enough. This will help support the trunk as well as providing added moisture and nourishment.

P. hastatum This is an attractive plant, with broad spear-shaped leaves, ideal for display. The stems of the plant must be supported with a stake.

P. 'Red Emerald' This hybrid has red stalks and stems. Its new leaves are totally red at first but, after a few weeks, the tops turn green.

P. scandens This is one of the easiest philodendrons to cultivate. Pinch out some of the growing tips regularly to stop the plant straggling.

P. wendlandii A non-climbing species, this has leaves arranged in the shape of a shuttlecock.

P. imbe A fast climber, this can reach a height of 8ft (2.5m) in a couple of years if it is supported securely. Its heart-shaped leaves are thin, but firm, in texture. They are carried on long stalks, which lead off vertically from the plant's stems, so the plant looks layered.

P. pedatum This is a slow climber, with shiny green leaves divided into five lobes.

This plant was produced by hydroculture.

Pilea

Many of these plants are compact, easy to propagate from cuttings, and not too difficult to manage. Cuttings can be taken at any time if suitable conditions are available. Sound pieces about 3in (7.5cm) in length should be taken from the ends of plant stems, and inserted in a peaty mixture at a temperature of 65°–70°F (18°–21°C). As an alternative to pure peat, the cutting can be inserted straight into 3in (7.5cm) pots filled with a good houseplant soil – at least five pieces should go into each pot.

Healthy plant Pileas come in creeping as well as upright varieties. They are popular for mixed displays because the different varieties encompass a wide range of size, colour and leaf texture. They look attractive when displayed with other small plants and they are suitable for bottlegardens. The *P. cadierei* or Aluminium Plant is perhaps the best known and it is relatively easy to care for. It can be distinguished by the silver patches on each leaf.

AVOIDING PROBLEMS

Light and position

Pileas flourish in shady surroundings and should never be placed near a bright light or in direct sunlight. They grow best in the summer, positioned at a short distance from a window.

Temperature range

Cool   Intermediate   Warm

These plants must be protected from cold draughts and they thrive in an atmosphere that is both hot and humid. It is not advisable to keep them in temperatures of less than 55°F (13°C) as they are unlikely to survive. Temperatures between 60°-70°F (15°-21°C) are much more suitable.

Watering

All varieties of pilea should be watered cautiously so that the potting mixture is damp throughout, without ever being sodden. The top half of the mixture or soil can be allowed to dry out before another watering is necessary. Pileas should never be completely immersed in water.

Feeding

Once they are well established, pileas should be fed each time they are watered. Although small, they are greedy plants, and they may need a stronger dosage than the fertilizer manufacturers usually recommend.

Seasonal care

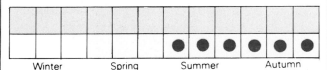

Winter   Spring   Summer   Autumn

Trimming and pruning should be done in the spring. However, the dead leaves should be removed regularly and the growing tips should be pinched out occasionally to ensure a bushy growth. Pileas may require slightly more water during the summer as this is the period of most growth. After three or four years these plants may become straggly and messy. When they start to deteriorate, cuttings should be taken and new plants propagated.

Soil

Potting mixtures without soil are suitable for pileas, and repotting should be done in the spring or summer. As small plants, they are displayed to their best advantage in half pots rather than full-size ones.

PROPAGATION

Remove 2½–3in (6–7.5cm) tip cuttings.

Gently remove lower leaf and dip into hormone rooting powder.

Gently dip cuttings into pot filled with seed and cutting compost.

Insert five cuttings per 3½in (9cm) pot.

Pilea is very easy to propagate: within a few weeks it is possible to produce a plant of worthwhile proportions. Although feasible to propagate from late spring to the end of summer it is better to propagate in mid- to late spring to produce a reasonable plant in a shorter time.

Pilea has a relatively low nutrient requirement; so it is possible to plant cuttings directly into a pot filled with seed and cutting compost. Using a sharp knife or pair of scissors, remove 2½–3in (6–7cm) tip cuttings. Dip the bottom of the stem into hormone rooting powder and insert five to a 3½in (9cm) pot. Although not essential, cover the cuttings to help improve their chances of taking if problems are encountered.

Maintain a temperature of 65–68°F (18–20°C) in a moderately lit position, keeping the compost hardly moist. Water when the compost begins to look dry, but do not allow it to dry right out or, conversely, to stay too wet.

Once rooting has started, within about a month, start to feed with dilute liquid plant food, increasing the rate to normal concentration after a further month or so.

To encourage the plant to become more compact and bushy the cuttings may be pinched back.

P. spruceana Two of the varieties in this strain are extremely popular as houseplants. The Silver Tree (*above*) is a short plant with upright growth, the common name deriving from the broad silver stripe of the leaf marking, (*left*). Markings on *P.s.* 'Norfolk' react quickly to the light, taking a warm tone in bright light and bluish when shaded.

VARIETIES AND PURCHASING

Fresh young plants should be selected in preference to larger ones. The latter may have used up all the goodness from the soil in which they are growing, and are more difficult to establish indoors.

P. cadierei Also known as the Aluminium Plant or Watermelon Plant, this is the most popular variety of pilea. It grows to approximately 1ft (30cm) in height, whereas the very similar dwarf variety, *P.c.* 'Minima' only ever reaches 6in (15cm).

P. involucrata This plant is more frequently called the Friendship Plant and it is thought by some to be identical to another pilea, *P. spruceana*. In the summer it should produce minute pink flowers, and it adapts to different conditions more easily than most of the other varieties.

P. mollis The leaves on this pilea have bronze markings, and are a brighter green than the leaves of *P. cadierei*. The rough surface of the leaves gave rise to the plant's common name, Moon Valley.

P. muscosa This pilea resembles a fern. It never grows higher than 10in (25cm) and usually blooms throughout the summer.

PESTS AND DISEASES

Pileas are not among those houseplants that are constantly prone to problems of this kind, but there are a few things that may trouble them from time to time. Although they are not particularly temperamental plants, strong, direct sun or cold draughts will inhibit them and cause damage. Leaves pressed against a windowpane during a cold winter are especially at risk and may turn black when chilled.

Mealy bug These are quite a common pest in pileas, mainly found among the lower stems of the plant. Left to their work, they will cause so much damage that in time the plant may lose its leaves completely. Mealy bugs are easy to see on the stems or under the leaves, being white against the green and brownish colouring of the foliage. Young bugs wrapped in their woolly protection are particularly visible. To treat the whole plant effectively immerse it in a bucket filled with malathion solution. If the infestation is very light, spray under the plant's leaves.

Red spider mite This is not usually troublesome but may occasionally be present and, when it is, must be dealt with immediately. Check regularly for spider mites by examining the undersides of leaves. Use a magnifying glass as the insects are tiny and easily missed. Because the foliage of a pilea is quite dense, immersion in a bucket of insecticide is the most effective treatment for this pest, as well as for the mealy bugs.

Botrytis This greyish-brown mould (*see illustration below*) attacks the leaves of the plant, causing them to rot. The whole plant may also become dusty looking. This fungal disease is encouraged by damp, cold conditions and exacerbated if dead leaves become trapped in the living foliage and start to rot. Treat botrytis by spraying the whole plant with dichloran, but first thoroughly clean away badly affected leaves and dead or rotten matter.

Botrytis This unpleasant fungus (*above*) has attacked a *P. cadierei* 'Nana', causing the whole plant to droop and have a generally dull appearance. Already the bottom leaves are grey-brown and rotting. Immediate spraying with dichloran is vital and rotted leaves must be removed.

241

PITTOSPORACEAE

Pittosporum

P. tenuifolium is native to New Zealand and is usually grown as a semi-hardy shrub, its foliage being used in the commercial flower trade as a useful material for including in flower arrangements. However, it is also an excellent potted plant, and there are numerous other improved varieties becoming available that should make these very fine foliage shrubs most popular. The pittosporum has woody stems and small leaves which are a glistening, glossy green, some with grey colouring in them, while others are overset with yellow, and many are attractively variegated.

VARIETIES

P. tenuifolium This has greyish green foliage. It develops into an erect, flourishing plant of about 5ft (1.5m).

P. garnetti This makes a neat ball of silver and grey variegated foliage. It is quite hardy outdoors.

P. eugenioides This may grow to 10–12ft (3–4m), but the grey leaves with white margins can be pruned back at any time.

PESTS AND DISEASES

Aphids These are not usually troublesome to this plant but they may affect new leaves. Spraying with malathion quickly controls them.

Red spider mite These are hard to spot underneath leaves but must be treated quickly with diazinon spray. Sooty mould can also cause problems (*See illustration below*).

Unhealthy leaves

Dehydration and exposure to bright sun through the glass of a window cause leaves to brown and curl at the edges (*left*). Water the plant and change its position if necessary. Sooty mould (*below*) is the result of secretions from scale insects. Wipe the leaves of the plant gently with malathion, or spray it on, and at the same time take steps to remove all the pests and their young.

AVOIDING PROBLEMS

Light and position

Good light, even quite bright sun, is necessary if the plants are to retain their leaves and keep their colour. Some protection may be needed if they are growing by the glass in a window, to prevent the leaves being scorched.

Temperature range

Cool · Intermediate · Warm

Avoid keeping a pittosporum in a warm atmosphere, it really prefers cool, airy conditions with a low temperature range of 50°-60°F (10°-15°C). Combining this with its need for bright light can be a problem in a hot summer, so if the plant usually lives in a window, remember to move it further into the room on very sunny days.

Watering

Water the plants thoroughly and regularly as they will suffer if allowed to become too dry. However, let the soil dry slightly before giving more water each time. A plant which is too dry will quickly revive again when it is watered.

Feeding

The plant can be given liquid fertilizer once a week in spring, summer and autumn, but reduce the feed in winter, giving it not more than once every three weeks.

Seasonal care

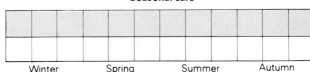

Winter · Spring · Summer · Autumn

Pittosporums are not the most demanding of plants and providing they get simple, regular attention throughout the growing season there is no reason why they should not do well. In summer, the plants can be placed outdoors in a sheltered place, but be sure to care for them as much as if they were indoors. Less attention is needed in winter, so reduce the frequency of feeding and watering.

Soil

Pot the plant firmly in loam-based mixture, but crock the bottom of the pot before putting in the soil. The pots should not be too large, to keep the growth in check, and by the time the plant has reached a 7in (17cm) pot it can remain there for three years.

Healthy plant Pittosporums are very attractive foliage plants, being bushy and strong when healthy. The glossy green leaves of *P. tenuifolium* are often cut for use in florists' arrangements. They can be bought at any time of year, and a better choice may be had from a retailer of outdoor shrubs, rather than a small houseplant shop. However, if the plant is at any time subject to a considerable change in conditions, try to break it in gradually or it may be unsettled. If the plant is kept in a light, airy place it will flourish. Some fairly new varieties of pittosporum have natural spots on their leaves, but the emergence of spotting during the life of a plant may indicate that it is being harmed by household sprays.

Pleomele

One of the finest of all foliage plants is *Pleomele reflexa variegata*. Commonly called Song of India, it produces short leaves that are congested on slightly twisting stems. The leaves are medium green when young but turn a rich golden-yellow as the plant ages. *Pleomele reflexa* is the green-leaved form. It is less branching in habit and generally less attractive.

Both *Pleomele reflexa* and *P. r. variegata* are very slow growing and will take upwards of 10 years to develop into attractive branching specimens 5ft (1.5m) tall. In early stages of growth, plants will grow on a single stem but will branch naturally as they age.

P. r. variegata needs a light location in order to retain its brightly coloured foliage. Plants need a minimum temperature of 65°F (18°C) and should be fed regularly during the summer. If soil is wet for long periods of time, plants will grow poorly and shed leaves. Pot on using a loam-based soil in early spring. Plants need free-draining soil, so place a few pieces of broken clay flowerpot in the base of the container prior to introducing the potting medium.

PLEOMELE

Light and position

Pleomeles need bright light out of direct sunlight. A position close to an east or west window is ideal.

Temperature range

Cool   Intermediate   Warm

A warm room temperature is essential for these plants. A minimum of 55°F (13°C) should be maintained throughout the winter months. Stand the pots on trays or saucers of moist gravel.

Watering

Keep the compost moist at all times, but reduce watering during winter. Let the top layer of soil dry out before rewatering.

Feeding

Give standard liquid fertilizer every two weeks during the active growing season—from spring to autumn.

Seasonal care

Winter   Spring   Summer   Autumn

Plants should be moved into pots one size larger every second or third spring. To propagate these plants, take tip cuttings or stem shoots and root in potting compost, using hormone rooting powder. Rooting plants should be kept warm and light for six months.

Soil

Use a loam-based soil mixture, with an admixture of one third rough leaf-mould and coarse peat moss.

Pleomeles (*above*) are very closely related to the dracaenas. The variegated form of this plant is particularly fine when displayed as a mature specimen. Good light is essential for growth.

Plumbago

The only species in the *Plumbago* genus that is grown indoors is *Plumbago capensis*. This plant produces lovely flowers throughout the summer and well into the autumn. Small leaves are attached to twiggy branches that grow rapidly if given suitable conditions and culture. Some support is needed, but the plant will rapidly cover a wall area, particularly if it has a free root run in the open border of the garden room.

The flowers of *Plumbago capensis* are a lovely powder-blue in colour, and there is also a white form, *P. capensis* 'Alba'. The latter is not quite so showy as the blue variety, but if both varieties are planted together the combination of blue and white is most attractive.

Overactive growth of the plumbago can be trimmed to shape at any time. At the end of the flowering season, cut the plant well back, down to a foot or two from the base of the plant if very vigorous; it will quickly refurbish itself in the spring. Pot on at that season, using a soil-based potting mixture. Unless fresh pieces of growth are needed for use as propagating material, all prunings should be burned.

Plumbago capensis (*above*) is a shrubby climbing plant producing clusters of trumpet-shaped, powder-blue flowers (*detail below*). The delicate colour of the flowers and the fact that it has a long flowering season make it a particularly pleasing houseplant.

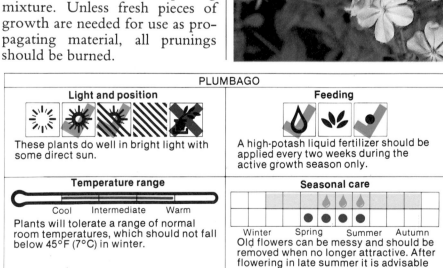

PLUMBAGO	
Light and position	**Feeding**
These plants do well in bright light with some direct sun.	A high-potash liquid fertilizer should be applied every two weeks during the active growth season only.
Temperature range	**Seasonal care**
Cool · Intermediate · Warm	Winter · Spring · Summer · Autumn
Plants will tolerate a range of normal room temperatures, which should not fall below 45°F (7°C) in winter.	Old flowers can be messy and should be removed when no longer attractive. After flowering in late summer it is advisable to cut stems down almost to pot level. Growth soon fills in again the following spring.
Watering	**Soil**
Keep compost moist at all times, but never allow plants to stand in water. Reduce watering during winter months.	Use loam-based soil when potting and re-pot when the plants are getting under way again in the spring.

Polyscias

Polyscias have small, rounded leaves attached to rather coarse, upright stems, which in the wild attain a height of 10ft (3m). However, plants rarely grow taller than 3ft (91cm) indoors, where they are prized for their decorative, variegated foliage.

There are several species of polyscias grown indoors, but the one most likely to be offered for sale is *P. balfouriana,* which has small, rather hard-looking leaves. These are attached to speckled, somewhat coarse stems. There are numerous varieties of *P. balfouriana,* differing mainly in the colour of the leaves. *P.b.* 'Marginata' has leaflets bordered in creamy white. *P.b.* 'Pennockii' has pale yellow-green markings along the veins.

Polyscias are not easy plants to grow. They have a marked tendency to shed lower leaves if watering is not properly controlled – the soil should be neither very dry nor very wet. The growing temperature should be at least 60°F (16°C), but if red spider mites are present, keep temperature under 70°F (21°C) to control them. Fertilize regularly during the spring and summer.

Polyscias are prized for their variegated foliage. *P. balfouriana* is the most readily available of the species that can be grown indoors, and *P. balfouriana* 'Marginata' (*above*) is a variety with leaf borders of creamy white. Care must be taken when watering these plants or they will shed their lower leaves.

POLYSCIA	
Light and position Choose a position in bright light, but out of direct sunlight, for these plants.	**Feeding** Standard liquid fertilizer should be applied every two weeks from early spring to late autumn.
Temperature range Cool Intermediate Warm These plants need warm temperatures above 65°F (18°C). You can maintain the right level of humidity by standing plants on trays or saucers of moistened pebbles.	**Seasonal care** Winter Spring Summer Autumn These slow-growing plants need little attention provided that their light and temperature needs are met. Repotting may be required every second or third spring, but plants should be examined for root development annually.
Watering Regular, but moderate, watering is advisable throughout the year. Let the top layer dry out before re-watering.	**Soil** A rich peaty mixture is suitable.

Primula

The wide variety of primulas have flowers that place them among the most delicate and beautiful of all the plants used for indoor decoration. Most are grown from seed, and will continue to flower for many months. *P. obconica* seems quite content to produce flowers throughout the whole year. However, it is sometimes known as the Poison Primula, because it can be a major problem for anyone with sensitive skin. It is possible for someone to become irritated by being in the same room as the plant, without actually touching it.

Healthy plant The best season for primulas is spring, and with their fresh colours and vibrant green leaves, they are appropriate symbols of the season. A group of plants with different coloured flowers makes a delightful display. To ensure that they are at their best, choose plants that are clean and fresh green in appearance with a few flowers showing and plenty of buds.

VARIETIES AND PURCHASING

There are many varieties of these most delicate and beautiful plants.

P. acaulis The flowers of this variety appear during the winter. They have no stalks and, nestling among the leaves, look very like primroses.

P. malacoides This is sometimes known as the Fairy Primrose. Slender stems above clusters of pale green leaves support the star-shaped flowers, which may be red, pink or white. The plants may grow up to 18in (45cm) tall.

P. obconica This is often called the Poison Primula because of its effect on people with sensitive skins who may come out in a rash after contact with the plant. However, for those who are immune, it is a very good houseplant, being quite strong and producing flowers almost continuously throughout the year. It is less delicate in appearance than other varieties.

PESTS AND DISEASES

Aphids The soft foliage of the primula is vulnerable to all sucking insects, but aphids are the most troublesome. They may be detected by the white 'skeletons' that they shed when moulting. If they are not dealt with rapidly, the flowers and leaves may become distorted and sticky. Any reliable insecticide will control them.

Red spider mite It is essential to inspect the undersides of the leaves regularly, as if red spiders go unnoticed for too long, they can do great damage. They are encouraged by hot, dry conditions, so if primulas are kept in a moist, cool environment, which in any case suits them better, they are less likely to attract these pests. If red spiders do infest the plant, it must be treated with a recommended insecticide immediately, with particular attention being paid to the undersides of the leaves.

Vine weevils These are sometimes seen on the foliage, but it is the maggots in the soil that do most of the damage. If they do occur, the soil should be drenched with an insecticide solution.

Botrytis (*see illustrations below*) Plants may contract this disease if they are in poor cultural conditions, particularly when there is poor air circulation. It causes wet patches on the leaves, or, if the plant is potted too deeply, its entire centre may be affected.

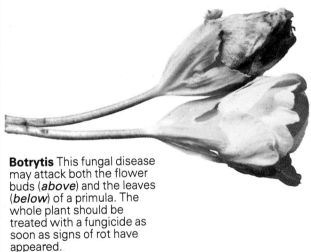

Botrytis This fungal disease may attack both the flower buds (*above*) and the leaves (*below*) of a primula. The whole plant should be treated with a fungicide as soon as signs of rot have appeared.

AVOIDING PROBLEMS

Light and position

Primulas need plenty of light but should be kept out of direct sunlight. As the plants should be kept moist, it is a good idea to plunge their pots to the rim in larger containers filled with moisture-retaining moss or peat.

Temperature range

Cool Intermediate Warm

Primulas like a fairly cool environment, between 50°-60°F (10°-15°C), especially when they are in flower. If the room temperature exceeds 60°F (15°C), the flowers are liable to fall more quickly. If the plants must be temporarily kept in a warmer environment, it is important to provide them with added humidity by standing them on trays of moistened pebbles and spraying their leaves.

Watering

Primulas thrive on plentiful supplies of water. Water copiously, ensuring that the potting mixture is thoroughly moist. However, care must be taken to ensure that the plant is not actually standing in water.

Feeding

From the time when the first flower stalks start to appear the plants should be fed every two weeks with a weak solution of standard fertilizer. This will extend the flowering period as long as possible.

Seasonal care

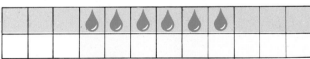

| Winter | Spring | Summer | Autumn |

Although sodden soil is harmful, plants should be kept moist at all times. It is possible to prolong the flowering period by picking the dead flowers as soon as they fade. *P. malacoides* is an annual but *P. obconica* can be potted on to flower more freely the following year. After *P. acaulis* has flowered it can be planted in the garden.

Soil

If on purchase the plants appear to be pot-bound, they should be repotted into larger pots immediately to give them room for development. Use a loam-based mixture and do not ram the soil into the pots too firmly.

248

Rhoicissus

The rhoicissus is among the toughest of all the dark green foliage plants, and when all else fails it could well be the best plant to try to establish indoors. It is a climbing plant with tri-lobed, glossy green leaves. Although it does not produce any flowers, it is invaluable for covering wall areas in difficult corners.

New plants are raised from 3–4in (7.5–10cm) cuttings and inserted in peat in a temperature of around 70°F (21°C).

VARIETIES AND PURCHASING

Look for a plant with full, unblemished, green foliage. Yellowing is a sign of poor culture.

R. rhomboidea This is the original Grape Ivy and is one of the toughest houseplants. It is ideally suited to climbing if you provide a framework.

R. rhomboidea 'Ellendanica' This recent variation has slightly waved indentations around the leaf margins.

Mealy bug The fluffy white young of the mealy bug are usually easy to see, looking like tiny lumps of cotton wool stuck on the stems or leaves of the plant (*below*). The adults have a powdery texture and resemble pale woodlice. If the infestation is not too advanced, treat the bugs with a sponge soaked in malathion, wearing rubber gloves to protect your hands. If there are many bugs, spray the plant thoroughly instead.

Healthy plant The rhoicissus is an elegant plant and really quite easy to care for; if it is allowed to climb or trail it will attractively fill an awkward corner where other plants have failed. The growth can be trained to a framework set in the pot, but as the plant can grow to 10ft (3m), it is very effective in a stairwell or supported against a wall. It is a resilient plant, and should it have suffered from poor culture or neglect, should recover quickly when given the right conditions.

PESTS AND DISEASES

Mealy bug These powdery white bugs and their young may infest congested growth in older plants (*see illustration above*). Spray the plant with malathion or soak a sponge with solution and wipe the bugs away.

Root mealy bug Similar to the leaf bugs, these attack the roots of a plant that has stayed in one pot for a long time. Water malathion solution into the soil.

Scorched leaf Browning at the tip is a sign of scorching or overwatering.

Healthy leaves The two rhoicissus varieties have quite similar leaves (*above*).

Scorched leaf Browning at the tip is a sign of scorching or overwatering.

AVOIDING PROBLEMS

Light and position

These plants will enjoy a bright or lightly shaded position, but cannot tolerate exposure to direct, strong sun. Provided it is not subjected to this or to cold draughts, it will do well almost anywhere.

Temperature range

Cool Intermediate Warm

The rhoicissus copes with lower temperatures but really prefers a range of 60°-70°F (15°-21°C). It will benefit from light spraying in summer, when warmer conditions are prevalent, but is extremely adaptable and in winter will even put up with fumes from oil or gas heating appliances.

Watering

Water the plant well in summer and during the period of active growth, but check the condition of the soil carefully as overwatering may damage the plant, causing the leaves to droop and even rot completely. Reduce watering in winter when the temperature is cool.

Feeding

Once established, the plants require frequent feeding. Give liquid food in the water at least once a week while in active growth. Reduce or discontinue the feeding when the plant is dormant in winter.

Seasonal care

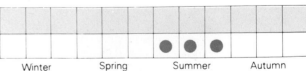

Winter   Spring   Summer   Autumn

The plants require no more than the usual care, with the soil kept moist but not sodden under any conditions. Untidy growth may be trimmed back in the autumn and if young shoots at the top of the stems are pinched out regularly, a healthy, bushy growth will result. Take cuttings in spring or early summer, using growing tips furnished with a couple of full leaves.

Soil

Annual potting is necessary, transferring the plant to a slightly larger container each time until the plant is in a 10in (25cm) pot. Then sustain the plant with regular feeding and change just the topsoil occasionally, using a loam-based mixture.

Saintpaulia

Although these plants are generally difficult to manage, this does not seem to be a deterrent, as worldwide they are among the most popular of all the potted flowering houseplants. The leaves are mostly rounded, hairy and attached to short stalks that sprout from soil level, forming a neat rosette that is a background for the flowers when they appear. Flowers of many colours are now available in single and double forms, and a collection of plants growing in ideal conditions will provide a display of flowers throughout the year. Plants can be propagated from individual leaves with stalk attached. These are put into clean peat in a propagating case in a temperature of not less than 70°F (21°C).

VARIETIES AND PURCHASING

The wide variety of African Violets available today vary in colour and in flower shape and formation. However, a few points should be borne in mind when buying. Select a plant with firm, non-drooping leaves, and, if possible, avoid purchasing from cold premises. Plants with blemishes on the foliage and sign of root or stem rot should always be passed over. Try to choose a plant that is in bud, as this will afford more lasting pleasure than one in full flower.

S. ionantha This is the only variety of African Violet in cultivation. All the many examples commercially available are hybrids of *S. ionantha*.

Healthy plant The African Violet (*above*) is one of the most popular flowering houseplants. It is available in a wide variety of colours and flower shapes. This example of *S. ionantha* 'Rococo' has pink flowers and double blooms.

251

AVOIDING PROBLEMS

Light and position

The African Violet requires good light and will tolerate direct sunlight so long as this is not magnified by the glass of a greenhouse or windowpane. It is important that this plant should be protected from all draughts.

Temperature range

Cool   Intermediate   Warm

A good nursery will not sell African Violets until the milder weather has arrived. They are plants which do not like being chilled and flourish in a temperature of 65°-70°F (18°-21°C). The warmth and humidity of bathrooms and kitchens provide ideal conditions for growth.

Watering

During the summer, spray plants occasionally with a fine mist of rainwater. Hard water causes white spots and patches on the foliage. In cold weather, water sparingly; if kept slightly dry plants will often survive in low temperatures.

Feeding

It is important that the leaves of this plant should be kept as dry as possible when feeding. Add a liquid fertilizer to the soil when watering, taking care to use a weak solution regularly rather than giving an occasional large feed.

Seasonal care

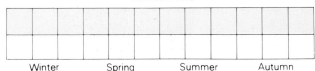

Winter   Spring   Summer   Autumn

The main difference in the care of the saintpaulia from season to season is in the amount of water required. Throughout the year, the plant should never be overwatered, but in cold weather it is even more important not to allow the soil to become too wet. Use tepid rather than cold water at all times. Remove dead flowers and leaves as soon as you notice them.

Soil

In general, small pots are more suitable than large ones. African Violets flourish in peat-based potting composts. A soil-less mixture is also suitable but if used it must be kept sufficiently moist.

Fungal diseases
Overwatering can lead to problems with African Violets, such as mildew (*above*) and botrytis (*below*). Never overwater. Treat outbreaks with fungicide.

PESTS AND DISEASES

The recent varieties of African Violet tend to be tougher than their predecessors, but care still needs to be taken when caring for the plants. Overwatering and wetting the leaves can cause problems.

Root rot Most types of root rot are aggravated by wet soil conditions, which prevent oxygen reaching the roots of the plant. Affected roots are brown and lifeless. In the early stages, treat by allowing the plant to dry out and to stay dry for several days. In an advanced state, the whole plant collapses and the leaves go limp. At this stage the plant must be destroyed.

Mildew This should be treated with a suitable fungicide such as dichloran.

Botrytis This fungus disease should also be treated with fungicide. If the attack is severe, destroy the plant.

Aphids These insects may attack the plant's soft, tender leaves. Treat with a systemic insecticide, and avoid wetting the leaves if possible. If the leaves are wet, do not place the plant in the sun.

Cyclamen mite Although generally uncommon, this pest can be fatal as there is no known cure. The plant should be burned so that the pest cannot spread.

Sansevieria

The common name of Mother–in–Law's Tongue is given to the best known of the these plants, *S. trifasciata* 'Laurentii', which has upright fleshy leaves that are mottled green in the centre and margined with a broad band of yellow. Occasionally plants will be seen without the yellow band, which indicates that they have been grown from a leaf section cutting, rather than from divided plants, which will retain the yellow leaf margin.

Young plants will retain their leaf colouring if they are propagated by removing well–developed plantlets from around the parent stem with as much root attached as possible.

Healthy plant *S. trifasciata* 'Laurentii', or Mother-in-Law's Tongue, is a tall-growing variety with striped, beautifully marbled leaves up to 3ft (1m) high. The leaves have spiny tips, which should not be damaged as this will prevent the leaf growing. The healthy plant will grow slowly but will last for years. It must be well rooted to save it from toppling over. The Mother-in-Law's Tongue will tolerate a wide range of conditions, enjoying high temperatures and direct sunlight. It should not be overwatered or overfed. Sansevierias are loved both because they are easy to care for and also because they create a simple and dramatic sculptural effect.

VARIETIES AND PURCHASING

Sansevierias are one of the most popular houseplants. They are long-lived, inexpensive and easy to care for, being well suited to thrive in rooms with central heating. They are also one of the simplest plants to use to dramatic effect – either by themselves or with a group of other plants. These plants originate in West Africa and are named after an eighteenth-century Italian prince, Raimondo di Sangro of San Severo. About 50 species are found in the wild but only five or six are grown as indoor plants, although new types have recently been created. The genus has two basic types – tall-growing and low-growing – all with stiff, pointed leaves, marbled or striped in green, golden-yellow or white. The tall-growing types easily become top heavy, and it is important to choose one that is well rooted, and potted in a heavy clay pot. All of these plants should have unblemished leaves with clean, sharp edges and the spiny tips of the leaves must be intact or they will not grow.

S. trifasciata Varieties of this plant are the best known of this genus.

St. t. 'Laurentii' This is the most popular variety. The tall, sword-shaped leaves edged with yellow and marbled with hues of green can reach 3ft (1m).

S.t. 'Moonshine' This is a quite new variety, which has apparently iridescent tall, pale green leaves edged with a very dark fine line.

S.t. 'Hahnii' One of the low-growing varieties, this has a rosette of stiff, sharply pointed leaves about 6in (25cm) in height.

S.t. 'Golden Hahnii' Also low-growing, this is more spectacular, with bright golden margins to its leaves.

S.t. 'Silver Hahnii' This has silver-green leaves lightly speckled with dark green. Three other species can be grown easily indoors: these are *S. cylindrica*, *S. liberica* and *S. zeylanica*.

PROPAGATION

Sansevieria Trifasciata Golden 'Hahnii'. This compact form of mother-in-law's tongue is a lower-growing variety which may be propagated from offsets or by leaf cuttings.

However, as the character of this variety could be adversely affected by splitting off offsets it is perhaps better to propagate by sections of leaves, even though this technique is certainly a great deal slower. Simply remove appropriate leaves with a sharp knife, taking care not to damage any other leaves and not to spoil the appearance of the mother plant. Cut the leaf horizontally to form 2in (5cm) pieces, and make sure you place them down the right way up to avoid propagating them upside down.

Dip the base of the cut leaf into hormone rooting powder and insert up to five or six cuttings in a 5½in (14cm) half-pot filled with cacti and succulent compost.

Keeping the compost barely moist, maintain a temperature of 68–70°F (20–21°C) in a well-lit situation. After several weeks, and perhaps even two or three months, each leaf should produce a new plantlet. When these are about 2in (5cm) tall, pot up singly in a 2½in (6cm) pot.

Gently remove plant from pot.

Carefully tease clumps apart to separate distinct plants.

Use sharp knife to cleanly cut and part the offset from the parent.

Dip base into hormone rooting powder and insert in 3½in (9cm) pot.

Remove leaf at base with sharp knife.

Cut leaf into 2in (5cm) pieces, cutting horizontally across leaf blade.

Take care not to invert pieces of leaf.

Dip base of cut surface into hormone rooting powder and insert five to six leaves

Sansevieria Trifasciata 'Laurentii'. Although, like *Sansevieria trifasciata* 'Hahnii', this variety of mother-in-law's tongue may be propagated from leaf cuttings (or rather sections of leaf cuttings) as well as from offsets, it is most unwise to propagate from sections of leaf. A plant successfully produced by this method will lack the yellow stripe that runs the length of the leaf on either side and will look far less interesting.

It is, therefore, preferable to propagate *Sansevieria trifasciata* 'Laurentii' from offsets. From late spring to mid-summer, when the plant is capable of withstanding a certain amount of disturbance, remove it from its pot and, by a process of careful teasing and cutting, remove offsets that are about 8in (20cm) tall or at least about half of the size of the parent.

Pot up each piece in a 3½in (9cm) pot of cacti and succulent compost, taking care to plant the offset at a similar level at which it was growing.

Keep the offset in a well-lit position and do not over-water, rather trying to keep the compost barely moist and allowing it almost to dry out between waterings.

A stable temperature of 65–70°F (18–21°C) will help the offset to establish reasonably easily.

AVOIDING PROBLEMS

Light and position

Sansevierias thrive in good light and will do well on a sunny windowsill in a bright room. They will also tolerate partial shade but will stop growing in complete shade. Plants that have been left in the shade for a long time should be moved into full sunlight by gradual stages.

Temperature range

Cool Intermediate Warm

These plants, natives of the tropics, thrive in summer temperatures of 65°-80°F (18°-27°C). They will also survive at temperatures of 55°F (13°C) but will not continue to grow below 60°F (15°C). Between 55°-60°F (13°-15°C) make sure that the soil is almost dry and, above all, protect these plants from extremes of cold.

Watering

In the growing period water Sansevierias in such a way as to moisten the whole pot but allow the top layers of the mixture to dry out in between waterings. In the rest period wait until the top half of the mixture has dried out before watering again. Do not overwater.

Feeding

Use a liquid fertilizer once every three or four weeks in the growing period but at only half the normal strength. Do not allow the feed to spot the leaves and take care not to overfeed.

Seasonal care

Winter Spring Summer Autumn

These very easy plants can be left alone in a warm room with a good light for the whole year with some water and very little feeding in the growing period. They will thrive at 65°-80°F (18°-27°C) all the year round without damage but should be protected from temperatures below 55°F (13°C) at all times. New plants can be grown in two ways. Either break away one of the offshoots with its section of rhizome and pot it or take a leaf, strip it into 2in (5cm) pieces, and plant them upright several to a pot.

Soil

Use a loam-based mixture and ideally use a heavier than usual pot as these plants will easily become top heavy. Place plenty of crocks, broken pieces of pot, in the base to ensure good drainage. Sansevierias like to be root-bound and will need repotting only when the pot breaks.

Dry leaf It is a great pity to spoil the elegant lines of this fine plant by simple errors in its care. The dried leaf (*left*) is quite rare because these plants usually thrive in high temperatures. Like all plants from tropical zones, however, they can suffer when too much direct heat is concentrated on a leaf. One way this can happen is if the plant is put where frosted glass focuses the sun's rays or immediately in front of a radiator. It may also be caused by the habit of these plants to become top-heavy and then topple over, touching the windowpane. Always give the plant a pot with a good solid base and water regularly, if sparsely.

PESTS AND DISEASES

Pests rarely attack these plants and most problems are caused by poor culture.
Basal stem rot This is caused by overwatering. The main stem of the plant becomes wet and mushy and if it is left untreated the plant will fall over and die. Reduce watering and keep the centre of the plant free from moisture.
Brown patches on leaves These are also usually caused by overwatering. Water less often but do not let the plant dry out.
Damaged leaf edges These suggest that the plant is not firmly fixed in its pot. Place the pot inside a large container and if the leaves are scorched move the plant away from the window.
Loss of colour This indicates a lack of light. Move nearer to the window.
Mealy bug Sometimes these pests attack this plant. Wipe off the white woolly patches with a piece of cotton wool dipped in methylated spirits or spray with a systemic insecticide or malathion.
Vine weevils If these start to eat away the edges of the leaves spray immediately with lindane insecticide.

Saxifraga sarmentosa

These are natural trailing plants that produce perfectly shaped plantlets on slender strands that hang down and give the plant its common name. 'Thousands' is a little exaggerated, but young plants are produced in large quantities none the less.

New plants are the easiest things in the world to propagate. Any plantlets should be allowed to develop into a reasonable size and then removed and put individually in small pots.

Healthy plant The Mother of Thousands is a popular and attractive hanging plant. It has rounded shaped leaves of different sizes and trailing reddish shoots.

AVOIDING PROBLEMS

Light and position

Ideally, these plants should be suspended in hanging pots or small baskets in a window area where they will get plenty of light. They must be protected from strong direct sunlight however, as this can burn the foliage. Larger plants also look very effective on slender pedestals with the plantlets trailing down.

Temperature range

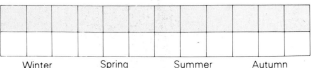

Cool   Intermediate   Warm

The Mother of Thousands grows well in cool conditions, but will survive in any temperature between 55°-75°F (13°-23°C). If the plant is being kept in fairly warm surroundings, a high level of humidity is advisable.

Saxifrages must be protected from draughts and will not tolerate continual shade. If they are never exposed to any sunlight the leaves will become discoloured.

Watering

These plants should be watered regularly, so that the potting mixture stays moist without ever being too wet. Less water is required during the winter period, as there is more danger of root rot at this time.

Feeding

Saxifrages benefit from a weak concentration of food whenever the plant is watered. Fertilizer in tablet form is the ideal nutrient for hanging plants. It can be pressed into the soil and will last for several weeks as long as the soil is watered regularly.

Seasonal care

Winter	Spring	Summer	Autumn

It is a good idea to remove any dead and dying leaves during the autumn period. The Mother of Thousands plant tends to become rather straggly by the end of the summer period, particularly if the weather has been very warm. In the spring months, these plants can be moved into larger pots as necessary. It is not worth preserving these plants for more than about three years as they become messy looking, and are very easy to propagate.

Soil

Soil-less mixtures are fine provided you do not forget to water the plants. Once they have dried out however, they are difficult to moisten thoroughly again, and for this reason a loam-based mixture is recommended for these hanging plants. This mixture should feel light and spongy.

VARIETIES AND PURCHASING

It is important to select plants that are free of blemishes. The underside of the foliage should be checked thoroughly for any signs of pest infestation. If the saxifrages are wanted for hanging pots, it is advisable to purchase several small plants and pot them together. Larger hanging pots are more pleasing as well as being easier to keep moist. *S. sarmentosa,* or *S. stolonifera*, is easily the most popular type of saxifrage available today.

PESTS AND DISEASES

Red spider mite The dark red colouring of the underside of this plant's leaf is perfect camouflage for this pest. Leaves should be inspected with a magnifying glass. It is difficult to spray the undersides of the smaller overlapping leaves, so immerse the affected plant in a bucket of insecticide for several minutes. Rubber gloves should be worn.

Mealy bug These pests are powdery white in colour and they wrap their young in a waxy covering resembling cotton wool. To ensure that the young of both spider mite and mealy bug are eliminated, it is advisable to repeat the immersing exercise at 10-day intervals until the plant is clean. Saxifrage plants may also suffer from botrytis or aphids.

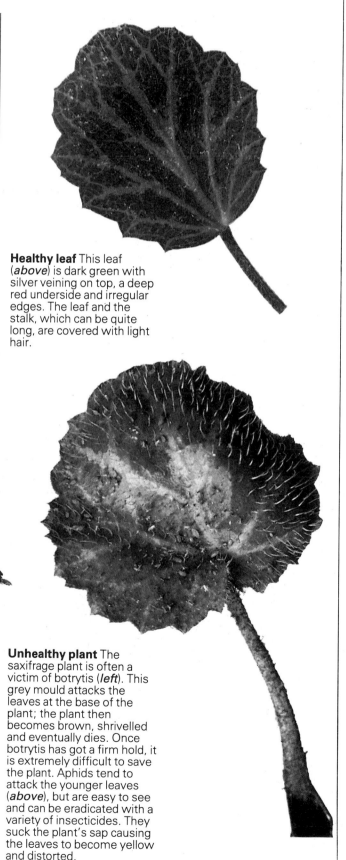

Healthy leaf This leaf (*above*) is dark green with silver veining on top, a deep red underside and irregular edges. The leaf and the stalk, which can be quite long, are covered with light hair.

Unhealthy plant The saxifrage plant is often a victim of botrytis (*left*). This grey mould attacks the leaves at the base of the plant; the plant then becomes brown, shrivelled and eventually dies. Once botrytis has got a firm hold, it is extremely difficult to save the plant. Aphids tend to attack the younger leaves (*above*), but are easy to see and can be eradicated with a variety of insecticides. They suck the plant's sap causing the leaves to become yellow and distorted.

Schefflera

Belonging to the same family as the heptapleurum, the schefflera grows in a similar way, but is a very much more robust houseplant. In some parts of the world it is known as *Brassaia actinophylla* while in Britaïn it is known as *S. actinophylla*. In tropical regions the schefflera grows to become a substantial tree, given the name Umbrella Tree because its foliage radiates like the spokes of an umbrella. These plants are strong growing and they may, in time, achieve a height of around 15ft (5m).

New plants are almost invariably raised from seed, which is started into growth in temperatures of around 70°F (21°C).

Healthy plant The schefflera is an excellent plant for people who are unwilling or unable to provide constant care and attention. Able to withstand most environmental conditions, in an ideal situation it will grow to a strapping height of 8ft (2.5m). When young, *S. actinophylla* can be quite unattractive, with spindly stems and over-sized leaves. When full grown, however, the plant becomes a handsome specimen with rich, glossy leaves exploding outwards from the top of each stem.

VARIETIES

Each type of schefflera is slightly different in size and appearance and should be purchased according to where it is to be situated. If, for example, the plant is to be the focal point of a room, then a full-sized plant is best because scheffleras can take a while to reach their full adult height. For all types, the health of the plant can be determined by the condition of its leaves. Purchase plants whose leaves are free of blemishes, firm and supple and not drooping. The leaves should be rich and glossy.
S. actinophylla This is the most common and largest variety available. Look for one that has well-shaped and proportioned leaves. Scheffleras today are often sold under the name *Brassaia*.

PESTS AND DISEASES

While scheffleras are prone to the pests and diseases common to all houseplants, they are also less likely to contract them.
Aphids Often a problem on young leaves, a commercial insecticide will clear up the problem quite easily.
Red spider mite This pest tends to be found on plants growing in hot, dry environments. Light brown leaf discoloration is a sign of their presence. To cure, use a recommended insecticide, which should be sprayed on the undersides of the leaves at weekly intervals.
Mealy bug This is mostly seen on older plants. Because the bugs are easily seen, they can be treated with a commercial insecticide.

AVOIDING PROBLEMS

Light and position

The Umbrella Tree is an accommodating plant that will tolerate many locations but prefers light shade or indirect sunlight. Young plants can be mixed in with other houseplants, but full-grown plants are best viewed when they are standing alone as a special feature.

Temperature range

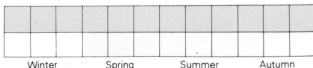

Cool   Intermediate   Warm

To keep the Umbrella Tree happy, reasonable warmth of around 60°-70°F (15°-21°C) is needed, 65°F (18°C) being about right. These plants also like humidity, so avoid dry heat. If the room in which they are situated is dry, place the plants in pots in shallow trays filled with pebbles and water.

Watering

The larger the plant, the more water it will require, except in winter when it becomes inactive. Keep the soil moist at all times.

Good drainage is essential. A pointed stick can be used to loosen the top of the soil to assist drainage.

Feeding

At all stages of development, a proprietary liquid fertilizer can be used with every watering. As the plant develops, two different fertilizers can be used to satisfy the plant's various needs.

Seaspnal care

Winter	Spring	Summer	Autumn

The soil of the Umbrella Tree should be kept moist at all times of the year, but only minimum watering is required during the winter months. The plants can be propagated in late winter from either seed or stem cuttings. Pot at any time except in winter when the plant is vulnerable to damage and radical changes in environment.

Soil

In four years' time, the robust Umbrella Tree may well need a pot 10in (25cm) in diameter. Once in a large pot, the potting mixture should sustain the plant for a number of years. A good mixture contains a fair amount of loam, but should not be too heavy.

PROPAGATION

Remove 3–4in (7.5–10cm) tip cutting.

Dip base of stem into hormone rooting powder and insert in 2½–3½in (6–9cm) pot.

Cover cutting with clear plastic bag.

The **schefflera** or umbrella plant may be propagated in mid- to late spring from seed, tip or stem cuttings.

If seed can be obtained it should be sown thinly in mid-spring in a tray or pan of seed and cutting compost, and germinated at about 68°F (20°C). Seedlings should be pricked out when large enough to handle, approximately 1–1½in (2.5–4cm), into a 2½in (6cm) pot of potting compost and grown on in good light.

Alternatively, tip or stem cuttings measuring 3–4in (7.5–10cm) should be removed with secateurs or pruning shears, dipped into hormone rooting powder and inserted one cutting per pot in a 2½–3½in (6–9cm) pot of seed and cutting compost.

Cover with a clear plastic bag and keep in reasonable light, but out of direct sunlight, at a temperature of 70–75°F (21–24°C). The compost should be moist, but not too wet, to prevent rotting off.

After approximately one month, when rooting should have occurred and new growth should have started, the plastic bag may be removed and the plant weaned and grown on sufficiently until a well-formed root structure has been developed.

The plant may then be potted on in a 5in (13cm) pot of potting compost and staked, if necessary, to produce a straight-stemmed plant.

Scindapsus

The scindapsus is one of the most remarkable foliage plants of them all. From being tender and difficult to care for a decade or so ago, they are now among the most rewarding of indoor plants. Obviously a tougher selected strain has been developed to make the radical change possible and today the scindapsus is a decorative plant with mustard and green variegation that is tolerant of a wide range of conditions in the home. Even when placed at the furthest point from the light source, the variegation is rarely affected – a quality that is unusual in most plants with variegated foliage.

Propagation is done vegetatively by inserting pieces of firm stem with two good leaves attached. A temperature of about 70°F (21°C) and a peat and sand mixture that is kept moist, but not waterlogged, are required.

Healthy plant There are about 20 species of scindapsus, each with a characteristic tendency to wrap itself around the nearest object. All the varieties can be grown either upright on a pole, or in a hanging basket.

VARIETIES

Scindapsus plants come in many shapes and sizes and most shops will have a selection. Some will be displayed as climbing, others trailing. Choose plants with firm leaves that stand out cleanly from the stem. Ignore any with curled, drooping leaves.
S. aureus (*above*). This is a green and mustard variegated plant, and probably the best buy. It may also be sold as Pothos.
S. a. 'Marble Queen' This plant (*above right*) has marbled white and green foliage. It is more difficult to care for than other types.

PESTS AND DISEASES

Some problems scindapsus is prone to include:
Botrytis (*see illustration below*). This causes wet, brown patches on the leaves. Remove any leaves that are infected.
Aphids These are found on the leaves of young plants. Wipe with insecticide.
Mealy bug Treat the bugs with methylated spirits.

AVOIDING PROBLEMS

Light and position

All scindapsus plants abhor strong, direct light. They also do not like shade, except for *S. aureus* which will maintain its distinctive yellow streaks if kept in low light. Bright, indirect light is ideal for most types. The plants can be grown in either a trailing or an upright fashion.

Temperature range

Cool   Intermediate   Warm

In their active period, these plants prosper in normal room temperatures between 60°-70°F (15°-21°C), 65°F (18°C) being ideal. In winter, a temperature of 60°F (15°C) will give the plant a chance to rest, and they can tolerate a temperature of 50°F (10°C). If the room is dry as well as warm, stand the plants in their pots on trays of pebbles and water.

Watering

The scindapsus does not like to be overwatered and should be allowed to dry out between waterings. During active growth water moderately. In winter, when the plant is dormant, water only enough to keep the potting mixture slightly moist.

Feeding

Being fairly sturdy, the scindapsus does not need large amounts of fertilizer. Small, established plants should have a weak feed with each watering. Larger plants will welcome a stronger dosage. During active growth, apply a liquid fertilizer every two weeks.

Seasonal care

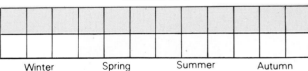

Winter   Spring   Summer   Autumn

Keep the potting mixture moist throughout the year by watering every four or five days in summer and every seven to eight days in winter. Prune in early spring. If a bushier plant is desired, prune the main growth well back.

Stem cuttings can be rooted in spring in either water or soil. The plants can be moved to a pot one size larger each spring. When the maximum size has been reached, replenish the topsoil rather than repotting.

Soil

Avoid putting plants in pots too large for their size. When repotting, the new pots should be only 1-2in (2.5-5cm) larger. Use a soil-based potting mixture with a small amount of loam added. When propagating, plant cuttings in a moistened mixture of peat moss and coarse sand.

Sinningia

This plant should really be referred to by its proper name, *Sinningia speciosa,* but its common name rolls off the tongue much more easily. Commercially, Gloxinias are raised annually from seed sown early in the year. As the year progresses the seedlings develop a corm and in time the plants find their way to a retailer. Following flowering indoors, the plant will die down naturally in the autumn and, if kept dry at a winter temperature of around 55°F (13°C), the corm can be retained until the following spring. Then it can be planted to produce a bigger and better plant. The corm should have all the dry soil removed from around it and be potted almost to its full depth in a houseplant potting mixture, with the rounded side of the corm going into the soil. This should be kept fairly dry until new growth is under way, when water can gradually be given more generously.

VARIETIES

S. speciosa This comes in many different forms. When the plants are fully grown they should have one or two of their spectacular, trumpet-shaped flowers open, but the chief thing to look for is an ample supply of buds that will flower during the coming weeks. To produce the maximum number of flowers, use a high potash fertilizer with each watering, rather than a nitrogen-based product.

Botrytis This is a fungus disease that often attacks plants that have been planted too closely together in dank conditions. The signs are wet blotches on leaves (*below*). If left untreated, the whole plant will rot and eventually disintegrate. Remove any infected leaves immediately and treat the plant with a recommended fungicide.

PROPAGATION

Sinningia Speciosa, commonly known as the gloxinia this spectacular, somewhat delicate plant may be propagated from leaf cuttings, division of the clump or from seed.

Commercially, plants are raised from seed and this method is probably the best technique to try, although plants can relatively easily be raised from leaf cuttings.

Division of the plant may be carried out in mid-spring, but this can be difficult as the plant is very fleshy and damage may easily be caused, resulting in a fungal infection which could cause subsequent loss.

Leaf cuttings taken in early summer should consist of healthy, developed leaves that are not too old or large. These should be carefully removed from the plant with a sharp knife, and the stem trimmed to a length of about 1½–2in (4–5cm). Once the base of the stem has been dipped in hormone rooting powder, the leaf may then be inserted in a 3½in (9cm) pot of peat-based potting compost.

The cutting should then be enclosed in a clear plastic bag and kept at 68–70°F (20–21°C) in reasonable light until rooted; this should take four to six weeks. A small tuber will then develop from which a plantlet will form. Grow on the plantlet, carefully weaning the plant out of its bag by gradually increasing the ventilation.

Leaf cuttings may also be propagated by inverting them on soft tissue and making clean cuts through the main veins. Where possible these should be reasonably spaced in four to six places. It is essential to use a very sharp knife or, even better, a scalpel.

The leaf may then be turned up the right way and laid on a seed tray filled with seed and cutting compost that is just moist, gently placing the leaf on the surface to ensure that contact is made with the compost. Take care not to crush tissue at any stage, otherwise rooting may occur. It may even be prudent to use a fungicidal spray of benomyl to help prevent rotting.

The leaf or leaves should then be enclosed within a clear plastic bag and kept at 68–70°F (20–21°C) for four to six weeks until rooted. Plantlets should then appear within a similar period; you should provide increased ventilation in the later stages to wean the plantlets. These may then be potted up singly in 3½in (9cm) pots of peat-based potting compost and grown on until large enough to pot into the final 5½in (14cm) half-pot in the same way as plantlets raised from leaf cuttings propagated by the first technique.

The gloxinia may also be raised from seed thinly sown onto seed and cutting compost in early to mid-spring. A 5½in (14cm) pan or small tray is ideal for this. Once sown, the seed should be covered with a piece of clear plastic or glass and kept at 70°F (21°C), ensuring that the compost remains moist. Germination should take about four weeks and may be patchy.

Once the seedlings are large enough to handle, probably after a further four to six weeks, they should be carefully weaned and then potted up singly in peat-based potting compost, in a 2½–3½in (6–9cm) pot first, and then later in a 5½in (14cm) half-pot.

Take care not to allow the compost to dry out at any time and also ensure that the plants are kept in a well-lit position out of direct sunlight.

Three problems The sooty mould (*above*) is a sign of an aphid attack, while the leaf marks (*above right*) are the result of red spider. Combat both with insecticide. Overwatering (*below*) leads to rot and botrytis.

AVOIDING PROBLEMS

Light and position

Find the lightest possible location for these plants, but avoid direct sunlight which can scorch the softer new leaves. Poor light will lead to thin leaves and the flowers will be weak and sparse. Protect from midday sun during the summer months.

Temperature range

Cool   Intermediate   Warm

A room temperature of around 60°F (15°C) during summer is best. In winter keep the corms dry and frost free at around 50°F (10°C). The maximum summer temperature should be 75°F (23°C).

Watering

In summer water generously two to three times a week. Water the plant at the soil level and avoid wetting the leaves or flowers. Gradually reduce watering in the autumn when the plant begins its dormant period. When growth has stopped, allow to dry out completely.

Feeding

No feeding is necessary as plants are becoming established. Those purchased in full growth should be fed with every watering. A weak feed is best, but for many flowers use a high potash fertilizer. Nitrogenous types will produce more leaves than flowers.

Seasonal care

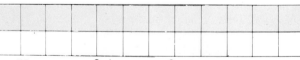

Winter   Spring   Summer   Autumn

Keep the soil moist while the plant is in flower, then gradually give it less water and keep it dry over the winter months. Pruning is generally not needed except to remove dead or damaged leaves and flowers. Young plants grown from seed or cuttings should be potted two or three times during the active growth period. Old tubers should be potted once in early spring. New plants can also be grown from seed at this time. Leaf cuttings can be taken when the leaves are mature in summer.

Soil

Any good household potting mixture will suit the Gloxinia. Repot in the first year only if the pot is smaller than 5in (10cm) in diameter. Do this on purchasing. Do not feed for six weeks after potting.

PESTS AND DISEASES

Given the right temperature and, above all, an adequate amount of humidity, *S. speciosa* will do well. Most pests are relatively easy to combat.
Aphids These are the most troublesome pest, but they are easy to identify. Treat with an insecticide.
Botrytis This is frequently the result of overwatering.

Remove infected leaves – the signs are wet blotches – as soon as they develop. Treat the healthy part of the plant with fungicide to prevent any further outbreaks.
Red spider mite These appear on the underside of leaves if plants are growing in too hot or dry conditions.

Solanum capsicastrum

Christmas Cherry

This plant gives it name to a very large family that includes the tomato and the potato. However, its chief use is as a decorative potted plant that bears attractively coloured berries at the latter end of the year. Plants are started from seed in the spring and, when established in their pots, they are placed out of doors until there is risk of frost. They are then taken into frames or greenhouses that offer cool conditions, to be grown on and flowered hopefully for Christmas trading. The plants have dull green leaves on twiggy stems and are nothing without their coloured berries.

Healthy plant The Christmas Cherry was originally brought from Brazil in the seventeenth century. It is a charming plant, whether placed indoors or in window boxes.

AVOIDING PROBLEMS

Light and position

The Christmas Cherry should never be placed in dark corners. If it is, it will shed its berries at an alarming rate, and its leaves will turn yellow and fall. Find the lightest location for these plants. Because they can tolerate cool conditions, windowsills are ideal.

Temperature range

Cool   Intermediate   Warm

A temperature range of 50°-60°F (10°-15°C) suits the plant best and will encourage it to produce more berries. A light and airy windowsill is ideal. In summer, the plants should be placed out-of-doors if possible.

Watering

During active growth, water profusely every other day. Do not let the soil dry out, even in winter. If keeping for a second season, make sure the soil is dry while the plant is dormant. After pruning, water every two weeks.

Feeding

Purchased plants will have been in their pots for some time, so regular weekly feeding with a fairly potent liquid fertilizer is necessary from the time they arrive indoors. No feeding is required after potting or pruning for about six weeks.

Seasonal care

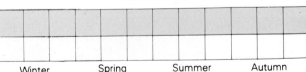

Winter   Spring   Summer   Autumn

Plants should be kept moist at all times, but on the dry side at the end of the active growth period. If kept for a second year, repot when the plant is pruned in spring. Cut the plants back to half their size in early spring and stand out-of-doors until the middle of summer. Restrict growth in autumn by pinching the non-flowering tips. Plants will easily germinate from seed in early spring.

A loam-based mixture should be used and plants should be repotted quite firmly. Large plants in small pots will suffer, so repot to 5in (12·5cm) pots at the outset.

Soil Seed-raised plants should be potted gradually from one size to the next. Never move a plant to a pot that is too large for it.

VARIETIES

Plants may be purchased in a variety of pot sizes, but whatever the size, select plants that have green foliage down to the soil level. Yellow leaves are an indication of root disorder. The plants may have green, orange, and red berries all at the same time. The berries are poisonous and should be kept away from children and pets.
S. capsicastrum The common variety with fruit about the size of a marble.
S. pseudocapsicum Commonly known as the Jerusalem Cherry, this has larger berries than *S. capsicastrum*.

PESTS AND DISEASES

The Christmas Cherry is prone to the usual problems of most houseplants.
Aphids These are usually found on young growth in summer. They are a nuisance and should be dealt with immediately with an insecticide.
White fly This problem is controlled only with persistent spraying with insecticide. Treat four times a day at four-day intervals for 16 days.
Botrytis This is not common but can be found in wet, airless conditions. Remove the affected leaves and treat with fungicide.
Red spider mite These cause discoloration.

Sparmannia africana

This plant's common name of African Windflower is derived from the unusual way in which its exposed stamens fold outwards when blown by a breeze of wind. The name Zimmerlinde is the lovely sounding German name for what in English-speaking parts of the world is the Indoor Lime. Surprisingly, these plants are not as popular as they ought to be, for they are easy to manage, grow at a prodigious rate and are not prone to many troubles in the way of pests. Its stems are erect and woody, and its lime-green leaves are large, with flowers appearing on the mature plant. Propagating new plants presents few problems as cuttings can be grown in temperatures of 70°F (21°C) at any time of the year as long as adequate conditions are provided.

Healthy plant A member of the lime family, the sparmannia is similar in appearance to the lime but it has softer leaves. When a fair size it bears white flowers with purple stamens which are sensitive to wind and touch.

VARIETIES

The African Windflower can sometimes be difficult to purchase. There is no particular season for the African Windflower, so if they are available they may be purchased at any time of year. If you buy a leggy and neglected plant, it will quickly respond to regular feeding and potting into fresh soil.
S. africana This is generally the only variety grown commercially.

PESTS AND DISEASES

Sparmannia is more prone to pests than diseases.
Red spider mite These will appear only when the plant is growing in hot and dry conditions. When first noticed, treat immediately with a recommended insecticide.
Symphalids These white pests can be eradicated by watering with a malathion solution. When watered the flies seem to jump around on top of the soil.
Sciarid fly These can cause a little damage to the root tissue of the plant. Treat by watering with a malathion solution.

AVOIDING PROBLEMS

Light and position

The African Windflower will benefit from good light, but guard against strong sunlight. Draughty windows can lead to an alarming loss of leaves. Because mature plants will have lost many of their lower leaves, they are best viewed when placed on the floor.

Temperature range

Cool　Intermediate　Warm

These plants enjoy fairly cool and consistent temperatures of 60°-65°F (15°-18°C). In winter, the plants can withstand temperatures as low as 45°F (7°C). If the temperature drops this low, keep the plant on the dry side and water only every 10 days or so.

Watering

S. africana should be watered profusely in the summer — once a day or at least every other day. Water in winter according to the room temperature. In normal conditions, once a week should be sufficient.

Feeding

This plant grows many roots, so regular weekly feeding with a fairly potent fertilizer is essential. Feed in winter only if the plant is producing new leaves. Regular growth requires regular feeding; no growth only needs minimal feeding.

Seasonal care

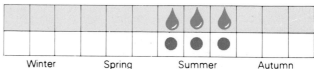

Winter　Spring　Summer　Autumn

Throughout the year, the plant should be watered sufficiently so that the soil does not dry out. During the first year of growth, the plant will probably need to be repotted two or three times. After this, annual repotting in the spring is enough. If the plant is left in its original pot, it will flower sooner. Prune in the spring. If the plant becomes very leggy, it can be cut back completely after flowering. Stem tip cuttings can be rooted in peat and sand in spring.

Soil

A new plant should have its roots inspected. If there is a mass of roots filling the pot, it will need new soil. Use a loam-based mixture and keep in a minimum temperature of 65°F (18°C). Water thoroughly after potting, then keep on the dry side until new growth begins.

Spathiphyllum

There can be few more simple or more effective contrasts than creamy white flowers set off against dark green foliage, and this is what the exotic spathiphyllums have to offer. The common name clearly derives from the manner in which spathe flowers are held erect on stiff stalks not unlike a sail. Although they belong to the same family as the anthuriums, the flowers of the spathiphyllum do not have the same lasting qualities when used as cut flowers. However, this is a small drawback as they will continue for many weeks if left on the plant.

Plants are propagated by the age old method of division. This simply means that the plant is removed from its pot and the clump of congested small plants is reduced to individual pieces or to smaller clumps that are potted up individually. The pieces should be removed with as much root attached as possible and they ought to be potted into 5in (12.5cm) pots using a standard houseplant potting mixture.

Healthy plants *S.* 'Mauna Loa' (*right*) is a pleasing, elegant plant. When choosing a plant, look for clean foliage and flowers that are in bud rather than full out. Drooping or discoloured plants are unhealthy. The spathe eventually turns green. It is still attractive for a few weeks, but after that time it is a good idea to remove it.

AVOIDING PROBLEMS

Light and position

Spathiphyllums like a sunny position but direct sunlight should be avoided. They are beautifully shaped plants and so are at their best advantage when they can be viewed from all sides.

Temperature range

Cool Intermediate Warm

Spathiphyllums should be kept at temperatures between 60°-70°F (15°-21°C). If they are kept at about 65°F (18°C) they should grow for most of the year. They do not like draughts and they need a humid atmosphere, so keep them on trays of moist pebbles or moss.

Watering

The spathiphyllum should be watered with moderate amounts – the potting mixture should never dry out completely. Avoid overwatering, as this could result in wilting.

Feeding

Use a standard liquid fertilizer and administer every two weeks while the plant is growing. Older and more established plants may benefit from a slightly stronger solution than the manufacturer recommends.

Seasonal care

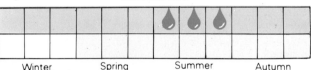

Winter Spring Summer Autumn

The plant grows fastest in summer and should receive greater quantities of water then. Avoid water-logging – worms in the soil may block up the drainage holes with their casts so check for these. Decrease the amount of food in winter. Avoid accidental spraying with household aerosols as this may cause spotting of the leaves.

Soil

The plants should be repotted every spring in a loam-based mixture. Ensure that they are properly drained by putting a few pieces of broken clay pots in the bottom of the new containers.

VARIETIES

These plants are normally only found in specialist retail shops as they need considerable care after they have been acquired.
S. wallisii The maximum height this variety achieves is 1ft (30cm). The leaves, which grow in thick clusters, are about 6in (16cm) long and 4in (10cm) wide. The flowers, on long stalks, appear in spring and sometimes again in late summer. This variety, however, is not often found in retailers' stock. The cream or yellow coloured spadix of each flower is enclosed by the white spathe, which gives rise to its common names, White Sails or Peace Lily.
S. 'Mauna Loa' This is a hybrid, and far more popular than the other variety. It has large green leaves and majestic flowers, which usually appear in spring. However, the plant does sometimes bloom at other times of the year. The flower stalks may be 15–20in long (38–50cm) and they give the flowers a very graceful appearance. The flowers have a fragrant smell, and altogether the spathiphyllum is one of the most attractive of houseplants.

PESTS AND DISEASES

Aphids These pests tend to attack the young, maturing leaves in the centre of the plant. As soon as they are noticed, steps should be taken to treat the plant, as they can cause considerable damage. Use an insecticide to get rid of them.
Red spider mite If the atmosphere is too hot and dry, the spathiphyllum may be attacked by red spider mite. It is wise to spray the leaves regularly, concentrating on the undersides. If the plant does become infested, use a

reliable insecticide and improve the growing conditions.
Mealy bug This pest is not a frequent visitor to the spathiphyllum, but the leaves should be checked for it occasionally as it tends to be hidden between the congested leaves. If there are only a few, they can be wiped away with a pad soaked in methylated spirits. Larger numbers can be removed by soaking with an insecticide such as malathion.

Unhealthy leaf (*above*). If the spathiphyllum is not given enough food regularly, its leaves will go patchy and the edges will become yellow and ragged.

PROPAGATION

Moisten compost thoroughly. Carefully remove plant from pot.

Gently tease clump apart to separate pieces with more than four mature leaves.

Place new plant in 4¼in (11cm) pot.
Fill pot with peat-based potting compost, taking care to avoid air spaces – but do not compact.

Gently firm to secure plant and water to settle compost.

Spathiphyllum wallisii is sometimes called White Sails bacause of the beautiful white spathe that surrounds a white- to cream-coloured spadix commonly seen as the plant's flower.

The plant may be propagated with extreme care by divison in mid- to late spring. Dense clumps may provide a number of new plants, but do not try to produce too many plants to the detriment of the parent.

Moisten the compost of the root ball well, and gently tease offsets of the main plant away, taking care to separate only those pieces with at least three to four leaves or more. Where there are less, try to ensure that these small plants are left attached to larger plants when separated.

Apart from teasing apart, use a sharp knife to sever the rhizome cleanly and try to keep as much root as possible with each new plant.

Pot up each piece in a 4¼in (11cm) pot of peat-based potting compost, or seed and cutting compost in which you may find plants will root more readily. Ensure that the plant is planted at the same level as it was when attached to the mother plant. A cane support may help to avoid root disturbance to large pieces.

Covering the plant for a few weeks with a plastic bag may also help plants that have a small or damaged root system, removing it once the plant starts to produce new growth. After the division process treat all plants with great care and keep them at about 68–70°F (20–21°C) in moderate light, misting occasionally with tepid water, as the plant thrives in a reasonably humid environment.

ASCLEPIADACEAE

Stephanotis floribunda

Madagascar Jasmine
Wax Flower
Floradora
Madagascar Chaplet Flower

These are natural climbing plants, with tough, leathery, evergreen foliage, whose main attraction is the almost overpowering fragrance of the waxy white flowers that are borne in clusters of five to nine. The individual flowers are trumpet shaped with short stalks, and are much favoured by florists for bridal bouquets. New plants can be raised from cuttings of older growth taken in the spring and placed in a peaty mixture at a temperature of around 70°F (21°C). Plants may also be raised from seed that is produced from large, fruit-like seed pods, which ripen in the autumn to expose small seeds attached to the most beautiful, silky white 'parachutes'.

Healthy plant The main attraction of these climbing plants is their mass of scented white flowers.

VARIETIES

Buy in summer, looking for healthy young plants that are fresh and green, with some flowers open and lots of buds on show. Avoid ones with yellowing foliage, or ones that have had such foliage removed. This is a sign of poor culture and root failure.
S. floribunda This is generally the only variety available.

PESTS AND DISEASES

The main enemies of *S. floribunda* are bugs and insects, but be careful not to water excessively or let the leaves become sun-scorched.
Scale insects These can only be eradicated by thorough application of malathion. Spray three times over 10 days.
Sooty mould This is a harmless black fungus caused by scale insects. Wipe off with a sponge dipped in insecticide or soapy water.
Root mealy bug Eradicate with an insecticide.

AVOIDING PROBLEMS

Light and position

Always place the plant in the lightest possible place. Full sun may scorch some of the leaves, but this is not unduly harmful. The

plant's natural climbing habit makes it essential that some sort of framework be provided for the plant to cling to.

Temperature range

Cool   Intermediate   Warm

A modest temperature of around 60°F (15°C) throughout the year is fine for these plants. In winter

keep them cooler at 55°F (13°C). In summer, do not let the temperature rise above 75°F (23°C).

Watering

In summer, water two or three times a week and in winter, once a week. Use lime-free, tepid water whenever possible. Spray

the plants once a week in summer but avoid wetting the flowers.

Feeding

Avoid giving excess food, but ensure that the plants have a weak feed with every watering

while in active growth. In winter, when the plant is not flowering, feeding is not necessary.

Seasonal care

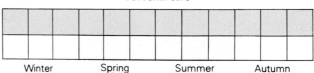

Winter   Spring   Summer   Autumn

Water stephanotis plants well during spring and summer but avoid too wet conditions by allowing the soil to dry out between applications. The plant can be trimmed to shape after

flowering in autumn, or the growing frame can be extended to cope with new growth. Stem tip cuttings should be made in spring.

Soil

Pot in the spring when the plants are getting under way for the new season. Never move plants into containers much larger than the

existing pot. Use conventional houseplant potting soil; peaty mixtures are not satisfactory.

Strelitzia

This genus contains one of the most striking of all flowers, *Strelitzia reginae*, commonly called the Bird of Paradise. Spear-shaped metallic-green leaves are carried on rigid petioles and may attain a length of 3–4ft (91cm–1.2m). Flowers are mainly orange and blue in colour. They bloom from an almost horizontal bract; the three-petalled flowers have a crested appearance and emerge over the course of several weeks. Plants may be anywhere from five to seven years old before they produce flowers, by which time plants should be in pots 10in (25cm) in diameter.

Strelitzias need bright light, with at least a few hours of direct sunlight every day. High temperature is not necessary, and plants may remain out of doors except when freezing conditions are expected.

Strelitzia reginae (*above and right*) is a striking plant that may be grown with reasonable ease from seed. However, it may take many years for plants to produce their flamboyant flowers.

STRELITZIA	
Light and position	**Feeding** 
These plants need a good bright position with at least three to four hours direct sunlight each day.	Standard liquid fertilizer should be applied every two weeks during the active growing season only.
Temperature range  Cool Intermediate Warm During spring and summer months, strelitzias will tolerate normal room temperatures. Cooler temperatures around 55°F (13°C) are needed during the autumn through winter.	**Seasonal care**  Winter Spring Summer Autumn Re-potting should be done in spring, but avoid the temptation to pot on too frequently: never repot before plants are well rooted in their existing pots. Mature flowering plants may stop flowering for as long as two years if displaced. Propagate by carefully dividing overcrowded clumps, or by removing a section with two or three leaves.
Watering Water moderately, reducing water during the dormant period.	**Soil** Use a loam-based mixture that is free to drain.

Streptocarpus

Indigenous to South Africa, the original Cape Primrose, *S.* 'Constant Nymph', with its profusion of delicate blue flowers, was for many years the only streptocarpus available. Now there are many fine hybrids offering a wealth of colour, and having the considerable added benefit that their leaves are smaller and very much less brittle. This makes it possible for the grower to pack them and get them to customers in a much better condition than was possible with the original variety. Its stemless leaves are coarse and they grow upwards with the plant's pretty flowers pushing up from among them.

New plants can be raised from seed, or particular varieties can be reproduced from leaf cuttings. These can be made by dividing the leaf up into sections about 3in (7.5cm) long, or by slitting firm leaves down the centre vein and placing them on their sides partially buried in peaty compost. The temperatures should be kept around 70°F (21°C).

Propagation This brightly coloured streptocarpus (*below*) has reached the stage where new plants can be propagated from leaf cuttings

PESTS AND DISEASES

Streptocarpus is prone to three main pests and diseases.
Aphids Either spray the flower stalks with insecticide, or remove by carefully running a thumb and finger along the stem.
Red spider mite This is not common, but can affect plants that are too dry and hot. Saturate the underside of leaves with insecticide.
Botrytis This is a result of dank, airless conditions, causing wet, brown patches of rot on foliage. Treat with a fungicide.

VARIETIES

Purchase in late spring to take advantage of the long flowering season. Select plants that are sturdy and fresh, with some flowers open and plenty of buds. Avoid any with damp leaves hanging over the side of the pot.
S. 'Constant Nymph' This long-established plant has attractive blue flowers, but brittle leaves that can be damaged easily.
S. 'Concorde Hybrid' This is a smaller plant, which comes in a wide range of colours and is less fragile.

AVOIDING PROBLEMS

Light and position

For the plant to continue to bloom throughout the spring and summer, it will need the lightest possible position, but not exposed to bright midday sun. During the winter months when not in flower, less light is tolerated.

Temperature range

Cool   Intermediate   Warm

Streptocarpus plants do not like heat, so an average temperature of 55°-60°F (13°-18°C) is best, with a constant of 60°F (15°C) being ideal. Should the temperature drop lower, keep the soil dry because the plant will become nearly dormant. In summer, a maximum of 75°F (23°C) is preferred.

Watering

Never let the plant stand in water or it will rot. In summer, water two or three times a week. In winter, water once a week or less. If possible, use soft, tepid water.

Feeding

Never feed the plant if it has just been potted, and feed sparingly during the winter. While in flower and well established, a greater number of flowers can be encouraged by using a fertilizer with a high proportion of potash.

Seasonal care

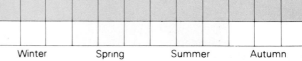

Winter   Spring   Summer   Autumn

Water thoroughly when in active growth and less in winter. At all times the soil should be allowed to dry out between waterings. Never clean leaves with chemicals. When not in flower, foliage can be cleaned by holding a hand over the soil in the pot and inverting the pot into a bucket of tepid, soapy water. Keep the plant out of the sun while it is drying.

Soil

While in small pots, a peaty mixture is best but when the pot reaches 5in (12.5cm) in diameter use a mixture that contains some loam. Good drainage is essential. Avoid putting plants in pots that are too large.

Tolmiea menziesii

These houseplants develop into neat mounds of pale green foliage, and produce perfectly shaped little plants in the area where the leaf is attached to the petiole. The plantlets can be removed and potted separately and they give the plant its amusing common name.

Healthy plant The Piggy-back Plant is compact and fresh looking (*above*). New plantlets grow out of leaf edges (*below*).

VARIETIES

Select plants that seem young and green. Those with a dry yellow appearance may well be suffering from red spider mites. Larger plants may appear good value, but the smaller ones adapt better to indoor conditions, and usually prove more satisfactory. It is a robust indoor plant, but is equally hardy outdoors. The *Tolmiea menziesii*, Piggy-back Plant, Youth on Age or Mother of Thousands, is the only known variety of this species.

PESTS AND DISEASES

Red spider mite These get onto the underside of the plant's pale green leaves, and are difficult to detect with the naked eye. Spraying the plant with insecticide is inefficient as the leaves overlap, making the operation difficult. It is advisable to immerse the plant for about five minutes in a bucket of insecticide. Rubber gloves should be worn.

Aphids These can be a problem on young leaves in the spring and summer months, but can usually be controlled by an insecticide.

Mealy bug These pests may occur among the congested foliage of older plants. As they tend to lodge in the more inaccessible places, plants again should be immersed in insecticide, rather than being sprayed.

AVOIDING PROBLEMS

Light and position

T. menziesii is not a fussy plant, and it can adapt to most locations apart from very sunny positions near the window. It should always be positioned in plenty of space so that the extra little plants can grow comfortably.

Temperature range

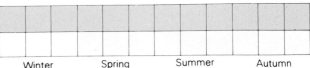

Cool   Intermediate   Warm

This plant abhors very hot conditions, which will also encourage red spider mites. It will grow well in temperatures between 45°-60°F (7°-15°C) although the leaves will become paler, the lower the light level. Piggy-back Plants must be protected from draughts, and do not thrive in continual shade.

Watering

Regular moderate waterings are required by these plants during the summer period. In the winter however, tolmeias should only be watered occasionally when the potting mixture has become dry.

Feeding

Weak liquid fertilizer should be applied with each watering, much less being required during the winter period. Alternatively, fertilizer in pellet form can be pushed into the potting mixture.

Seasonal care

Winter   Spring   Summer   Autumn

Excesses of very wet and rock hard soil should always be avoided. Piggy-back Plants should regularly have all their dead leaves removed. New baby plants can be removed by hand at any time in the spring or summer period and potted again separately. They will grow very rapidly reaching a respectable size after only a few months. Tolmieas require considerably less food and water during the winter months.

Soil

Shallow pots are the most suitable for Piggy-back Plants, and they rarely need to be larger than 5in (12.5cm) in diameter. If the plants outgrow these, it is advisable to divide the plant or to start again with easily rooted plantlets. Loam-based mixtures are the most suitable for tolmieas.

PROPAGATION

Tolmiea menziesii, the Piggy-back Plant or Mother of Thousands is another plant that lends itself well to being propagated readily. From mid-spring to late summer the plant may be propagated by either of two methods. Use whichever you find to be most successful.

The easiest way is to fill a 3½in (9cm) pot with seed and cutting compost and to place one of the leaves with an already formed young plantlet onto the surface of the compost. Do not cut the leaf from the mother plant, but leave it attached. Ensure that the leaf stays in contact with the compost by anchoring it down with a long-shanked staple or opened-up paper-clip to secure the stem close to the leaf.

Rooting should occur within a month, after which the new plant may be separated from the mother plant with a sharp pair of scissors. Leave the young plant to develop a little more before removing the clip and, if required, the old leaf, which can simply be carefully cut off.

Another way of propagating tolmiea is to cut off plantlet-bearing leaves, complete with 1–1¼in (2.5–3cm) of stem. The leaf stalk should then be inserted in a 3½in (9cm) pot of seed and cutting compost, taking care to ensure that the base of the leaf is in contact with the surface of the compost. The plantlet should root within a month.

Whichever way you choose to propagate the plant, ensure that the compost is kept just moist and not too wet, and that the plantlet is provided with a well-lit position out of direct sunlight, at least for the first few weeks. Tolmiea should root well at 65–68°F (18–20°C). Once rooted, it should be grown on and fed with a liquid fertilizer before being finally potted up into a 5½in (14cm) half-pot of potting compost.

Tradescantia

The numerous varieties of tradescantia are among the easiest to grow and the least expensive of all the indoor plants.

During the summer months, cuttings about 3–4in (7.5–10cm) in length taken from the ends of sturdy growths will root easily in any good houseplant soil mixture. Up to seven cuttings should be inserted in each small pot, and both pot and cuttings should be placed in a sealed plastic bag to reduce transpiration, so encouraging rooting.

TRADESCANTIA RELATIONS

Among the tradescantia, there is a small selection of slightly more difficult plants that are only occasionally offered for sale.

Most plants are propagated from cuttings, but are a little more difficult to rear than the common types, needing slightly higher temperatures in the region of 65°F (18°C). Also, if black leg rot is to be avoided on cutting stems where they enter the soil, particular attention must be paid to watering, which should be minimal until rooting has taken place. The siderasis is propagated very easily by dividing clumps and the rhoeos either from cuttings or seed, which is not difficult to germinate in a temperature of around 65°F (18°C).

Healthy plant The tradescantia, also called Wandering Jew or Inch Plant, can be displayed in a hanging basket (*left*) or in a wall pot. The trailing stems can grow as long as 1ft (30cm). If a tradescantia is properly cared for, its leaves should be a striking combination of cream and green stripes.

PESTS AND DISEASES	VARIETIES
Aphids These do not often attack this plant, but they may occasionally get onto soft new leaves and cause discoloration. There is a variety of insecticides that should control them. **Red spider mite** These may be troublesome. To cure, spray with malathion. Red spider will cause discoloration. Another possible cause of this is root rot from overwatering (*see above right*).	It is advisable to buy tradescantias during the spring. ***T. fluminensis*** This has striped leaves with purple undersides. ***T.f. 'Quicksilver'*** This variety is tougher and grows faster than *T. fluminensis*. ***T. albiflora* 'Albovittata'** This form has a silvery foliage. ***T. a. 'Tricolor'*** The leaves of this plant are striped white and purple.

PROPAGATION

Remove 3in (7.5cm) tip cuttings.

Gently insert in 3½in (9cm) pot of seed and cutting compost.

Insert five cuttings per pot taking care not to crush stems or leaves.

Instead of inserting in compost simply insert directly into rooting gel or water.

Tradescantia can be rooted readily in compost or water, using whichever method you find to be the most successful.

This plant tends to grow quite lank and should be renewed or pinched back regularly, especially from mid-spring to late summer, when not only can the mother plant be allowed to re-generate, but the 'trimmings' may also be propagated.

Pinch off, or cut with a sharp knife, tip cuttings up to 3in (7.5cm) in length, ensuring that the base of the stem is cut cleanly and not crushed to avoid any likelihood of disease.

Insert five cuttings in a 3½in (9cm) pot of seed and cutting compost and keep at 65°F (18°C) in a well-lit position out of direct sunlight. Maintain the compost at just moist, taking care to ensure that it does not become too wet.

Within two or three weeks roots should have been produced, and the plant can be grown on with further water and liquid fertilizer added as required.

Cuttings may also be rooted in water. When the roots have grown to approximately 1½–2in (4–5cm) in length they may then be potted up five to a 3½in (9cm) pot of potting compost and grown on accordingly.

AVOIDING PROBLEMS

Light and position

For tradescantias to retain the variegated colours of their leaves, it is essential that they are placed in plenty of light but protected from very strong sun. They are often positioned so that they can trail over shady windowsills.

Temperature range

Cool   Intermediate   Warm

Cool conditions are ideal for this plant, 50°-60°F (10°-15°C), but it cannot tolerate draughts, very cold areas or continual shade. It is also advisable to keep tradescantias well away from all heating appliances. They will survive in dry surroundings, but grow better in a more humid atmosphere. Chilly temperatures may cause leaf discoloration.

Watering

Tradescantias should be watered regularly, but the colours of the leaves will become dimmer if the soil or potting mixture is allowed to become too wet. Less water will be required during the winter period when the plants are not so active.

Feeding

These plants will respond well to feeds of weak liquid fertilizer at every watering. Obviously this will be less frequent during the winter months, but it is important that feeding does not stop completely during this time.

Seasonal care

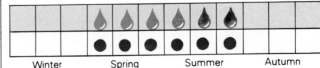

Winter   Spring   Summer   Autumn

The green shoots that occasionally appear on tradescantias should be carefully removed, as they are very vigorous and will quickly lose their variegated colouring, so marring their appearance. If the leaves become at all dry and shrivelled, they should be taken off the bases of the longer stems. Less water is needed in winter when the plants are less active, especially as during this period they are more prone to root rot from over-watering.

Soil

There is a belief that these plants thrive on little nourishment but this is not the case. Young tradescantias must be potted with great care if they are to do well. A good houseplant mixture should be used, and ideally it should be loam-based.

Yucca elephantipes

In tropical South America, one or other of the almost indestructible yuccas is often used to mark out boundaries – hence its common name. Only recently have they become popular as indoor plants, being elegant individual plants for important locations. Stout stems of the yucca are imported, cut down and shipped almost as if they were miniature tree trunks. On arrival at their nursery destination, the various-sized stem sections are propagated in beds of peat at a temperature of around 75°F (23°C). Amazingly for such large and solid sections, almost all of them produce roots and leaves, which is a testimony to the tough character of these plants.

Healthy plant Yuccas are easily identified by their sword-shaped leaves and very thick stems.

PESTS AND DISEASES

Scale insect These may attack the Yucca plant, clinging to the foliage, and occasionally the stem, like miniature limpets. They suck the plant's sap.
Sooty mould This is a messy though harmless fungus that settles on the excreta of the scale insects leaving an unsightly black deposit. Scale insects and sooty mould can both be wiped off with a sponge soaked in soapy water.
Stem rot This may set in if the yucca is overwatered. As the base rots, the plant will start to keel over.

VARIETIES

All plants should have bright green foliage that is firm to the touch. The cost will vary according to the height of the plant and the number of stems in the pot.
Y. elephantipes The Spineless Yucca, has much softer leaves than other varieties.
Y. aloifolia Spanish Bayonet has extremely sharp leaves, hence its name, so it should be touched and moved with caution. There are several varieties of the *Y. aloifolia* such as *Y.a.* 'Variegata' and *Y.a.* 'Marginata' that have white and yellow markings.

AVOIDING PROBLEMS

Light and position

Yuccas must be given the lightest possible surroundings and will tolerate full sun. If the leaves are too close to the glass however, there is a danger of discoloration through scorching.

Temperature range

Cool　　Intermediate　　Warm

These plants are both versatile and resilient. Any temperature between 50°-70°F (10°-21°C) will suit them, providing the soil is not too wet when low temperatures are anticipated. If the surroundings are not well lit, yuccas should be kept as cool as possible. They are tolerant of a very dry atmosphere.

Watering

Yuccas need plenty of water but should never be overwatered or left to stand in water or botytris may set in. They should be kept fairly dry during the winter period

Feeding

Once they are well established in their pots, these plants should be fed with liquid fertilizer at each watering. Fertilizer in tablet form can be pushed into the soil at intervals recommended by the manufacturer.

Seasonal care

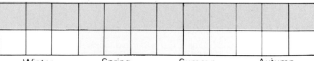

Winter　　Spring　　Summer　　Autumn

During the summer months, the yucca plant may remain out-of-doors in a sheltered position, with watering and feeding going on as normal. Leaf tips may occasionally become brown as a result of excessive watering. The plant must be positioned carefully so that it gets sufficient sunlight each day. Older plants may produce cream coloured flowers in the summer.

Soil

Peaty mixtures are quite useless as this is a robust plant. It will overbalance very easily if it is not provided with the anchorage that a loam-based mixture offers. Clay pots are more suitable than light plastic ones.

Zebrina pendula

Similar in habit to the tradescantias, this is one of the most attractive of the common indoor plants. Its foliage has an overall silvery sheen when the plants are well grown, and the undersides of the leaves are a rich shade of burgundy. They are perfect hanging basket plants that are best prepared by potting five or six small plants in the basket in spring. The earlier growing tips should be pinched out to encourage branching and fuller, more attractive growth. In fact, the ends of each stem can be removed at a length of some 4in (10cm) and inserted in potting soil as cut-tings that will root readily in spring and summer.

Healthy plant Another type of Wandering Jew, zebrinas are admired for their variegated leaves. They grow very quickly, but must be fed and watered regularly and kept in suitable surroundings. If these plants are neglected (*right*) they will thin out, becoming brown and withered.

AVOIDING PROBLEMS

Light and position

Zebrinas require well-lit surroundings, but should never be left in direct sunlight. Ideally, they should be positioned at head height in hanging baskets or suspended pots, so that they can be cultivated with ease.

Temperature range

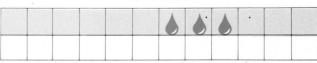

Cool   Intermediate   Warm

Extremes of temperature should be avoided, but anywhere between 55°-65° F (13°-18° C) is suitable. These plants must be kept out of draughts and away from all kinds of heating appliances. At lower temperatures they will grow more slowly, and chilling may cause the leaves to drop.

Watering

Regular watering is essential, and most hanging plants tend to get neglected in this respect. The potting mixture should be moist throughout but never too wet.

Feeding

It is not advisable to starve Inch Plants in an attempt to improve the leaf colour. Zebrinas thrive on weak liquid fertilizer applied each time the plant is watered.

Seasonal care

Winter   Spring   Summer   Autumn

To prevent plants from becoming straggly and unattractive as they age, it is wise to trim back untidy growth periodically. The growing tips of any shoots that appear to be outpacing their neighbours shoud be pinched out. When large plants start to deteriorate new cuttings should be taken. It is not necessary to feed plants that have been newly potted.

Soil

Use a loam-based mixture, potting plants in larger containers as soon as the existing ones are filled with roots. Unless zebrinas are going into hanging baskets, they will rarely need pots larger than 5in (12.5cm) in diameter.

PESTS AND DISEASES

Aphids These are sometimes a problem if there are a lot about, and they may cause spotting. They can be eradicated with an insecticide spray, or if there are only a few, simply remove between finger and thumb.
Red spider mite These may attack zebrinas, but they are very hard to see with the naked eye. Leaves that are affected will start to take on a very dry and lifeless appearance, but insecticide spray containing dicofol or malathion should cure the plant. On the whole, zebrinas tend to stay free of pests and diseases if they are kept clean.

VARIETIES

Avoid buying tired old plants with long straggling strands of growth. They may seem good value, but the younger ones are more likely to be free of blemishes and leaf damage.
Z. pendula This is the best-known plant with its purple flowers and silver striped leaves.
Z.p. 'Quadricolor' This is similar, much less common, and has reddish-brown, green, silver and pink striped foliage.
Z.p. 'Discolor' This has leaves with a brown tinge that are narrower than those of the other varieties.
Z.p. purpusii This plant has purple leaves.

Glossary

A

Aerial root A root that grows up above the level of the soil, often seen in philodendrons and the *Monstera deliciosa*, which can extract moisture from the air.

Alternate An arrangement of leaves on a stem in which they grow singly on opposite sides and at different levels.

Annual A plant that completes its whole life-cycle within one year of being grown from seed.

Aquatic This term is given to a plant that lives wholly or partially in water.

Axil The angle between a leaf or leaf stalk and the stem on which it is carried. A growth from the axil is called an axillary bud.

B

Biennial A plant that flowers and seeds in the year following its own growth from seed, thus completing its life within two years.

Bloom This term is often used to mean a flower but, more specifically, refers to a waxy or powdery coating on the leaves or fruits of certain plants. This coating is usually white or has a pale blue tinge.

Bract A modified leaf, shaped like a leaf or flower petal. Bracts are often highly coloured, as in the Poinsettia, and may support a less showy flower.

Bromeliad A member of the Bromeliaceae, or pineapple family. Bromeliads are epiphytic plants and can be grown supported on tree bark rather than in soil.

Bulb A fleshy bud growing underground which stores food and protects new growth within its overlapping layers.

C

Capillary action The upward movement of liquid in areas of confinement. This principle is used in watering from below, the water rising through spaces in the soil.

Chlorosis A condition when the leaves of a plant become pale or yellowed due to lack of chlorophyll. This may be caused by insufficient nutrients in the soil.

Compost In the context of houseplant growing, this term means a mixture of soil and other ingredients in which the plant is potted, otherwise called a potting mixture.

Conservatory A room with specially controlled heat and humidity, in which houseplants are grown.

Corm The swollen base of a stem formed underground which protects new growth and stores food, and is used for propagation.

Creeper A plant with trailing growth which puts down roots at intervals along the growth.

Crocks Broken pieces of a ceramic pot, or stones and ceramic material, placed in the base of a pot to allow free drainage through the soil.

Crown The part of a plant from which the roots and stems grow, forming the base of the plant.

Cultivar A term for a plant that has been bred in cultivation, rather than originating in the wild.

Cutting A piece of a plant that is used to raise a new plant, such as a leaf or stem tip, which may be potted to develop roots.

D

Deciduous A term describing plants that shed their leaves when inactive, usually during the winter.

Division A method of growing new plants by splitting the root-ball of a mature plant and potting the sections separately.

Dormant period A temporary period in which a plant ceases to grow at all. This often occurs during the winter months.

E

Epiphyte A plant that can derive moisture and nutrients from the air or decaying plant matter and therefore does not need to grow in soil, but can support itself when growing in bark or shallow moss.

Evergreen A plant that keeps a mass of foliage throughout the year, shedding a few leaves at a time.

Exotic This term strictly refers to plants foreign to the country in which they are being grown, but is also commonly used for brightly coloured, succulent or unusual plants.

F

Floret A single, small flower that is one of many making up a large compound flower head as in a daisy or cineraria.

Foliage plant A plant that is grown indoors to display the beauty of its leaves. Although some bear flowers, these are usually insignificant.

Foliar feed Fertilizer that is sprayed onto the leaves of the plant and can be rapidly absorbed.

Frond An alternative term for the leaf of a fern or palm.

Fungicide A chemical used to control disease and destroy fungus growths on a plant.

Fungus A parasitic form of plant life including microscopic organisms that cause such houseplant diseases as mildew and botrytis.

G

Genus A term that refers to a group of plants with similar characteristics which can be sub-divided into separate species. Several genera of fundamentally similar plants make up a family.

Germination The earliest stage in the growth of a plant, when seed begins to sprout.

Grafting A means of joining a stem or shoot of one plant to another plant that is still rooted.

Growing shoot A shoot that extends the growth of the plant from a stem tip.

H

Habit The normal growth pattern of a plant, whether trailing, creeping, bushy or climbing, for instance.

Half-hardy A term for a plant that can adjust to cool conditions but cannot survive in extremely cold temperatures or wintering out of doors.

Hardy A term describing a plant which can withstand prolonged exposure to cold temperatures and even frost.

Honeydew The sticky secretion left on plants by insects such as aphids and whitefly.

Humidifier A piece of equipment that will maintain or increase the level of humidity in a room.

Humus A substance consisting of decayed organic matter which can be used to make a rich topsoil.

Hybrid A plant that is bred by cross-fertilizing two plants of the same family, although not necessarily of the same genus or variety.

Hydroculture A method of growing plants without putting them in soil. Instead, the pots are filled with pebbles and the plants are fed nutrients when they are watered.

I

Inflorescence A term commonly applied to a cluster of flowers, a head or spike growing on one main stem, but also a general term for the flowering of a plant.

Inorganic A word descriptive of a fertilizer or chemical that is not derived from living matter.

Insecticide A chemical or organic substance used to control any insects.

L

Lateral shoot A shoot growing sideways from a main stem at any point below the tip.

Leaf cutting Part of a leaf or a whole leaf used to propagate a new plant.

Leaflet A small, single leaf that is one of a number growing from a stem to form a compound leaf.

Leaf mould A component of some potting mixtures which consists exclusively of rotted down leaves.

Leggy A term describing tall growth of a plant when the stems become spindly and bear fewer leaves, especially at the lower ends.

Loam A high-quality soil used in potting mixtures, which contains a good balance of clay, sand and decayed matter.

M

Margin The edge of one section of a plant, most usually applied to the edge of the leaf.

Midrib the main rib of a leaf which divides the length centrally. The midrib usually stands out from the surface of the underside of a leaf.

Mouth The open end of a tubular or bell-shaped flower.

N

Node A joint or swelling on the stem of a plant from which leaves, buds or lateral shoots appear.

O

Offset A small, new plant that develops naturally from its parent and can be detached and propagated separately.

Opposite An arrangement of leaves on a stem where they grow in pairs, one on either side of the stem.

Organic A word describing matter such as fertilizer or compost that is derived from living tissue.

P

Palmate A term for a leaf consisting of three or more leaflets radiating from a single stalk in an arrangement resembling an open hand.

Peat Also known as peat moss, this is a substance used in potting composed of partially decayed organic matter. It is particularly valued for its air- and moisture-retaining characteristics.

Perennial A term applied to a plant that lives indefinitely. In houseplants, this means surviving through at least three seasons of growth, and often much more.

Petiole A stem or stalk that carries a leaf.

pH balance A means of measuring the acidity or alkaline content of the soil.

Photosynthesis The process in a plant by which the leaves are nourished. For effective photosynthesis plants require water, air and adequate exposure to light.

Pinching out This refers to the procedure in which new growing tips are removed by pinching them between the fingertips to encourage branching and bushiness elsewhere on the plant.

Pinnate The term for a compound leaf in which the leaflets are carried in pairs on opposite sides of the stem. In plants where there is a further division of each part of the compound leaf, the arrangement is called bipinnate.

Plantlet A small plant produced on the runners or stems of a parent plant.

Pot-bound The condition in which the roots of a plant are crowded inside the pot. This usually prevents healthy growth, although some plants do well if slightly pot-bound.

Potting on Transferring a plant to a larger container to allow continued growth of the roots.

Propagation Techniques of forming a new plant by means of cuttings or divisions of a mature plant.

Pruning Cutting back the growth of a plant selectively to encourage bushiness, a compact shape and better flowering.

R

Repotting Transferring a plant to a new container or renewing the soil in the pot to revitalize the growth.

Resting period A season in which there is little or no new growth in the plant. This period is not necessarily accompanied by decline or falling leaves.

Rhizome A thick, horizontal stem, usually growing underground, from which buds and roots are grown.

Rootball The dense mass of matted roots and the compost trapped in them visible when a plant is removed from its pot.

Rosette The name given to an arrangement of clustered leaves radiating from a central area, either carried on a single stem or on separate stems.

Runner A trailing stem that runs horizontally along the soil and roots at intervals to form new plants.

S

Sharp sand A coarse sand, free of lime, sometimes used in potting mixtures.

Shrub A plant with branching, woody stems that remains relatively small and compact in growth, unlike a tree.

Spadix A fleshy spike that carries small flowers embedded in its surface.

Spathe A large bract, often brightly coloured, that acts as a protective sheath for a spadix.

Species A sub-division of a genus of plants forming a grouping of plants that can fertilize each other and grow from seed without being specially cultivated.

Sphagnum moss A spongy bog moss, useful in cultivating houseplants becaue of its high capacity to hold water.

Spore The reproductive cell of a fern or moss, acting in the same way as a seed from a flowering plant. Ferns usually carry spores in raised cases on the undersides of the fronds.

Sport A plant variety that arises as a natural mutation from the parent plant.

Strike The term used to describe the rooting of a stem or leaf cutting.

Succulent A plant that can withstand a period of very dry conditions, having fleshy stems and leaves, which are able to store moisture.

Systemic A term describing an insecticide or fungicide that is absorbed into the tissues of the plant though the soil or leaves and poisons the organism or insect living on the plant.

T

Tendril A fine, twining thread arising from the leaf or stem of a plant that clings to a frame or surface, enabling the plant to climb.

Terrestrial A plant that grows in soil in its natural habitat, as opposed to an epiphytic or an aquatic plant.

Top-dressing Freshening the soil in which a plant is growing by replacing the top layer, rather than repotting the whole plant.

Transpiration The natural process in which water evaporates through the pores in leaves.

Tuber A swollen stem, usually underground, that stores food and produces new growth.

V

Variegated A term that refers to plants with patterned, spotted or blotchy leaves. Most common variegations are green broken by cream, white or silver, but some plants have brighter colours on the leaves.

Variety A member of a plant species that differs from the others by a natural alteration such as in the colour of the leaves or flowers. The term is often applied to plants bred in cultivation, which strictly should be called cultivars.

Vein A strand of tissue in a leaf that conducts moisture and nutrients. Large veins may be known as ribs.

W

Whorl A radiating arrangement of three or more leaves around a node on a plant's stem.

The common name of plants are cross-referenced to their botanical names. All page references are listed as the botanical name, even if the common name is used in the text. Page numbers in italic indicate illustrations.